Understanding Technological Change

This book is dedicated to the Polish Solidarity Movement; for having given meaning back to words.

August 1980

Understanding Technological Change

CHRIS DE BRESSON
with Jim Petersen

BLACK ROSE BOOKS

Montréal-New York

Chris DeBresson with the assistance of Jim Petersen.
Edited by Deborah Seed.

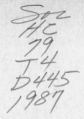

Black Rose Books No. 0 106

Canadian Cataloguing in Publication Data

DeBresson, Chris
  Understanding technological change

ISBN 0-920057-26-8 (bound). – ISBN 0-920057-27-6 (pbk.).

1. Technological innovations – Economic aspects.
2. Technological innovations – Social aspects.
I. Petersen, Jim. II. Title.

HC79.T4D42 1987   331   C86-090227-7

Cover design: J.W. Stewart

Black Rose Books

3981 boul. St. Laurent
Montréal, Qué. H2W 1Y5
Canada

340 Nagel Drive
Cheektowaga, N.Y. 14225
USA

Printed and bound in Québec, Canada

Contents

III. CRITICISM AND PROPOSALS FOR CHANGE

Chapter 14
THE WAY WE THINK 155

Steam fitter, Pennsylvania Railroad, 1930. (Lewis Hine)

PREFACE

Because our world is so complex, it is difficult to fully understand the phenomenon of technical change. Improvements in technology alone cannot explain the number of technical changes that mark our society. Social, economic and political factors have also played a major role in bringing about technical change. These factors at least are fairly easy to grasp.

This book is meant to serve as a general reference guide for college students and working people who want to understand the forces behind technological change. It was originally prepared for an evening course on this subject that included participants from labour unions. Their response to the material convinced me that information about technological change has a broad appeal.

Working people are usually the first users of a new technology, either on the job or at home. When they use an innovation they develop a keen and intimate sense of what it may offer. They experience the social advantages it may bring about, as well as the health hazards and stress that may ensue. Working people, therefore, are ideally suited to assess the innovation's social value.

In the workplace, organized workers are especially well placed to act upon their judgment of a technical change, to control its application and to modify its impact. To do this, they must begin to think about the overall design of a technology. All too often, however, technological change is either left totally to the employer's discretion or resisted across the board. Unions must therefore develop explicit policies regarding technological change, based on a critical analysis of how that change occurs and what its effects may be. This book should provide them with a critical overview to help them develop such policies.

The mass media often imply that any resistance to technological change is a strike against progress. Workers who react negatively to change are accused of neglecting the best interests of society. They should not be deterred by such accusations: the critical examination of any technical change is everyone's duty, especially that of working people. When industrial workers object to the long-term effects of a specific technology, such as nuclear power, they focus attention on the adverse effect it may have not only on their own health and livelihood, but also on their children and society. Their viewpoint is just as valid as the judgment of investors who wish to promote the new technology.

Scientists look at the general principles that make a technology work; engineers modify techniques and processes but rarely have to work with their designs; and investors reap the financial rewards without necessarily understanding the scientists' principles or the engineers' designs. Workers, as the first users of changes, have a crucial vantage point. They must be heard, because they are often intuitively correct, even though their impressions are sometimes partial, fragmented and unclearly expressed. When recurrent problems prompt formal research on technological change, their misgivings are usually found to be legitimate.

When a society embarks on a technological course, it should have well-substantiated reasons that are acceptable to all its members. This is rarely the case, unfortunately. Carelessness and omission are the rule rather than the exception. To change this trend, we must recognize that the worker's first response to a new technique represents its initial social evaluation. We can start controlling other new techniques that are being developed on the basis of the worker's evaluation.

Eventually organized labour will have to participate in the design of such techniques. This has already occurred in social settings as diverse as that of the Lucas Areospace plant in the United Kingdom and the Shanghai First Machine Tool Works in China. Hopefully the pattern will be followed elsewhere. The goal of organized labour should not be limited to preserving jobs; it must also comment on the quality and social utility of jobs. As technology continues to have even further-reaching effects beyond the workplace – as the 1986 nuclear accident at Chernobyl dramatically shows – the workforce will be challenged to rethink its social vision and play a part in the development of technologies.

In the process, organized labour will have to initiate its own research on technical change. Research that is geared to the potential users' needs stands a good chance of being implemented rather than being relegated to a dusty shelf. Moreover, those who make use of this research are best able to clearly identify the specific needs and problems worthy of examination. "One is never as well served than by oneself" is a valid precept in this regard. Organized labour followed this principle in setting up pension funds and credit unions; now it is time to acknowledge the need for new areas of research. This book was conceived as a means to promote such research – because technological change will proceed with or without union input.

College and university students should also find this book useful as a general introduction to technological change. They do not have the time to plough through all the contributions to the subject made by social scientists. Besides, there are no comprehensive texts, because each social science seems intent on focussing on its own contributions while ignoring those of other disciplines.

The narrow focus found in the different social sciences derives from the fact they are so isolated from one another. Engineers don't generally speak to economists, who in turn can't understand sociologists and psychologists. Most historians ignore all social sciences, claiming they are too theoretical. The search for an interdisciplinary approach or a broad understanding of a topic is no longer even considered realistic or worthwhile.

Such specialization has a devastating effect on the understanding of technical change. Historians who specialize in technology explain techniques by referring to other techniques and so are called internalists. Industrial engineers, on the other hand, combine techniques and work organizations. Economists examine the effects of relative prices, as well as the influence of economic demand and investment in machines. Scientists examine how science affects technique, while political scientists look at how governments bring about technical change. Few researchers even bother to study how the military influences change. Yet each group assumes that all the effects beyond their field of research are the result of "technology." In short, what they don't study or understand is attributed to technology.

Technology, however, is a material culture that is affected by prior techniques, economics, science, culture, and politics. To be understood fully, we must examine all these aspects. This book attempts to do just that.

Finally, much of the language about technological change is obscure and laden with references for specialists. My aim here has been to cut through such jargon to explain the causes and effects of technical change to the layperson.

Structure

The best literature on technical change is found in case histories. I have therefore drawn many examples from the best of this material. However, it is not known to what extent these cases represent overall trends because they tend to be specific to a given industry or a given trade. After each example, I have tried to show how general the patterns seem to be. I have approached these case studies, usually written by industry specialists, as a generalist, contrasting various features common to industries, technologies, periods, and places.

The first part of the book, "Technical Changes and Society," is designed to supply the reader with an overall analytic framework for understanding technical change. In this section, consisting of four chapters, I have tried to demystify the issues and get beyond the jargon. My focus here is on the underlying causes explaining technical change. Chapter 4 in particular deals with microprocessors.

The second part, "Evolutionary Constraints," contains Chapters 5 to 13. It examines the seven major forces that motivate and shape technical change: working knowledge and learning, technical adaptation, economics, science, politics, culture, and the search for status.

The final section contains both criticism and proposals for change. Chapter 14 examines some of the myths about technology and progress, while Chapter 15 suggests how we can act to control and direct future technological change. The book also has an appendix that includes some of the best contemporary documents I have found on the subject. These documents, supplied by labour, should offer the reader many valuable insights into how social movements have confronted the challenge of technological change.

I
TECHNICAL CHANGES
AND SOCIETY

CHAPTER 1

BEYOND THE BUZZ WORDS

There is no such thing as Technology with a capital T; there are only specific technologies and particular techniques. Management will often refer to the new technology without being specific. It will invoke a vague technological change as a reason for not being able to give in to a union's demands. The mere reference to technological change is supposed to create a scare, because Technology is supposed to be uncontrollable.

Like managers, journalists and social scientists often invoke the term without specifying precisely what they are referring to. Technology has thus become one of the most popular buzz words we use today. The imprecise manner in which it is used tends to mystify the key issues.

What do cooking, gardening, sewing, hunting, fishing, smelting metals, chemical processing and bio-engineering have in common? Yes, these are all technologies, ways of doing things. Besides the label they share, do they have any other similarities? They don't in fact, because different branches of industry and even different trades within the same industry are difficult to compare. Researchers on industrial innovation thus find it very hard to make any generalizations across industries. Yet we are supposed to talk about "technology" as if it were one thing.

Both this term and the word "technique" refer to ways of doing things. The two words have different connotations, however: "technology," because of its "ogy" ending, refers to a science or body of knowledge. "Technique," on the other hand, has a more concrete connotation, referring to a working practice – to how one does things. Usually, people prefer to use the word "technology" instead of "technique" because the former sounds more important.

There is another important difference in the contemporary connotations of these terms. Increasingly, people invoke technology to designate tools and instruments rather than the human procedures. Technical hardware, called "technics", is seen as representing the "hard" content of technology; the knowledge to make the hardware work is viewed as being secondary, as being "soft." The latter is called software in the computer industry, and working knowledge or procedures in others. (We can thank IBM for these value-loaded images that shape our perceptions about technologies, techniques, and technological change.)

Hardware – the machines and tools – are easier for social scientists to observe and quantify. In isolation, however, the hardware makes no sense; only the way humans use the machines or the tools make them understandable. To study any technology, then, it is necessary to start with human practice and know-how, without abstracting it from its human purpose. The hardware is not a neutral artifact which can be used for anything. On the contrary, although some technical artifacts can be applied differently to meet divergent social goals, they usually bear the imprint of the society which produced them.

The First Tool: Hand Axe

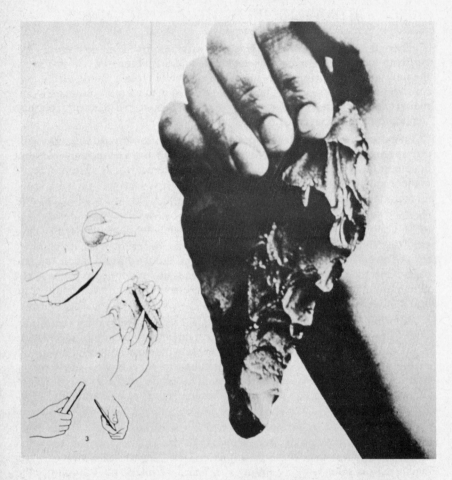

The earliest all-purpose hand tool, the hand axe, over a half million years ago was used to flint blades off other stones, bore holes, cut wood, carve animals and fight other human beings. In these early times knowing how to use this revolutionary tool was the essential component of technique.

Throughout this book we will use the term "technology" only when a technique is linked to a scientific field, as in the chapter on science and techniques.

Human Technical Knowledge

A crucial part of any technology is the knowledge of those people who operate its hardware. For reasons we will detail later, economists, who always think in terms of the exchange of goods, represent the world upside down. On the one hand they call human skills and technical knowledge "disembodied technical change"; on the other hand they label the machines incorporating that knowledge as "embodied" technical change. Such thinking has to do with the fact that machines can be exchanged as goods, whereas human knowledge is more difficult to trade. Such jargon, however, should not dissuade us from putting technical knowledge first in a study of technical change. In fact, this component must come first.

For example, a technical change can be brought about without even modifying the hardware, as people who work in processing plants well know. Many money-saving technical changes result from suggestions made on the shop floor. Take the national historic site that will be opened in Stevenson, British Columbia, for instance. This site will exhibit a fish cannery belonging to Canada Fish and feature the canning machinery it used until only a few years ago.

One of the processing lines in this cannery was set up for herring. It separated the meal from the oily liquid. Since herring oil is so precious, much care was taken to separate the oil from the rest of he liquid. At first the liquid was put through centrifugal separators, then through the boilers, and finally rerouted through the centrifugal machines. One day, the company chemist decided this process was the wrong way around: when the process was reversed, its efficiency increased fifty percent. None of the equipment had to be changed.

The importance of human technical know-how, compared to technological hardware, is best understood, however, if we adopt an historical perspective. Early human activity relied mostly on know-how and little on hardware, or instruments. The tools themselves did not change that rapidly, but the ways in which they were used did.

In the early Stone Age, stone tools were not likely saved from one day to the next. The very idea of saving a tool for future use was in fact slow to emerge. Technical change was basically limited to modifying current human practices regarding those tools.

Since the Stone Age, different elements have been added to the equation. But the processes of technical change still incorporate this same feature: we discover the use of a tool somewhat each day. In New Caledonia today, there are still groups who split rocks as our early ancestors did. Today we have incorporated the primitive practices into our more elaborate procedures. We rely, however, much more heavily on other components – on equipment, as well as the oral and written memory of how to use this equipment.

Still, we initiate most technical changes through experimentation at work.

And often the future tool is only at first seen as an ad hoc aid we devise to help us solve a particular problem we think is unique. Scientific instruments, for instance, are usually invented by experimental scientists who do not find suitable equipment for their needs; they then try to adapt the tools at their disposal. Later scientific equipment may be adopted by all industries, as in the case of welding.

Human knowledge is not merely a sufficent condition for technical change; it is always a necessary condition. It is concretely based on productive activity and it is also collective in nature. Finally, it is a crucial prerequisite for any modern technology.

Techniques have to be learned and assimilated both by individuals and groups. In today's world, multinationals span the world, often transferring their technologies and machines from one country to another. If a new machine and process are to work successfully elsewhere, however, the firm must ensure that people in the new location will have the technical skills to be able to use the machinery. It makes no sense to transfer simply the equipment.

All production processes, even the most rudimentary, are based on a certain understanding of natural phenomena. This understanding is rooted in the practical experience gained by working with materials. As such, it constitutes the primary form of knowledge. Formally educated managers and engineers tend to discount this fact, yet it is a prerequisitive for maintaining any production process.

The primary form of technical knowledge, then, comes from productive action. This knowledge may not have been verbalized for thousands of years. Even today mechanics often discover that something works without being able to first articulate why. Such a conviction is nevertheless solid, experimental, and proven by repeated experience. Historically, this form of knowledge problably precedes all forms of verbalized knowledge; in one's life experience, it remains the first form of knowledge, the one against which verbalized forms should be tested and sanctioned.

Take woodworking, for example. There are many ways to apply percussion to wood: obliquely or at a right angle, in the direction of the wood fibre or at a right angle to it, etc. Various instruments are best suited for each movement.

Out of this practice one gains the knowledge of the material, the tools used to work it, and the interaction of the two. You learn about a material by changing it. We call this technical knowledge. We might only have an inkling about how we acquire such familiarity, yet we rely on it all the time.

The language experts who compile our dictionaries have defined technology as the application of scientific knowledge to production. Such a definition excludes practical knowledge, however. The dictionaries are wrong here; the largest single source of a technology is the combination of experience and knowledge, not simply the application of formal science. Significantly, in ancient Greek, one word alone designated both science and technique: "techne."

Technologies, then, have to be assimilated personally and collectively. It is insufficient to have just one person who understands how a machine functions. The reasons are obvious: the machine process usually requires more than one person to run it. What would happen if that one expert became sick? How could the factory set up multiple shifts? There are also other, less obvious reasons for not relying on a lone expert. Technical improvements usually occur when people interact and exchange their ideas. If too few workers understand the technique, there is little likelihood it will be improved. On the other hand, when a shop-floor culture develops, when workers share their practical know-how, they might very well make changes for the better.

Any work process also involves some division of labour. One logger will cut off the branches of a tree, then saw through the trunk; another might attach the grapple to it; an operator might drag it to the yard; yet another person will load it onto a truck, and so on. Each operation depends on the next operation; each individual has to know something about the other's job. Such knowledge about the overall work process increases the group's efficiency.

In an artisan trade or small machine shop setting, a single worker is like only one finger on a hand. To put the entire hand to use, all the workers have to cooperate in an endeavour to assimilate the necessary steps in the process. And when the labour becomes even more specialized, they have to cooperate still further to put the entire body to use.

Historically, in fact, techniques evolved in this manner – as collective practices rather than individual skills. Keeping the fire burning, hunting, planting, and irrigating were all collective human endeavours. Hunting is one practice that has continued throughout the ages. In the case of hunting for mammoths in prehistoric times or hunting for caribou in our century, entire groups of people must be involved. Details about the animals' movements, reactions and sounds, together with the effects of human movements, have to be shared. Even if some individual hunters perform the crucial act of killing the animal, they need to depend on others to do so. Accordingly, the shared skills and knowledge form the foundations of the culture.

Technical knowledge did not become fragmented among people until very recently. The metal workers, who produced the tools to be used by others, are one of the first examples of this fragmentation. Nevertheless, their specialized skills depended on a pool of knowledge about how to use the special products. They had to cater to the many who would use the improved instruments. Furthermore, the exercise of the specialized trades depended on a score of shared survival skills, which allowed for the creation of a surplus, thereby enabling the metal workers to dedicate all their time to their trade. The common stock of shared technical knowledge thus constitutes the basis of material life and culture.

The examples we have taken – woodworking, rock splitting, and hunting – are fairly primitive techniques compared to today's machine technology. Yet technical know-how is a prerequisite for the development of modern technology as well for three basic reasons.

First of all, the primitive techniques have been incorporated into the modern ones. Even in the most advanced industrial societies, the process of cooking food has not altered much since the dawn of civilization. It is based on the application of fire, even though different types of heat have been used from one culture to another. The actual cooking utensils – pots and pans, burners and ovens – have likewise gradually diversified. Interestingly enough, though, the centuries-old Chinese wok is still considered the most energy-efficient and nutritious way of cooking vegetables.

Similarly, gardening, a technique many North Americans pursue as a hobby, also relies on the same basic principles as early agriculture: moving the earth, acquiring a water supply, ensuring the plants get enough sun, and so on. Despite the paraphernalia of modern instruments and aids, the basic principles have remained the same.

Collective Hunts

Like monkeys, since the earliest times human beings have acted collectively, dividing up the tasks in order to reach a common end. Collective know-how, everyone understanding what, when and why the others are doing different things and how that fits in with one's own share of the work, is key to production.

Secondly, one's ability to use instruments to work materials does not proceed from scientific knowledge; it builds on the knowledge supplied by handling the materials, as we saw earlier with the example of woodworking.

Thirdly, manufacturers must understand both how and where their new products are going to be used before they mass-produce them. For instance, small fishing boats were equipped with refrigerators only after a fisherman had figured out how to adapt the refrigeration process. Researchers employed at the federal fisheries research laboratory in Vancouver had vainly tried to use freon; they switched to the "champagne" process after a local fisherman explained how salt water could be used instead.

In paternalistic companies a few decades ago, foremen often dropped by work stations to show the rank and file how to do their jobs better, faster, or more energetically. The workers would look on with contempt, knowing that they wouldn't be able to do a full eight-hour shift if they followed a foreman's advice. Today's managers and engineers who are not trained on the shop floor no longer usually intervene in such a manner.

Contemporary managers, however, often tend to forget that there is more to production than simply running the machinery. If a company installs a sophisticated piece of equipment in a mine or lumber camp, yet fails to employ skilled tradespeople on the site to run it, the company will inevitably have to transport such individuals from the urban centres to debug and repair the machine. It will spend even more money paying idle workers when the equipment fails.

Do Robots Do Away With Workers?

In the case of robots, it would appear that human technical knowledge is dispensed with altogether. Robots work alone. Their performance matches that of topnotch welders. Indeed these robotic welders probably produce higher-quality work at a more consistent rate than human welders do.

The apparent absence of human knowlege, however, is illusory. Programmers have to write a series of programmes to record a skilled worker's performance, to decode this information, and finally to recode it for the machine. The robot in fact repeats the performance of the highly skilled human worker. The robot's performance depends on several different human skills – those of the welder, whose performance it is modelled after, and those of the programmers who code a multitude of instructions to make it work.

Robots that are programmed on the basis of the recorded operations of skilled tradespeople apparently work best. Other types of numerical control machine tools (NC machine tools for short) have been invented, but with less success. When the U.S. Air Force wanted to promote high-performance machining for its equipment, it tried to skip the recording stage. Instead, researchers decided to get mathematical descriptions of the work to be done by the machine tool. They opted to rely solely on the mathematicians, programmers and computer systems. At Lynn, Massachusetts, one of the operators at a General Electric factory almost lost his life as a result.

In this system, the operator was handed a programme to insert into the NC machine tool. He did not know how the programme or the control mechanism worked. One day, due to a bug in the programme, the NC machine tool started hurling lathe tools around the room. The man had to take cover, but luckily was not injured. According to the procedures, he was not supposed to communicate directly with the programmers. He handed in the programme to his immediate supervisors, explaining that the machine didn't hold the tools. (He did not want to appear "irrational" by describing what had actually happened.) The programme was fixed.

A few weeks later the NC machine tool again threw lathes around the room. This time the operator decided to disobey the procedures: he asked the programmer if the latter was trying to kill him. In the end, the programmer instructed him in how the commands operated. To be on the safe side, the operator also started studying programming. Subsequently, he always checked the programmes before feeding them into the machine; he even requested that some of the commands be changed for safety reasons.

No numercial command machine tool has yet worked successfully without relying on informed operators. And even when they do rely indirectly on the operators' skills, they have run into problems. This technology, like all others, then, cannot dispense with human know-how.

TOOLS AND MACHINES

The role of human knowledge varies, however, with different technical implements. Distinguishing between different types of equipment will help us understand this notion.

Hand Tools

Hand tools are simply extensions of the hand's and arm's actions. They have evolved considerably over the years. Because we admire what the latest tools can do, we tend to overestimate their importance in our daily life. And yet, many fancy gadgets sold at hardware stores are not really all that different in design than their early counterparts. This is certainly true of gardening tools, or instruments for preparing and cooking food. As people attempt to do different jobs, working with different materials, they gradually adapt their tools. The term "manufacturing" is in fact derived from the Latin roots "factur" – to process – and "manu" – hand. Manufacturing has evolved a multitude of different tools for every type of production and material.

The diversification of tools has been matched by a proliferation of techniques, depending on the environment. The more tools, the more techniques. But it is difficult to understand how a particular tool functions unless we have of drawing of someone **using** it.

The tools we no longer use remind us of the lost power of our hands. When we replaced this power with the energy supplied by domestic animals (horses, oxen), then later with motive power (water, wind, steam, explosives, fuels, electricity), tools became more simply designed. The crude power source could not shift its direction as easily as the hand. Mechanical transmission systems thus required simple standard tools.

CHECKLIST
How to Evaluate Changes at the Workplace

This checklist is designed to help you find out what new technology and equipment management is trying to introduce. It doesn't attempt to cover all aspects of technological change; however, it should help identify the scope of the change.

  1. What is being changed–the product or the process?

Product Change
  1. What products are being made? What are the varieties?
  2. What is the job?

Process Change
  1. What processing is being used?
  2. What is the primary material?
  3. What variety of feedstock can the process take?   (cont'd on page 10)

Understanding How it Works

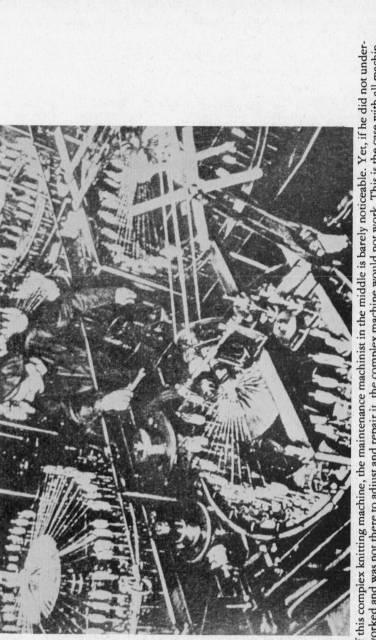

In the maze of this complex knitting machine, the maintenance machinist in the middle is barely noticeable. Yet, if he did not understand how it worked and was not there to adjust and repair it, the complex machine would not work. This is the case with all machinery, even computerized machines.

CHECKLIST (cont'd)

4. What tools does the process use?
5. What type of power is used?
6. What type of fuel is used?
7. What mode of power generation is there – combustion or fusion; internal or external combustion?
8. What feed and guide system is there?
9. What transmission system exists?
10. What control mechanism is in operation – human, mechanical, hydraulic, electrical, or electronic?
11. What changes occur in the sequence of jobs?
12. What changes occur in human functions?

Answer these questions so that you can decribe what is in operation now. Then ask the same questions regarding management's suggestions for future changes. What exactly will change? Can you think of any alternatives?

Power Tools and Machines

How do power tools differ from machines? The essential difference is that they are driven by a motor and need to be guided by the human hand. Chain saws, tractors, four-wheel skidders and whole-tree harvesters are all classified as power tools. Indeed, some are in fact highly sophisticated tools.

Machines, on the other hand, perform the work with minimal human guidance. They require a transmission system to direct the motor's energy in one direction . They also require a control mechanism, whether it be mechanical or electronic, to transmit the energy to the piece to be worked. This same control mechanism also commands machines to start, stop or repeat actions. In more sophisticated machines these mechanisms can regulate the rhythm of production or ensure quality control. (The computerized control mechanism in paper or newsprint processes is one such example.)

Once calibrated and started up, the machine will then set the pace of work, dictate the proportions of various feedstocks and fuel to supply it with, process these feedstocks, and relentlessly churn out the same product. The absence of human participation may lead us to think that machines don't need people. But this is an illusion: people have to invent the machines in the first place, and calibrate and repair them when they break down.

Types of Equipment

Mechanization is a never-ending process. Various segments of production processes have been automated since the Industrial Revolution, while other segments have remained manual. Periodically, each time a new process becomes automated, it frightens workers, who believe they will be totally excluded from the new setup. This has been a recurrent pattern since machines were first introduced. Yet new automatic machines never do away with labour completely.

Such may be the dream of managers and the fear of workers, but the total elimination of work is impossible. Granted, some designs do aim to reduce

---

CHECKLIST
How to Determine the Levels of Change

This checklist is designed to help you determine which levels of change are being proposed.

1. Is the improvement to be incremental without replacing the process itself?
2. Is the component to be changed or the materials?
3. Is the change to occur within a function, motive source, transmission, feed, guidance, or control?
4. Are the entire job and product to be altered?
5. Is the entire process going to be changed, or only some steps in it?
6. Is the change going to occur in the core technology or in the ancillary support techniques?
7. Is the whole technical system (i.e. blast furnaces) to be altered?
8. Will there be changes to the social organization?

---

human work to a minimum. They can also divide society into two groups—those who conceive the work and those who execute very specialized tasks—with the result that human prodcutive capacities are limited to a dangerously small number of people. Some utopian dreamers have even visualized a world without work. While not having to sell one's labour for one's survival is a reasonable goal, work is probably as essential to humans as social activity. Although wage labour may perhaps disappear one day, other forms of work will likely never disappear.

Many people believe that automation is the direct result of electronics and the computer chip. Indeed the microprocessor is a very efficient and inexpensive control mechanism. Yet dozens of control mechanisms precede the microprocessor. These include mechanical techniques, as well as hydraulic, chemical, electronic and optical ones. The laser is one of the most recent.

Similarly, equipment can be classified by its motive power (human, animal, steam, gasoline, natural gas); by the type of movement created (rotative or alternative); and its combustion (internal or external). Equipment can also be categorized by its power transmission system.

Technologies, including their artifacts – tools, machines, and control mechanisms – are best understood by their purpose. In specifying a technical change, one should start with the job design, because it will clarify the purpose of technical change.

CHECKLIST
Determining the Impact of Change

1. Are there to be more or fewer workers for the same output? Does management intend to hire any new workers?
2. What qualifications will be needed?
3. What know-how will be required?   (cont'd on page 12)

CHECKLIST (cont'd)

4. What change will occur in the learning process?
   a. Is formal training to be necessary?
   b. Is there any educational requirement of any kind?
   c. Is there to be an apprenticeship?
   d. Is there any on-the-job training?

5. What is the number of operations per workers?

6. What is the speed of the work and the output? How many shifts and breaks are there?

7. What impact would the change have on noise, heat, air quality, and circulation?

8. What changes would occur to the location of work stations? Will there be the same number of work stations?

9. What human backup is there?

10. What about stress and monotony?

SUGGESTED READINGS

CHILDE, V. Gordon. (1946) *What Happened in History*. New York: Penquin Books.
—— . (1941) *Man Makes Himself*. New York: Watts.

KRANZBERG, Melvin, and GIES, Joseph. (1975) *By the Sweat of Thy Brow*. New York: G.P. Putnam's Sons.

CHAPTER 2

SOCIAL FORCES BEHIND TECHNOLOGICAL CHANGE

When labour expresses its concern about the possible impact of a technological change on either the work process or jobs, it is inevitably accused of selfishly looking to its own interests. It is accused of a prolabour bias, which prevents it from objectively evaluating the changes. (The proponents of the new technology apparently are not subject to a similar bias.) Such criticism assumes that a technology can be socially neutral – that it exists independently of human needs and interests.

In fact, the essence of a technology is the social purpose for which it is designed. The literature on the subject tends to claim that all technological change is progress, implying that one should let the natural selection process decide which are the fittest technologies to shape our future. The natural selection of techniques is considered superior to human selection.

The writing on technological change rarely specifies whose lives will be improved. It tells us that technological progress is rational; that technology has its own rationality which is independent of people's needs; that workers – or any other members of the community – who contest the wisdom of a given technological change are illogical. Granted, some contemporary analysts have admitted that some technologies, which they deem useful for advanced industrial societies, are not necessarily suitable for developing countries. But they talk about the appropriate technology without specifying for whom it is suitable.

In later chapters, we will examine how these ideas about progress came about, what grain of truth they feed upon, and what effect they have on our perceptions. In this chapter we will merely show that they are false.

Who Determines Technical Choices?

A technology always belongs to someone. A machine or factory usually belongs to a private industrialist or a corporation, while the technical knowledge to operate that equipment belongs to the workforce. Similarly a technology always serves someone's purpose. A technical change cannot occur unless an individual initiates it. In the overwhelming number of cases, the initiator has the necessary financial resources to bring about change. When managers have accumulated profits or an entrepreneur has saved enough to start up a business, then they may propose a technical change. More often than not, the savings and investment are a necessary precondition for that change.

This doesn't mean that technical change will automatically occur each time there is an investment. Usually, new investments will be devoted to modifying current techniques to improve the work processes. If the workers, such as contruction workers, own their working tools, they can introduce minor changes in the production techniques as they use them. If the workers don't own their tools, they might modify how a technique is applied, without changing its overall purpose, design, or effects on the division of labour. These broader changes will occur only if management decides they are beneficial to its own interests, or if the work force imposes them on management.

Only the largest investors indeed have the power to choose a major new technology in a given society. This holds true not only in an industrial capitalist society but also in societies with planned economies. For example, in the U.S.S.R., the government bureaucracy alone makes the investment choices. No matter which society is concerned, the capital investment to start up any production process is considerable. What other group, besides the government, could then have the savings required to introduce a new technology?

At the end of the Middle Ages, it would have been impossible to bring numerous craftspeople together to work in a manufacture around a new source of power without the surplus money provided by trade. No matter which society we are discussing, technical change is brought about by those who control the surplus production, wealth and savings. Technical change is basically controlled by the haves rather than the havenots.

CHECKLIST
How to Determine the Backers

Here are some questions to help you clarify who owns the technology.

Design
  1. Who invented or designed the new technology?
  2. Who is promoting the design?

Ownership
  1. Who owns the present hardware?
  2. Who owns the instruments of production?
  3. Who is investing in the new technology?
  4. Where does the money come from?
  5. Whose savings are being invested?
  6. Who will own the new technical instruments?
  7. Who will reap the economic benefits, get the proceeds from the sales, benefit from the production costs savings and new markets?
  8. Who will make the decisions in the new organization?

Use
  1. Who has the technical know-how to operate the new equipment?

The number of people who contribute to making technical choices varies, depending on the political system. This affects the degree to which technical power is democratic or autocratic. Under Roman slavery, for instance, the slaves would be fed at the end of the day no matter how much work they did. They used their knowledge to reduce their workload but they didn't have the incentive to suggest labour-saving improvements. Thus in the the slave state, the power to initiate and bring about technical change is concentrated in a small group of slave owners.

Such power, however, does not have to be confined to an autocratic elite. In the Middle Ages, there were many centres of technical designs – monasteries, feudal castles, towns, and new settlements. Many rival technical options were developed by different social groups: for example, peasants used a hand mill to make flour, while monasteries and lords favoured the water mill. Thus the degree to which economic and political power is concentrated in a society will affect the degree to which technical choices are concentrated.

SLAVES, MULES, AND MACHINES

Social systems profoundly influence how technical implements are designed. Before we examine this influence, let us first specify how one can distinguish between social systems.

One useful concept is that of production modes. An idea developed by late eighteenth century philosophers, it was coined in the nineteenth century by Marx. He defined production modes in terms of their property relationship. (The major property relationships have been summarized in the adjacent box.)

Modes of Production: Property Relations

Slavery: Landlord owns human beings; has the right to sell or put them to death; owns the newborn slaves.

Feudalism: Lord has the right to a number of work days from the serf; serf has the temporary right to use lord's land.

Capitalism: The worker (proletarian) is free and rents out his hours of work to industrialists who own the land and tools of production.

Aside from the modes of production Marx defined, there are many other variants. Marx stressed the property relations between classes. As we will see later, however, within a given system of property relations, there are many different ways to organize work, which in turn affects technical changes.

Under slavery, agricultural tools were made to be simple, heavy and sturdy; fragile horses were replaced by more resistant mules. Adam Smith, the great English classical economist, explained why: "If a slave had proposed...an improvement, his owner would think that this was because he was lazy and wanted to reduce his own work for his master. The slave could only expect insults and perhaps a beating as a result of his initiative."

The slave would be fed at the end of the day whatever work he or she did. The fear of being sold to a worse slave owner was his only incentive to work well. Paradoxically, slave mine owners paid relatively equal attention to their slaves, their mules and their machines. The owners had a vested interest in keeping their slaves healthy: they were valuable property, and certainly more agile and easier to train than mules.

Capitalist owners of mines operated by free wage earners, however, have paid more attention to equipment than to the hired hands. In the event of a cave-in, they would suffer a capital loss if the equipment and mules were destroyed. Other workers could always be found. The owners' incentive in keeping workers was to draw on their skills and intelligence, and their willingness to take risks.

Mines operated by slaves have never run as well as those worked by miners, since the slaves refused to take any risks. Miners, however, were induced to take those risks if they wanted to get their pay.

The choice of a mining technique, therefore, has to be seen within a broader social context. The nature of the social organization – a mine operated by slaves versus a mine run by paid workers – should show why one technology is chosen rather than another.

The reverse is likewise true: a chosen technique perpetuates a given social organization. One group usually benefits more than others in any given social organization. This same group usually promotes the technology that supports and extends the organization from which it draws its benefits. As John Kenneth Galbraith has noted in **The New Industrial State**, technology manifests the desire for power on the part of the accumulating classes. It likewise reflects their attempts to institutionalize these power relationships and to seek acknowledgement for their creative and progressive role. In this regard Galbraith's view corresponds to that of Marx, who observed that a given technology reveals how social relationships are formed in production.

The acquisition of a new technology is the means by which a new property relationship develops. For example, anthropologists have reconstituted how the migrant population was transformed into sedentary farmers in Madagascar. Such a transformation occurred at the same time as the adoption of wet rice, since its cultivation required sedentary agriculture. The long-term results of this transformation were both technological and social: when the migrants became farmers, they also stopped hunting with their kinship clans and sharing scarce resources. Patriarchal tribes developed, whose members intermarried to accumulate greater private wealth in the form of land and slaves. The tribes no longer shared property with one another.

This example suggests why the grain storers in emerging agrarian societies had a direct interest in promoting irrigation and sedentary agriculture. Such a production system had to be accompanied by an elaborate hierarchy to ensure the proper monitoring, control and regulation of water levels. This irrigation system maintained the grainholders' power. Their power could be further strengthened if they rigorously controlled and stored the surplus food and taxation. Irrigation, canal systems, pottery, basic arithmetic, as well as brick for the homes, were the technological results of the agricultural revolution promoted by the grain storers.

Motivations of Industrial Entrepreneurs

For labour, it is crucial to understand what motivates managers or entrepreneurs into introducing technical changes. This will help explain the particular orientation the change will take; it will also help reveal the biases inherent in the technical design chosen.

The basic motiviation for introducing technical change is of course profit. It is a special type of profit, though. Joseph Schumpeter called it entrepreneurial profit (3); Everett Rogers, windfall profits (4); Karl Marx, extra surplus value (1). Whatever the label, it results from the profit the company makes by producing a product – or by replacing a product – at a lower cost than it takes the entire industry to produce efficiently. Another way to reap profits is to turn out a product that has the same function or performs much better than its rivals. These are called substitutes.

The price of the new product will be determined by the balance between supply and demand. The price varies around the average production cost of this product in the industry. In other words, if some factories produce a pencil for 30 cents apiece and others for 50 cents, and if pencils are produced for an average of 40 cents, then the price will vary around 40 cents. If hundreds of people suddenly need pencils but there are none to be found, their price might rise. Conversely, if there is a glut of pencils on the market, their price might decrease.

If I introduce a new production process, such as word processing, my cost for typing the same job will be lower than that set by my competitors, who use typewriters, due to my savings in labour. However, the price of the typed page on the market won't be immediately affected. And if my typing business is the only one to use a word processor, the average production time in the industry won't be affected either. Consequently, I can still sell each typed page at the normal price, thereby gaining the normal profit my rivals get, as well as tap an additional profit because of the new technique. As soon as other typists adopt word processing, though, the average cost of producing a page will drop, which will in turn lower the price. At this point the margin for extra profits between the market price and my costs will disappear.

Graph 2.1
Diffusion of Standardized Innovation

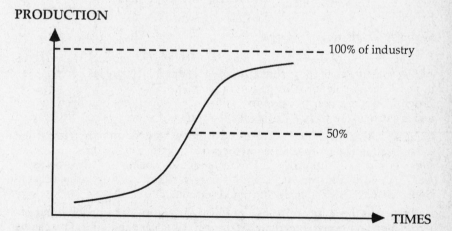

PRODUCTION

100% of industry

50%

TIMES

This example suggests why the initial diffusion of a standardized technique tends to be rapid. In the later stages of diffusion, entrepreneurs will adopt the new technique to ensure that their private costs are not higher than the average costs in the industry. They also will want to get the same profits as their rivals.

There is an advantage, then, in preventing competitors from learning about the new technique. The entrepeneur can either try to be very discreet or apply for a patent. The patent will give him a temporary monopoly over the use of the new technique for approximately 17 years. However, obtaining a patent may not prevent others from using the new process. Should they try to do so, they can be asked to pay the inventor some royalties; in theory, the inventor even has the right to demand that the government halt the imitator's production. Few take this route, though, because of the high legal costs. Instead, they will use the patent as a bargaining tool with their competitors.

Unable to effectively block the widespread adoption of the new technique, the entrepreneur will nevertheless try to take advantage of his exclusive rights while they last – by rapidly increasing the production volume, reducing the price, and taking over the competitors' markets. The goal here is to increase the volume and speed of production as soon as possible. Management economists have labelled this "economies of scale and speed."

Economies of scale do not always entail the most rational and efficient production, from the viewpoint of using energy and primary materials. The goal is simply to obtain the largest sales figure and profits for the company, which means that the volume and speed of production have to be increased to gain a temporary edge over the competition.

Economies of scale go together with economies of speed. The time during which a firm has a technical edge over its rivals is limited. Soon after adopting the new technique, it will usually introduce three eight-hour shifts and other measures to avoid down-time. From the point of view of profit making, these steps are quite logical. If the firm is reaping a 20-percent profit for every thousand dollars it has invested, it will try to turn a profit as fast as and often as possible. Work more and work faster is thus the ethic of industrial capitalism. Time is money; overtime means "progress." Prosperity means 24 hours of stress. Growth becomes an end in itself, whether consumers need the products or not.

Gender Division of Work

Compared to all the technical divisions of work, the gender division is the one we take the most for granted, as being "natural." Having children is seen as the woman's role; producing goods, the man's. Biologically, of course, reproduction is the woman's province, since only women are equipped to bear and breastfeed the young. Caring for the young, however, is another matter.

In primitive societies, mothers and women hunted with the rest of the tribe. Gradually they specialized in the work of gathering the produce, creating agriculture in the process. The technique of hoeing and the hoe itself, weaving and its instruments, breadmaking, ovens and pottery are all inventions that have been mostly attributed to women.

As long as the family remains a productive unit, the division of labour between men and women need not be distinct. Childcare and education can be shared by the entire group, and often are the grandparents' responsibilities.

The separation of the home from the place of work is in fact a very recent historical phenomenon. The confinement of women to the home is even more recent: this first appeared with industrialization, when men began commuting to factories located far from their homes. This gave rise to our present nuclear family.

Our consumer society is presently geared to meet the needs of this small family unit. Today's family lives in a single-family dwelling, complete with a car, washing machine and dryer, oven, lawnmower and television. Such families are ideal consumers for the products of industrial capitalism. There is obviously no economic logic to having all these durable goods used only a few hours each day by one unit.

Yet there is another logic to this seemingly inefficient pattern of consumption. It becomes apparent in the choice of consumer products, drugs, and their design. It is nicely reflected in the advertising that promotes the consumer lifestyle – advertising that is geared to the female buyers who purchase the family's products.

Industrial capitalism has created a small, tightly knit nuclear family overseen by a female custodian. Women assume the responsibility of the family's reproduction, its subsistence, its members' health, and their emotional and social needs – even if the women are employed outside the home. Indeed, many of the paid jobs women hold are simply extensions of these family functions: they are teachers, nurses, childcare workers, social workers, or secretaries. In addition, they are expected to donate their free labour to numerous volunteer organizations.

This nuclear family is the system that supposedly regenerates the labour force day after day. It shapes the designs of technologies as much as industrial capitalism does. All three variables – family unit, technology, and capitalism – are in fact closely linked.

Take the production of fast foods, for instance. The first fast-food civilization actually surfaced during the Industrial Revolution in the United Kingdom. Street vendors sold meals to workers near the mines and factories in the Midlands. The production and sale of fast food were related to changes in family life. At the time, children were separated from their families to work in the mines. Women, too, worked in the mines. Sexual licence was rampant among working people. The period was marked by a decrease in gender hierarchy but an increase in gender strife, with the result that families were broken up.

CHECKLIST
Economic Motivations of Promoters

This checklist is designed to clarify the goals of the promoter of a new technology.

1. Will this new technology increase the profit, the absolute amount of profit, or the profit rate?

2. Will the promoter get ahead of competitors? If so, how long will he or she stay in the lead? If not, is the promoter an early or late imitator?

3. Will the new product or substitute mean a less costly process?

Gender Bias in Advertising

*It's up to
the woman
to keep
love
beautiful*

from an advertisement in *Modern Bride*

> Advertisements reflect the values of an epoch and also the social intent of the promoters of a technology. These advertisements reflect, willingly or unwillingly, the male bias and discrimination against women.

Another pertinent example of how these three variables are linked has to do with contraceptives. The extensive use of contraceptive methods has separated the reproductive functions from the sexual, so that sex no longer needs to be linked to pregnancy. Yet most contraceptives are designed for women: it's up to women "to keep love beautiful" as one ad slogan says. The messages found in ads for contraceptives remind women of their responsibility; they are ads written by men to tell women about reproduction, and how to control it.

The production of fast foods, which free women from cooking, the sale of contraceptives, which remind women of their duties, and countless other examples are all geared to maintaining the nuclear family. This family unit may have only had a short history – it may in fact be evolving into something else entirely – but it is now being maintained by our present techniques and products, just as other family structures were sustained by other techniques.

During feudal times, the wet-nurse industry and the use of the cervical cap were likewise the technical vehicles to promote gender and social strife. Female serfs were enjoined by the Church to bear more children, thereby producing more farm labourers. They were also expected to bear and nurse their lord's illegitimate children. Many women used the cervical cap to limit the number of children they could have. Only the seigneur's wife was exempt from nursing or caring for children.

The split between male and female work is similar to the division between intellectual and manual labour, or the division between conceivers and doers. Such constructs are linked to the divisions between the decision makers and the followers. Although none of these divisions of labour are irreversible, they do affect the shape of technology today.

Effects of Machine Designs on Work

It is vital for workers to pay particular attention to the way their jobs are designed. Shifts in organization and job designs are bound to have dramatic effects on technical designs.

In the nineteenth century, German and American engineers apparently realized that they could use semiskilled labour more efficiently by making some basic changes in the design of machine tools. Semiskilled labour could be made as productive as craft labour; a liability, in short, could be turned into an asset. The answer lay in tapping a cheap and abundant source of labour represented by the semiskilled workers.

Between 1890 and 1900, new lathes were designed with gearboxes, thereby allowing the speeds and feeds to be changed. Older methods had involved changing gears by hand – literally by taking out one gear and putting in another, or by sliding a belt up and down a conical drum or some other crude device. Changing the gears before the gearbox was invented required specialized training; only the craftsmen were able to perform this task, which took a long time to learn.

Tool setting used to be, and still is, one of the most archaic elements in the machinist's job. During the deskilling drive at the turn of the century, the turret lathe came into its own. It was an American device, which appeared first in the 1850s in New England. In principle, the time required to set many different tools in a lathe could be reduced by setting them all at once in a turret. The turret was turned around to access the tools need for a particular operation. Such an invention eliminated the need for skilled craftsmen.

The above example shows how industrialists' motivations can influence which machine design gets adopted, as well as the social consequences of that design. Basically there are several factors that reflect underlying biases when it comes to machine design. They are worth examining one by one.

1. Machines tend to process as much volume as possible to ensure economies of scale.

2. Machines are designed to run continuously to ensure economies of speed. Their parts are likewise designed to be interchangeable so that the entire machine isn't put out of commission when one piece needs to be repaired. The machine is also designed to run at full capacity by finding resistant materials, discovering auxiliary materials, and using control mechanisms. (Managers likewise try to reduce the time it takes to move the product around the plant.)

3. An ideal process, from the viewpoint of an industrial capitalist, is the continuous fluid-flow process of the chemical industry: the feedstock materi-

als (such as petroleum) enter at one end, while diverse chemical products exit at the other. Another ideal process is the assembly line: the conveyor belt ensures that production keeps moving all the time.

4. An attempt will be made to standardize any new product to allow for its mass production in an assembly plant or continuous production setting. The most famous example of this tendency towards standardization is the Model T Ford. Originally Henry Ford designed the Model T in 1909 to be as simple as possible; once he started mass-producing the car, he cut the price. This also was the case of Singer's sewing machines.

Rigorous standardization is one of the secrets of mass production and economies of scale. It also ensures that service costs are reduced by rapidly replacing standardized parts.

5. A machine's life is designed to be relatively short. Another, more efficient process will be introduced before a machine is worn out. Often, even if a machine is fuel-efficient and profitable, it will be retired because another process has been invented that provides larger profits. The previous machine is declared obsolescent even though it works perfectly well; it is earmarked for the junkyard if it makes fewer profits than its newer counterpart. The entrepreneur can't afford to wait too long before switching to a more economic process, especially if he risks losing the opportunity to make extra profits. The profit motive, then, accounts for the planned obsolescence of machines.

6. The search for a new product to replace the old becomes an end in itself. The entrepreneur's goal here is to obtain a new market and displace the competitors. Better still, the new product is designed to become obsolete after a short period so that the industrialist can tap the same market over and over again. The consumer thus is encouraged to purchase a new car every three years.

The same search is made to invent minor product differences to lure new buyers. Different car models may deliver the same engine performance, but this is disguised by the bewildering array of brand names and specification sheets.

7. In striving to mass-produce a product, industrialists will also look for ways to replace highly skilled workers, who command good salaries, by semiskilled workers, who receive lower salaries. When parts become standardized, the skilled craftspeople, whose broad knowledge enables them to adjust to diverse tasks, can be eliminated.

A good example of this deskilling process is the case of the Numerical Control Machine Tool, according to David Noble, an historian specializing in technical change (5). Early in the 1950s, some firms experimented with what was called the record playback machine tool. The principle was simple: a skilled worker would operate the machine tool and a tape would record the operations, then play them back. Human skills were thus recorded and interactively reproduced. (The most reliable of today's Numerical Control machine tools have come back to this principle.)

The U.S. Air Force, however, which was sponsoring the research into machine tools to produce more sophisticated aircraft, wanted to rely on computer designs rather than on human skills. At great expense the Numerical Control of production operations was developed: programmers would simulate the skilled worker's operations and translate them into machine language. Although the machines didn't perform very well, the U.S. Air Force opted for the design.

On the whole, industrial capitalists will tend to choose techniques which are relatively intensive in equipment and material and less intensive in labour. Economists call this phenomenon "capital-intensive" technology. An improvement designed to increase efficiency will affect the relationship between the machines, material and labour that yield the end product. Of course, each time any new process is introduced, it will increase production; the absolute volume of labour will also expand. But in the long run, each product will be produced with relatively less expenditure in wages than in equipment and materials.

Production Modes

As we shall see in a later chapter, there are different ways to organize work. The three major production modes are called custom, batch and line. Each mode implies different types of relationships between the workers and machinery. Each also imples different types of technical designs.

Institutions

Institutions also affect technical design because they too have their preferences. For instance, B.C. Hydro in 1979 decided to build two 500 kv alternating current transmission lines between Cheekeye substation near Squamish and Dunsmuir station near Qualicum, on Vancouver Island. They opted for this instead of building a smaller 230 kv transmission, or producing electric power on the island by means of gas turbines, which were both viable and preferable alternatives according to the B.C. Energy Commission. Such a decision reflects the biases of monopolies: they tend to set production units larger than what strict technical efficiency would call for.

CHECKLIST
Advantages of a New Technique

What are the advantages of a new proposed technique over the previous one?

—maximum volume of production

—continuity of production

—speed of output

—flexibility in changing product

—energy efficiency

—reduced consumption of primary materials

—fewer wastes

—fewer lemons

—less reliance on skilled labour

REFERENCES

1. MARX, Karl. (1960) *The German Ideology*. New York: International Publishers.

2. GALBRAITH, John Kenneth. (1978) *The New Industrial State*. Boston: Houghton Mifflin.

3. SCHUMPETER, Joseph. (1962) *The Theory of Economic Development: An Inquiry into Profits, Capital, Interest and the Business Cycle*. New York: Oxford University Press.

4. ROGERS, Everett. (1983) *Diffusion of Innovation*. New York: Free Press

5. NOBLE, David. (1984) *Forces of Production: A Social History of Industrial Automation*. New York: Knopf.

SUGGESTED READINGS

NOBLE, David. (1984) *Forces of Production: A Social History of Industrial Automation*. New York: Knopf.

CHAPTER 3

THE SOCIALLY CONTESTED OUTCOME

Now that we have seen how technical designs can contain biases, let us take another tack. This chapter will look at the social forces which affect the choice, direction and mode of diffusion of technical change. Although many students of technology have analyzed the effects of technical change on society, few have looked at the other side of the coin – the effects of social change on technical change.

Among the myriad techniques available, investors determine which few will be tried out. Techniques are not the result of a natural selection process. Before the Agricultural Revolution of 6,000 B.C., the constraints of survival may have been so rigorous that the technological options were indeed limited. By the time of the Agricultural Revolution, however, humans had learned to cooperate to provide for their livelihood. Other forms of social organization besides the simple family appeared, according to V. Gordon Childe, author of **Man Makes Himself** (1). This marked the beginning of humanmade history as distinct from simple evolution. From this point on, collective choices – politics, wars, culture – all become factors of the human condition.

Technology is a part of culture, since it is fashioned by humans. A technique is likewise a form of human cooperation, whether this cooperation is voluntary or involuntary. A technique essentially refers to how human beings relate to one another and to the material world.

But why does a certain technique come about, we may wonder. What purpose does it serve? Any technique has a purpose or a "telos," as philosophers would put it. This motivation has to be clearly understood before one examines the evolutionary constraints that determine why it comes to be selected.

One of these factors has to do with the social relationships at work. They condition the choice of technique, the subsequent direction of technical change, and the rhythm of diffusion of this change throughout industry. Many historians of technology have already looked for the connections between technologies and social relationships. Even technological evolutionists concede that there is a link between technological and social systems, as does Bertrand Gille in **Histoire des Techniques**, and that technology is a social product (2).

My view of technical change differs from theirs, however, in that I believe that the organization of work is not merely a dependent factor, but also a controlling factor. Social organizations choose techniques which reinforce them. This offers humankind the opportunity to control technology. We do not have to assume a passive role in the drama of technical change: we can write the script.

This chapter will first examine how the organization of work controls the choice of techniques and the direction of technical change. In particular, it will show how a few core technologies are used by a given social system to establish its leaders' prerogatives in production, organize society and divide the work among people. It will then examine the many ways in which work has been, and still is, organized today. (The multitude of existing social options are greater than we usually want to imagine.) It will also briefly review the extent of social influences that exist within a technical system. Finally, it will examine how techniques always remain the object of a mute power struggle between social groups in society.

Interaction Between Social and Technical Systems

How does a social organization control the orientation of technical activities? It does so mainly through technical systems. As we saw earlier, a technical system is a set of interdependent techniques. Around a core technique – for instance, the car's internal combustion engine or the snowmobile's sprocket wheel and double tread – revolve many other ancillary technologies. The core technique limits the direction of technical activity, thereby creating the illusion that social forms are predetermined. This illusion is so widely held that historians have argued that flood control led to the rise of oriental despotism or that the steam engine led to the development of capitalism.

Graph 3.1
Direct and Indirect Consequences of the Adoption of Wet Rice Growing in Madagascar

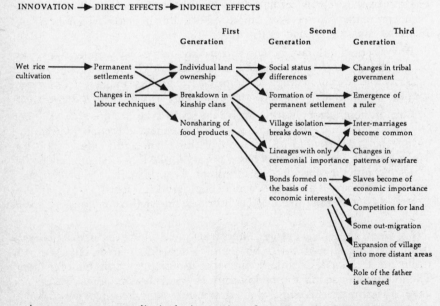

Arrows represent causality in the interaction of wet rice technology and society as described by Ralph Linton in Kardiner and Linton, *The Individual and His Society*, New York: Columbia University Press, 1955.

The potential for technical activities, however, precedes the development of different social systems. For instance, long before the Agricultural Revolution of 6,000 B.C., migratory tribes cut wild wheat around Sumer (now Iraq); women sowed grain, "produced" the wheat, and "discovered" or "invented" agriculture. The agricultural technique did not start the Agricultural Revolution; it merely made it possible. This productive potentiality, however, was not perceived for centuries. A nomadic civilization which lived off hunting, collecting wild vegetation and, perhaps, controlling the hunt, could not benefit from this technical potential. Only after nomads had decided to become sedentary, focus on agriculture and control water for irrigation, did agriculture and irrigation become the core technique of a new social system. Then a number of ancillary techniques were added, such as storing grain and building houses out of brick.

To a certain extent, one group must have instigated the social change despite the opposition of others who wanted to continue to live as nomads. From this point of view, V. Gordon Childe's definition of technique as a "cooperative association," on a voluntary or involuntary basis, is appropriate. Certain social systems are well suited to specific techniques: sedentary life with agriculture, workshops with machines, etc.

Because the technical potential always precedes the social change, one might be tempted to conclude that a technique always causes such change to occur. This is not necessarily true, however. Both the machine and the workshop preceded the development of capitalism by many centuries. As we will see in a later chapter, the crankshaft existed for many centuries even before the concept of the machine developed. Then during the fourteenth or fifteenth centuries, the crankshaft and the idea of a machine seized the Renaissance imagination. Later these notions captured the imagination of the traders who invested in workshops.

In this sense, although opportunities precede social change, the major inventions are social: adopting a sedentary life, the workshop, the manufacture, the factory, the assembly line.... With each of these social changes, human beings contract new social relationships and a hierarchy. A core technique and technical system stamp an order on these individual interactions.

We should not then mistake the form – the technical artifact – for the context – the relations between people. Technical systems are the chosen instruments to regulate interpersonal relations. The clearest example of this is the conveyor belt. "The chain drive [continuous assembly] proved to be a very great improvement," wrote H.L. Arnold after studying Ford's car plant in 1914. It hurried the slower men, held the faster men back from accelerating the pace, and acted as an all-around adjuster and equalizer (3). What is true of chain drives is true of other technical systems; they regulate the workers, making the different jobs compatible.

The existence of the assembly line is due to investors, who decide who works for them; they also decide how employees will work and relate to their coworkers. In this regard, they enjoy a distinct technical power, enabling them to pick one of several ways work and people are organized in the labour force. Beyond class or property relations, investors determine the internal relations within the working force. And with the same million dollars, they can make many different choices in that respect, even if they should profit from all of them. By choosing to shape the internal relations within the working class, investors in turn shape much of its material culture.

The Different Organizations of Work

In Das Kapital, Karl Marx suggested that the history of technology – the material basis of all social organization – could reveal how man acts upon nature and the productive process of his material life. Therefore it also reveals the origin of the social relationships and corresponding intellectual ideas and concepts. Few of his doctrinaire disciples, who tend to prefer rhetoric and an authoritarian exegesis of his word to the painful work of analyzing reality, have followed his advice and written such a history of technology. V. Gordon Childe, Joseph Needham, and the French historian Marc Bloch are probably among the few who have followed his advice seriously, despite the difficulties of the task. It is insufficient to simply describe the advent of a technology and conclude that it automatically triumphed because of its intrinsic advantages. When historians have examined a technology, their work has only just begun. Their next step is to show how the specific technology reflects the most intimate structure of the society in which it appeared.

The organization of work in the last few thousand years has changed dramatically. Techniques and tools have changed at the same pace. In the last 300 years, the organization of work, as well as technology, have changed at an even more dramatic pace. But our perceptions of these changes lag behind the facts. And they continue to be rather fuzzy. We talk about revolutions: the Industrial Revolution; the scientific and technological revolutions; the first, second, and third Industrial Revolutions, and so on. The term "revolution" has become as meaningless for economic historians as for South American generals. If the term still means something, however, it should refer to a change in the dominant way people are organized in production. Instead of revolution, I have opted for the term "social transformation" because it is more descriptive and less rhetorical.

What does the organization of work actually mean? According to the American historian of technology, Melvin Kranzberg, it refers to the way in which men and women group themselves and their tools to produce the goods and services necessary to maintain life in society and reproduce it (4). These social relations determine the framework for all subsequent technical activity.

The mechanical crank is an extraordinary case to show the link between new social organizations and technical systems because of the almost unbelievable delay in using it. It may have existed as early as the ninth century in Europe. Sketches of crankshafts dating from the fourteenth century have been found, yet there is no evidence that any of these designs were actually built. Nevertheless, the sketches show that the idea of the crank was finally beginning to arouse the European mind. By around 1430, the compound crank had been transferred from the carpenter's brace to a novel type of machine design, judging from the notebook of a German military engineer of the Hussite Wars. First, the connecting rod, a mechanical substitute for the human arm, was applied to cranks. Then double compound cranks appeared, which were also equipped with connecting rods. Finally, the flywheel was applied to these cranks to get them over the dead spot, the chief difficulty in mechanized crank motion.

Students of applied mechanics have agreed that the technical advance specifically characterizing the modern age is the one from reciprocating motions to rotary motions. The crank is the condition of that change. The appearances of the bit-and-brace in the 1420s, together with the double compound cranks and connecting rod about 1439, mark the most significant single step in the late medieval revolution in machine design. With extraordinary rapidity, these devices were absorbed into Europe's technological thinking and used for the widest variety of operations. How can we explain the delay of so many centuries not only in the initial discovery of the simple crank but also in its wide application and elaboration?

At the heart of feudalism was a cluster of central techniques supporting the entire system. The use of the steel plough, the axe, the stirrup, the harness, and the field rotations of crops were the core techniques which enabled people to clear the forests, erect subsistence settlements and defend them. Emerging capitalism in the fifteenth century towns used the available sources of power – the machines and concentrated labour power of the cities. Capitalism then used the workshops, leading to the birth of a new organization of work. In the power workshop, the crankshaft flourished, enabling the machine culture to emerge. All other techniques were to revolve around the machines and a power source.

At some historical juncture, the entire direction of human technical endeavour has been drastically redirected by such new productive organizations. The technical preoccupations of a migrant agrarian population are not the same as those of a sedentary one. A feudal serf might be concerned about the durability, resistance, and the depth of reach of his plough, or the yield of his two yearly crops to feed his family. Capital-intensive agriculture, on the other hand, might be concerned only with the year's marketable product yield in comparison to the products and work put into the earth at the beginning of the season.

Many of us don't usually speculate on social systems different from our own. We take ours for granted, just as we take for granted the customs and laws that maintain it. We also assume that it is difficult to change a given social order. Yet history abounds with examples of different ways of organizing people for work. Labour has always been collective in one form or another, whether it consisted of watching the fire, herding caribou, reclaiming the Nile swamps, irrigating Sumer or China, minding the children, or working on the assembly line. The organization of work has always been the organization of collective labour.

Investors are the ones who have taken the initiative to organize other people's work. There lies the material source of power over people. (This stands even for decision makers who claim they decide in the name of working people, such as in the Soviet Union, Cuba, China or Yugoslavia. A state bureaucracy in these countries is selected as the basis of ideology and privilege, thereby giving those chosen the right to organize other people's work – and to accumulate and exercise power.) Organizing people's productive labour is done around a given technique and its implements (the dam, the plough team, the power mill and machines, etc.).

The way productive labour is organized also determines a society's reproductive labour. In the extended rural families of the feudal system, for instance, the elderly took care of children, who in turn worked in the fields. In an industrial capitalist and consumer society with its nuclear families, the mother alone performs childcare with the assistance of schools. Reproductive social relationships are almost as varied in history as productive relations. And yet, little research has been done on the subject; our knowledge is still sketchy. If we look simply at the work relationships on farms, the Bengali development economist A.K. Sen has described over eight pure forms.

Graph 3.2
Property Relationships in Farming

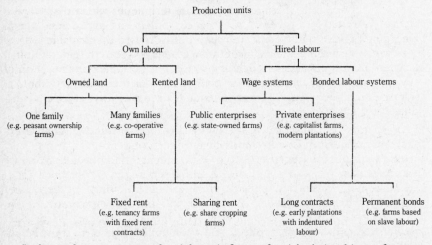

In the two bottom rows are the eight main forms of social relationships on farms as described by the development economist A.K. Sen.

Finally, the property relations in production are of crucial importance. The fact that industrialists own the machines and materials but wage earners own only their labour is crucial to the choice of techniques. Marx was concerned mainly with these social relationships of production as property relations because they defined social classes. But there are also finer, more subtle social relationships in production which affect technology. For example, class relationships (such as wage differentials) do not tell us whether you are confronted with a manufacture or a modern factory.

A business historian, N.S.B. Gras, has distinguished between the many forms of social relationships that exist in industry according to the use of the final product (5). People who produce for their own use (usufacture) are first distinguished from those who produce goods for sale. Within the latter group, we must separate handicraft (manufactured) products, which are made for immediate retail sale in the local market, from those which are

---

CHECKLIST
Property Relations

What property relations exist at your workplace?
Who owns:
- the plant buildings?
- the power?
- the machines?
- the tools?
- the fuel?
- the primary materials?
- the skills?
- the labour force?
- the work at the end of the day?
- the sales facilities?
- the transport facilities?
- the retail outlets?
- the consumer credit facilities?

---

made for a wholesale trader. (This last category has been called the "cottage industry"). In it are found the merchants. They may also concentrate all their workers into centralized workshops, thus taking advantage of available power sources and reducing the number of hired hands.

Still further variations of industrial organizations exist. Within the usufacture (production for one's own use), labour can be brought into the family on a temporary basis, as in the case of sewing or housework, or on a more permanent basis, as in the case of indentured immigrant workers. In the past, members of a community could rent the local olive, sugar, or cider press or the local baking facilities, and operate them by themselves. Similarly, today one can rent the facilities of a neighbourhood U-fix-it mechanical or welding shop. Or one might bring one's primary materials – cloth or grain, for instance – and have the work done by someone else.

It is easy to understand how each of these social relations creates a different mentality. People who sell only their skills do not worry about machines or materials, nor do they make money the same way as the supplier. Millers, for instance, were always suspected of hoarding some of their clients' flour, just as goldsmiths were suspected of keeping some of their customers' gold. The ring belongs to the wearer, but the gold belongs to the goldsmith, according to the saying. The goldsmith could devise a method of saving the gold and mixing it with other metals without the client being able to notice any difference in the ring.

Retail producers have motivations different from those in wholesale production. In retail production the profits come from sales margins and quality goods; sales are made by the product's reputation with little marketing effort. In wholesale manufacturing, on the other hand, the profits depend on the quantity of products made and the low unit price. Since the producer and buyer do not interact, the producers must consciously plan and execute marketing strategies.

If we narrow our focus even further to how production is organized, it is possible to designate three different types: custom, batch and line. You can choose to produce five items, one after the other, in custom mode; or, you can choose to produce them all at the same time. Similarly, you can choose to produce a few hundred items in large batches or in line production.

Although these production modes do not differ by fixed quantities, they are nonetheless qualitatively different. This difference is most notable in the relationship between the market and production on the one hand, and the organization of work on the other. In a customized production, the English tailor makes a made-to-measure suit according to the client's order. In batch production, a manufacturer produces on order a set of parts and assembles them; and he might make a few extra parts in case there are some that are defective or because he anticipates further demand. The cost of a few extra units is not that great compared to the cost of manufacturing a faulty part over again; also, the opportunity for rapid earnings through the sale of additional units provides him with a further incentive.

Line production requires the manufacturer to predict what the market will be. The mass producer will also try to shape the market by product design and publicity, capture some of it through a preestablished sales network, plan to finance an inventory of components, and invest in specialized production equipment.

CHECKLIST
Production Modes

What type of production system do you work in?
1. Is it a job shop?
    – Do you work to specifications?
    – Do you do custom work or does your production anticipate demand?
    – How many items of a product do you produce at a time?
    – Are these products on order?
    – How often do you set up your equipment for new products?
2. Is it batch production?
    – How large are your batches?
3. Is it line production?
    – Are you working on an assembly line?
    – Is it continuous or semicontinuous?
    – Is the process fluid-flow?

What technical division of labour exists in your plant, office, or store?
How many job categories exist in production?
How many different skills are there?
How many different pay scales exist in the plant?

The technical efforts are quite different in the three systems. In custom and small batch production, the attention will focus on the product's performance. The production cost and the product's price are less important than the item's quality and performance. But in the line production of a standardized good, price, uniformity and reliability will be crucial. The technological demands will thus be very different, depending on whether we are in a single stage or multiple stage process with continuous or intermittent flow.

Understanding the technological demands of the production system depends on your understanding the production mode in the workplace. Here are some questions the worker can ask.

Two-thirds of industrial production units are still in custom or batch production mode. The modern factory and assembly line still remain the exception in industry. Today it is seen as the desirable norm for modern industry both in the United States and the U.S.S.R. It is the only production mode that enables employers to establish a hierarchy of line production. This will of course condition possible technical improvements in the future.

According to J.R. Bright, there are six distinct steps in the mechanization of production lines:

1. Mechanization of manually performed operations.

2. Arrangement of machinery into a production-operation sequence in which all the operations are done at approximately the same rate so that continuous flow can be achieved.

3. Combining of several functions into a single machine base (i.e., a compound machine).

4. Integration of all machines with automatic work feeding, work removal, and material handling devices (between machines) so as to create a work movement system that is nonmanual.

5. Changes in the product design to permit mechanical manipulation, assembly, and other forms of nonmanual working in production operations.

6. Changes in material to permit mechanical manipulation(6).

The Reverse Effect of Technical Systems

Social organizations are a controlling factor that affect the design, choice and diffusion of techniques; technical systems, however, are not just the passive carriers of these social organizations. Technical systems, in their turn, orient social activity in a certain direction. The effect of technical systems on social change is indeed well known. Many researchers have done studies on it.

One of the first such researchers was the American sociologist William Ogburn. In the 1930s he wrote about the transforming effects of technology. Under Franklin Delano Roosevelt, Ogburn's participation on Congressional commissions transformed his personal beliefs into a social creed: technology was the primary force that changed society. Later, as a professor of sociology at Harvard University, Ogburn wrote many textbooks which influenced thousands of students to accept the idea that technology is one of the major instigators of social change (7).

One of Ogburn's most famous case studies was on the radio's social effects. He found no less than 150 direct influences of radio on social life. Probably its most important influence was to greatly accelerate the scope and speed at which ideas were spread. It did so by creating greater homogeneity, although the multiplication of various radio stations, in particular community radio stations, has diluted this homogeneity since Ogburn's time.

Ogburn's analysis, however, is somewhat mechanical and simplistic. He attributes the social effects to the radio itself rather than to the intentions of radio promoters.

The Direct Social Influence of Radio

I. **On Uniformity And Diffusion**

6. Isolated regions are brought in contact with world events...
12. Cultural diffusion among nations, as of United States into Canada and vice versa.

II. **On Recreation And Entertainment**

23. With growth of the reformative idea, more prison installations...
26. Entertainment on trains, ships, and motor-cars...

III. **On Transport**

28. Directional receivers guide to port with speed and safety...
30. Greater safety to aeroplanes in landing. Radio system also devised now for blind landing...

IV. **On Education**

38. Broadcasting has aided adult education...
50. Provision of discussion topics for women's clubs...

V. **On Religion**

66. The urban type of sermon disseminated to rural regions...
69. Churches that broadcast are said to have increased attendance...

VI. **On Industry And Business**

76. Some artists who broadcast demanded for personal appearance in concerts...
81. An important factor in creating a market for new commodities...

VII. **On Occupations**

90. A new provision for dancing instruction...
92. New occupations: announcer, engineer, advertising salesmen...

VIII. **On Government And Politics**

95. Censorship problem raised because of charges of swearing, etc...
117. Campaign promises over radio said to be more binding...

IX.   On Other Inventions

119.   Development stimulated in other fields, as in military aviation...

121.   Television was stimulated by the radio...

X.   Miscellaneous

137.   Growth of suburbs perhaps encourage a little bit...

142.   Additions to language, as "A baby broadcasting all night"...

Extracts taken from W. Ogburn, *Recent Social Trends*, pp. 153-156.

Technical Change as a Social Struggle

Organizations are the outcome of social history, as are techniques. They may appear to be external forces outside the historical realm, but this is an illusion.

All societies are made up of many different classes of people. Each class may prefer one technology over another. Even within a given class, groups may favour different technical options, which they then promote to further their own interests, either against previous production systems, or against the class of people they are trying to subordinate. A social group can also serve its own interests by promoting a technique that organizes the labour of other groups in a particular way, although the result of such an attempt is far from automatic. In general, social groups create industries, trades and cultures; specific groups, organized according to gender, for example, promote specific techniques. Class struggle by means of technical change is easier to illustrate in an historical perspective than by looking at isolated examples.

One of the most famous economic and social historians, Marc Bloch, has vividly shown how technologies were part of the social and economic struggle in the Middle Ages. The period he studied ranged from the end of slavery to the end of the Middle Ages, the triumph of the towns over the feudal lords.

CHECKLIST
Level of Mechanization

Take, for example, your factory. What level of mechanization does it have? Ask yourself the following:

1. What operations are still manual?

2. Is the work on different machines at different work positions done at a coordinated pace to allow a continuous flow?

3. Are there some compound machines combining a few operations?

4. Is the work fed manually or mechanically?

5. Are the product and its components standardized?

The slave-owning societies around the Mediterranean knew about the water mill and the animal harness, but did not need to resort to their use. The availability of slaves acted as a disincentive against the use of animal chattels. It was the feudal lords who turned to these techniques in their struggle against slave owners. They were aided by ex-slaves (serfs), who, understandably enough, wanted to transfer the harness to animals. The lack of a sizable work force made such techniques necessary: animal and water power had to be harnessed to control the land. The water mills and the harness thus were the instruments that helped promote the new social order: feudalism.

In a later stage of feudal society, technical change was likewise the source of conflict between lords and serfs. Peasants used portable hand mills, called querns, to mill their own grain. The lords campaigned to have these mills destroyed so that peasants would be forced to come to their water mills. In this way the lords could control the production and levy their share of flour.

Another conflict developed over the use of tools for cutting wheat. The feudal lords favoured the scythe, which cut the wheat stalk at the base of the plant, providing hay for their livestock. The peasants, on the other hand, preferred the sickle, which cut the wheat at the top of the plant. The village livestock would then come to graze on the commons.

The Sickle and the Scythe

Peasants liked to cut the wheat with a sickle at the top of the stem, bring the grain home and mill it with hand querns, and let the standing hay be used for communal grazing. But the lords preferred that the peasants cut the wheat with scythes at the foot, and bring the grain to their water mills so that the hay would be available for their livestock. The above Stubbs painting gives an example of a technical compromise: peasants use a sickle but cut at the foot — while the landowner watches.

Another source of conflict developed over the rotation of crops. Feudal lords wanted the crops rotated three times a year, thereby enabling the growth of different grains for their livestock.

As these three examples show, one group may promote a tool or a technique in a bid to gain power or to organize the work of others. Few historians who have looked at technical change have followed Bloch's examples, however. There is one exception: David Noble's history of the intellectual and institutional struggle between the promoters of the Numerical Contol machine tool and the Record Playback system. In this case, too, the outcome was the result of a social struggle.

Technical Power

In conclusion, the right to choose a technology is a source of power. Like political and economic power, it enables those who wield it to have influence over other people's lives. In particular, it allows them to choose techniques that will affect the way people interact.

Although technical choices are often made at the same time as investment choices, they do not necessarily have the same effect. With the same million dollars an investor can choose among several several machinery systems. The investor is also not the only person who is involved in choosing new techniques. In liberal democracies, in fact, the right to choose techniques has not been explicitly attributed to anyone. (Technical rights have not been incorporated into our decision-making process.) Producers who use the techniques daily have as much right to participate in the selection as private investors or governments. The final choice of the dominant technical system, then, will have to result from a social agreement. Today, disputes over technical choices are the object of a legal battle, since no one knows who has the right to do what.

The notion that organizations of work can orient technical activity is thus important. The creation of a new form of work organization may reorient the direction of technical change. Radically redirecting technologies is therefore possible.

REFERENCES

1. CHILDE, V. Gordon. (1941) *Man Makes Himself.* London: Watts, p. 52.

2. GILLE, Bertrand. (1978) *Histoire des techniques: technique et civilisations, technique et sciences.* Paris: Gallimard, p.1250

3. ARNOLD, H.L., and FAUROTE, L.F. (1915) *Ford Methods and the Ford Shop.* New York: The Engineering Magazine Company, p.114.

4. KRANZBERG, Melvin, and GIES, Josheph. (1975) *By the Sweat of Thy Brow.* New York: G.P. Putnam's Sons, p.212.

5. GRAS, N.S.B. (1930) *Industrial Evolution.* Cambridge: Harvard University Press.

6. BRIGHT, James R. (1958) *Automation and Management.* Boston: Division of Research, Graduate School of Business Administration, Harvard University.

7. OGBURN, William, and NIMKOFF, M.F. (1947) *A Handbook of Sociology.* Boston: Houghton Mifflin Company.

SUGGESTED READINGS

BLOCH, Marc. (1963) "Comment et pourquoi finit l'esclavage antique," in BLOCH, Marc, *Melanges Historiques* (vol.1), pp.261-285. Paris: S.E.V.P.E.N.

——— . (1963) "Les transformations des techniques comme problème de psychologie collective," in BLOCH, Marc, *Mélanges Historiques* (vol.2), pp.791-799. Paris: S.E.V.P.E.N.

——— . (1963) "Avènement et conquêtes du moulin à eau," in BLOCH, Marc, *Mélanges Historiques* (vol.2), pp.800-821. Paris: S.E.V.P.E.N.

——— . (1963) "Les inventions médiévales," in BLOCH, Marc, *Mélanges Historiques* (vol.2), pp.822-832. Paris: S.E.V.P.E.N.

DEBRESSON, Chris, and LAMPEL, Joseph. (1985) "Beyond the Life Cycle: Organizational and Technological Design." *Journal of Product Innovation Management*, 3, pp.170-195.

CHAPTER 4

THE CASE OF COMPUTERS AND SEMICONDUCTORS

In the 1980s, a microprocessor chip the size of a fingernail can perform operations in a fraction of a second which took minutes to perform in a room full of electronic equipment in the 1950s. In the 1930s the same task took several mathematicians, equipped with desk mechanical calculators, days to execute. The amazing combination of increased speed and miniaturization marks the computer revolution we read so much about today. In many ways, it is similar in magnitude to the transportation revolution that occurred between 1800 and 1920. The latter reduced the time to travel around the globe from one year to a single day.

The scope of the changes marking the computer revolution has made computer chips synonymous with technology. Today when we refer to technological change, we think of computers in one form or another, just as people in the nineteenth century thought of the steam engine as the epitome of technical progress. For those of us working in hospitals, banks or supermarkets, semiconductors have already changed our lives; they are already in the process of leaving their mark on schools and other sectors.

Let us examine briefly the major technical changes involved. Basically they represent the combination of two techniques: computers and semiconductors.

Computers

Calculating machines have existed at least since the seventeenth century, performing addition, subtraction, and multiplication. Some computers, referred to as analog computers, approximate these calculations; digital computers, on the other hand, employ arithmetic and Boolian algebra, using only "yes" or "no" answers and dividing problems into a long sequence of questions. The mode of recording data has gone from punched cards to magnetic disks and electronic support from vacuum tubes and transistors, just as the computing techniques have evolved from being mechanical to electronic. With electronics, the speed allows the user to solve problems sequentially with multiple operations, even though the number of these problems is multiplied by their reduction to binary logic. Standard logical operations are programmed into the memory and later into the hardware itself. Machine-level instructions are initiated by higher-level programming languages. The computer's speed and capacity, of course, depend on its memory, the electronic bits that retain information.

Semiconductors

Some materials conduct electricity; others isolate it. What interests us here is the materials that conduct electricity in one predictable direction only.

EMPLOYMENT BY OCCUPATION

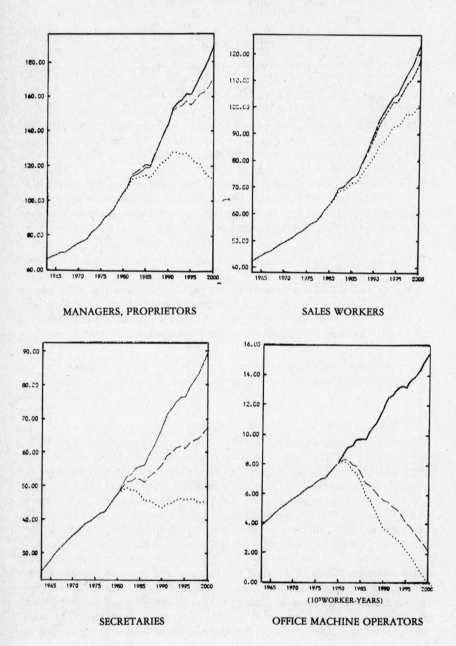

MANAGERS, PROPRIETORS

SALES WORKERS

SECRETARIES

OFFICE MACHINE OPERATORS

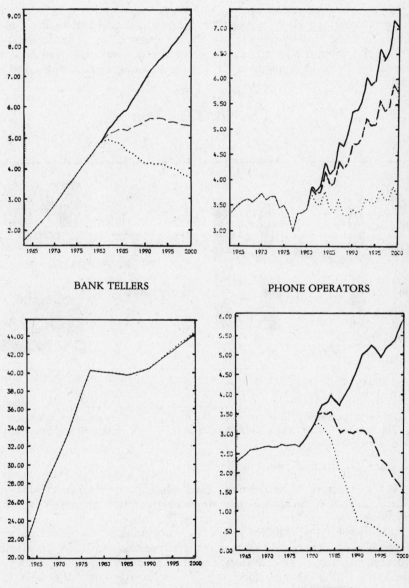

BANK TELLERS

PHONE OPERATORS

TEACHERS

DRAFTERS

These materials, called semiconductors, have atoms which carry electrons under the stimulus of a small charge. For example, an atom of silicon in solid state has four electrons, two of which are shared by two atoms – hence the semiconductor properties of silicon. A transistor is simply a semiconductor device.

By stringing semiconductor devices together, one can simulate simple logical operations. By designing the four basic functions of the computer into the silicon chip (input, output, memory, operations), semiconductors become the hardware for the computers. The two techniques, then, have merged to form microprocessors.

The First Transistor

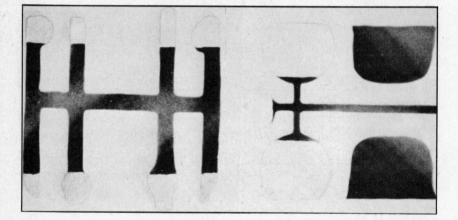

The first transistor of William Schockley in 1951 in an enlarged photograph. The semiconductor device is the basis of today's microelectronic and information technologies.

Impact on Employment and Skills

What impact will these technical changes have on employment and skills? Wassily Leontieff, the Nobel Prize-winning economist from New York University, has attempted to estimate this in **The Impact of Automation on Employment, 1963-2000** (1). Some of the results of his predictions are shown in the following graphs: teachers, draftpersons, secretaries, retail sales workers, office machine operators, bank tellers, phone operators, and even managers will be the most affected by the technology. Like all predictions, however, Leontieff's must be qualified. He makes many assumptions, each with only a certain probability of coming true.

In a way, his predictions underestimate the impact of change because they only consider microprocessors and not the run-of-the-mill technical changes that will occur in various industries because of their own momentum, as well as because of the stimulation of microprocessors. His study also makes assumptions about technical diffusion rates. Some of these are overestimations and some are underestimations, which ignore the jerky stop-and-start aspect of technical diffusion.

Leontieff's method, based on an input-output analysis, earned him the first Nobel Prize ever granted in economics. Its strength is that its forecast is consistent for all industries. The end results, however, are predicated on the assumptions. Without going into the details of input-output economics, it is necessary to nevertheless specify one assumption. Each industry is given a set of "input coefficents": future material feed stocks, labour, machinery, or equipment requirements. They are estimated per dollar of product output. (For instance, for every dollar of paper produced, there may be 50 cents of wood chips, 20 cents of electricity, 20 cents for salary, 5 cents of chemicals and 5 cents for depreciation of equipment. In this case 50 cents would be the wood-chip input coefficient for paper.) These future coefficents are estimated according to the present state of things in the technical literature.

Although this literature is vast and its quality uneven in connection with such issues, Leontieff has only drawn on a small number of sources. For example, he estimates that the use of robots will create technical jobs but will displace six other worker categories. Similarly, he assumes that the Numerical Control machine tools will reduce the need for machine operators and tool and die makers, implying that the machinist's job won't be upgraded to NC specialist. The creation of a new category of work and displacement of other categories, however, depend on negotiation, whose outcome cannot be foreseen.

Interestingly, he also assumes that management functions will diminish. Using an article published in **Business Week**, he suggested that as more top managers realize that much of the information once gathered by middle managers can be obtained faster, less expensively, and more thoroughly by computers, they will conclude that the middle managers are redundant. The same conclusion could be applied to managerial functions in general. Microprocessors could make these functions obsolete by allowing workers control of production, thereby giving them the opportunity to overcome the traditional division of labour. This would allow for a decrease in overhead and the operational costs of manufacturing.

These two examples show that the end results shown in the graphs are inherent in the assumptions which Leontieff makes about the future technical coefficients of these industries. In other words, the predictions about employment and skills in different industries are only as good as the assumptions.

Social action in the near future may determine the final outcome of these technological changes. To effect such change, though, we need a better understanding of how changes have occurred so rapidly in the computer industry. It is difficult to isolate them for an objective scrutiny because they are so recent. In addition, many of the books on computers are written by participants in the field and tend to be quite partial. And since the dissemination of computer technology is still going on, we are all actors in the historical process. There are, however, some factors that are worth our attention.

Some General Characteristics

There are several major factors that are crucial to technical development in general and to computers in particular.

1. Technical knowledge accumulates, building endlessly on past achievements. Since the idea of a digital computer was conceived in the nineteenth century, various components of technical knowledge have combined to make its production possible. Vacuum tubes, Boolian algebra, the use of a card computer for the U.S. census in 1911, the scientific understanding of semiconductor principles in the 1920s – all these elements, and many others, have made computer developments possible.

2. The accumulation of technical knowledge occurs, as one would expect, in the process of working with a technique. Working systematically at a technique means an even greater probability of a chance discovery.

For example, Walter Brattain, the coinventor of transistors at Bell Laboratories along with Walter Brainard, discovered point-contact transition by accident. They were looking for a transistor effect at the surface of semiconductor materials. But it occurred elsewhere as they closely spaced two electrodes on a germanium crystal, an amplificator.

Technological development seemed to progress well at the Bell Laboratories because the researchers were given quite a bit of freedom over their own work. Brattain has in fact stated that Bell Laboratories are proudest of the things that were achieved in spite of management. The greater innovativeness of small companies in transistor technology has been attributed to a similar factor: inventors and development engineers are more in control and don't have to deal with as much red tape as their counterparts elsewhere.

Today production workers, instead of inventors and engineers, still help to determine the reliablity of technological success. Improvements evolve from practice and production. One rule of thumb in the industry is that average costs go down by 20 to 30 percent every time the total accumulated production doubles. Following this rule, Motorola signed a contract with Chrysler to supply silicon rectifiers for automotive alernators for less than half the actual cost. It knew from experience that because of the volume of the order, the cost could go down. Initially Motorola did not cover its costs, but production techniques improved as the order was being filled, enabling the company to make money on the contract.

In the early stages of transistors, the increase in productivity was due to on-the-job experience and very unsophisticated methods. Women would make transistors with tweezers and manipulate components under microscopes. The manufacturing problems were so numerous and severe that there seemed to be a mythical element to success or failure.

The makers of transistors often relied on their intuitive knowledge to improve the end product. Making good transistors seemed to depend on the individual disposition of the material. In particular, there seemed to be a recurrent cause for failure: makers called it "deathium" for a long time, not realizing what this material really was. It turned out to be copper.

There are recurrent patterns that one can discern regardless of which technique one is discussing. These are listed below, along with a relevant example drawn from computers.

3. A technical dead end or stalemate in one technique helps focus the search for a solution using another technique. For example, vacuum tubes, also called valves, which were developed for light bulbs, were uses as amplifiers for high frequencies and energy before transistors came along. But they were large, bulky, expensive and fragile; they would also burn out easily and needed to be heated to start working. Such problems provoked research on semiconductors.

4. The parallel development of two similar technologies occurs frequently. Computers were developed first with punch cards, then with vacuum tubes and shortly afterward, with transistors. Germanium and silicon semiconductors were worked on more or less at the same time. Once the technical function is identified, techniques develop in tandem until it is determined which applications are best served by which technique. The parallel use continues even after the predominance of one form has been established.

5. Concentration on one avenue may retard progress in another. The use of germanium as a semiconductor material retarded the use of a cheaper substance, silicon, which was more abundant; the use of silicon in turn has retarded the use of gallium arsenide, a superior semiconductor. However, this doesn't mean that parallel routes aren't tried.

6. Discoveries often occur simultaneously. Just as Newton and Leibnitz developed calculus at the same time, Descartes and Fermat fused Greek geometry and algebra into analytical geometry. And Atanasoff, employed at Iowa State University, and Mauchly, at the University of Pennsylvania, were more or less contemporaries in conceiving the idea of a digital computer based on vacuum tubes, while Konrad Zuse developed a computer in Germany for the air force. Similarly, Brainerd, while employed at Bell Laboratories, heard his colleagues, Bray and Bergen, from Purdue University describe an experiment to the American Physical Society in 1948 which had led him a month earlier to discover point-contact transition. When all the components are present, and an identified need motivates the effort, it is only a queston of time before an invention is made. Because the transistor was an idea whose time had come, 25 organizations could have made the discovery in the United States, England, France or the Netherlands.

7. Technical breakthroughs occur through trial and error. In 1939, Schockley and Brattain tried copper oxide to develop a transistor, while other scientists tried silicon and still others, germanium. Eventually breakthroughs were made.

8. Incremental improvements in a technique enable new users to adopt it. Because the transistor had a higher tolerance to heat, and was smaller and consumed less energy, it served as a substitute for vacuum valves in most operations.

More applications of a technique become possible as the technique is improved. Initially, transistors were used only for hearing aids; computers, for ballistic purposes. Now their uses are countless.

9. Variations of a technique are adapted to different jobs. Between 1956 and 1962, 6,000 types of transistors were made available. Three quarters of these are still available.

10. Invention often occurs through cumulative synthesis. Third-generation transistors and the logic of computers were merged into circuited memory, so that the hardware performed the standard logical operations. Thus, in 1969, Buscom of Japan and Intel, an offshoot of Fairchild in the United States, developed the microprocessor – a chip which performed the computer's four functions.

11. Various techniques combine into systems. Semiconductors, software, magnetic tapes, and video display systems make up the information system – one that is comprised of several interdependent technologies.

12. Resistance to a new technique is partly due to habit. Electronic engineers in the 1940s and 1950s had been trained in valve technology rather than in the solid state physics world of transistors. They expected canned, hermetically sealed devices, not the rough materials of semiconductors.

13. The new technique must adapt to the old. Just as the steam engine worked alongside the waterwheel, the first contract for a commercial computer by the Prudential Insurance Company had to accommodate the IBM punch card system which Prudential was then using.

In subsequent chapters, we will analyze some of these factors in greater depth.

REFERENCES

1. LEONTIEFF, Wassily, and DUCHIN, Faye. (1984) *The Impact of Automation on Employment, 1963-2000*. New York: Institute for Economic Analysis.

SUGGESTED READINGS

BRAUN, Ernest, and MACDONALD, Stuart. (1978) *Revolution in Miniature: The History and Impact of Semiconductor Electronics*. New York: Cambridge University Press.

II
EVOLUTIONARY
CONSTRAINTS

The next eight chapters will look at all the nontechnical factors that help to explain why techniques in general evolve – the role played by economics, politics, and science, as well as other factors. These different factors act as evolutionary constraints on technical change. In evolution, the analyst must start by explaining what cannot exist in order to limit the scope of the possible. Negative constraints can be technical, economic or political. They all exclude some technical options.

Once the field of technical possibilities is explained, the historian is still left to ponder why one option was chosen as opposed to others.

CHAPTER 5

LEARNING BY WORKING*

The primary factor leading to technical change is the assimilation of a technique on the part of workers. No change can be implemented without their intelligent consent. Thus working people are the go-betweens who mediate all the formal knowledge – in scientific and technological information – necessary for production. Workers select only the information they need in production. In so doing, they help raise the overall productivity. As they gain more experience, they also substantially increase their own productivity, without incurring additional costs.

In this sense, working experience offers a primary source of innovative ideas. Job skills are acquired by on-the-job problem solving and by the oral exchange of ideas and solutions gained through generations of experienced workers. Working knowledge differs from the formalized literate knowledge of engineers and managers; whereas workers probably can learn their managers' formal knowledge, it is questionable if the reverse can happen.

Applying New Techniques

The first constraint of technical change is obvious: a technique must be implemented before it can become a reality. Production workers make the decision whether to apply the new technique or not. If they choose to assimilate and master the new technique, they will no doubt modify it. All techniques require some fine tuning. In this process of practical application, whoever is involved in the work process ends up perfecting the new technique.

The validity of this theory becomes obvious whenever workers decide to no longer support a particular application. In cases of work slowdowns, for example, workers withdraw their consent and adhere to the formal rules, with the result that the process breaks down.

Positive scenarios, on the other hand, make more interesting case studies. But there have been few studies about how technological know-how is assimilated and transformed through workers' experience. Perhaps this is because analysts tend to focus primarily on relations between people and machines rather than on groups interacting with one another and with the natural world. Yet the social aspect of work probably plays a greater role in determining the evolution of a technology than do purely technical factors. Some researchers who have worked in industry – notably Donald Roy, Michael Burawoy, Ken Kusterer, Joe Townsend and James Petersen – have highlighted this point.

---

*Much of the text for this chapter was generated by James Petersen. Some of it appears in "More News from Nowhere: Utopian Notes from Hamilton Machine Shops" in Labour/Le Travailleur, in press, and in his thesis on gold mining in Canada (1, 2).

Despite the fact that Marx saw work as the basic historical act and fundamental condition of all history, his followers have paid more attention to the ideas of managers and capitalists than to the working process itself. Braverman, for instance, uses mostly management sources in his conclusions to **Labour and Monopoly Capital: The Degradation of Work in the 20th Century** (3). He says that all working skills have been taken away from the work force, as management intended. This is surely not the case; and in our view, his conclusion represents a manager's impossible fantasy.

It should be obvious that modern industry would not operate unless labourers agreed to participate; they must be willing to learn improved methods and processes. Employers buy more than raw manpower when they pay wages; they also purchase the good judgment of labourers, which makes the labour power worthwhile. The system would grind to a halt if workers withdrew their judgment. One of the best indicators of the degree to which workers consent to an industrial system is the extent to which they give employers the benefit of their good judgment.

The importance of such judgment has been noted by Eugen Kogon in **Der SS Staat** written in 1947 (4). Summarizing the labour experience in Nazi slave camps during World War II, Kogon wrote that prisoners in SS-operated factories carried out a simple but effective programme of passive resistance. (What else could they have done when they could have been shot for the slightest infringement of rules?) The prisoners withdrew their judgment, reducing production as much as 80 percent. In 1982, Polish Solidarity recommended a similar "stupid" passive resistance to General Jaruzelski's martial law. Solidarity supporters obeyed all instructions to the letter. The problem was that these instructions, issued by bureaucrats who had never worked themselves, were absurd.

Labour relations in North America seldom sink that low, however. Michael Burawoy, a British industrial sociologist now teaching in the United States, made an important study of a machine shop in Peoria, Illinois, during the midseventies. His study is noteworthy because he actually worked in the shop as a machine operator for ten months. Coincidentally, by a quirk of fate, he chose to examine the very same shop a fellow sociologist, Donold Roy, had studied thirty years earlier.

In **Manufacturing Consent,** Burawoy argues that the North American labour force is induced to participate in a consenting relationship with management by means of a set of gamelike interpersonal moves that regulate labour-management relations (5). This is the only reason why it is improper to speak of the "rape of labour by capital." Management seduces workers into applying their judgment to their work in order to "make out," or win incentive points. The stakes are dollars. But the game is far more complex. A worker can opt out of playing the game by deliberately not making bonuses when wages are unfair.

Burawoy also stresses the importance of basic rules agreed to by both labour and management. These are not the official company rules distributed to employees so they may learn which ones they can break with impunity. The real rules are not written down; often they are not even consciously expressed. Since employers consider it essential that the game end in profit, they accept any rules that bring about this result. The game's value lies in its capacity to engage the workers' intellect so they will learn their work, master it and even improve on it without feeling exploited. In fact, it should even be possible for them to win the game sometimes. It breaks down when they cannot; they then feel cheated, as they chronically do.

In Canada this feeling of being "had" is often dissipated by strikes. Although strike action is occasionally useful in changing working conditions and creating more class solidarity, one must admit that workers often strike just to let off steam. They seldom succeed in reaching major improvements by strikes.

Boredom figures highly in industrial work games. Workers sometimes complain to one another when a job is too easy, even if they can make good incentive payments by doing it. The most interesting game occurs when it is doubtful whether an operator can "make out." Thus it seems that both workers and owners enjoy being on the frontiers of applying a new technique, especially when big gains as well as big losses are possible. Whenever the uncertainty is too great, though, both workers and investors withdraw support.

On-the-Job Knowledge

The learning strategies people use on their jobs ultimately determine what they will assimilate. They learn only those things that exert a practical effect on the specific tasks they must do. Their knowledge can be divided into three parts: the coded information given in formal, on-the-job training sessions, the informal knowledge passed on by coworkers, and the knowledge they acquire by experience in overcoming job problems.

Obviously there is a strong element of randomness to a person's working knowledge, because the range of problems that come up during work are unique. Problem solving is the principal source of valid working knowledge. In this respect both trades and production workers are equal, since both groups acquire problem-solving skills on the job. However tradespeople also possess a "literate," formal knowledge with which they can access technical literature. The relative weight of literate knowledge distinguishes the tradesperson from the production worker. At this stage let us simply note that literate knowledge is unrelated to most on-the-job learning.

The American sociologist Ken Kusterer, who was first a printer, examined the working knowledge of production workers. He began by studying the sociology of science and then Thomas Kuhn's philosophy of science. He concluded that the knowledge of skilled trades, like printing, is organized in the same manner as scientific knowledge. His conclusion may surprise us, because people commonly assume that science produces a higher form of knowledge radically different from that of the working world. Conversations with many friends who held "unskilled" jobs led Kusterer to the further hunch that knowledge paradigms exist for every job, not just for those of scientists and skilled workers. (Thomas Kuhn loosely defines a paradigm as a pattern of relevant scientific questions introduced by certain schools of thought. After Copernicus, for example, the paradigm, or set of scientific questions about stars and planets, shifted, since the earth was no longer considered the centre of the universe, as in Ptolemy's astronomy.) Kusterer claimed that analagous paradigms, or sets of relevant problems, evolve from working situations.

In his study, entitled **Know-how on the Job,** Kusterer highlights the operation of making paper cones in a large New England factory (6). About a thousand women perform this semiskilled work in the factory's lowest paid department. A team of 33 tradesmen and one woman trainee back them up and service other departments as well. All the socially recognized skills in a shop of approximately one thousand workers are thus concentrated in the hands of fewer than 50 people, which inevitably reduces labour costs.

The cone machine works as follows: operators "tend" the machine by keeping its critical surfaces clean, do basic troubleshooting when the machine acts up, perform quality checks on cones, pack them into boxes and cases, and label cases with a number to identify the machine that produced it.

The formal troubleshooting procedure is simple. Either the machine starts to produce defective cones or it gets jammed, stopping production entirely. In the first instance the operator must shut down the machine, then clean it to see if that helps. In the second case the operator must call a mechanic or ink-man. No operator is ever supposed to try to repair a machine; a hierarchy of mechanics will help the operator whenever serious mechanical trouble occurs.

But the rule barring operators from doing mechanical work exists only on paper, since the department could not maintain production if it were obeyed. This is an example, then, of an informal transfer of technical responsibility. The company first formally removes a responsibility from operators, then turns a blind eye when workers are forced to assume it. (The company, of course, does not increase the operators' wages.) Such a procedure is necessary because many mechanical problems of a production machine are idiosyncratic, that is, peculiar to that one machine. Thus the most efficient place to store information about a specific machine is with the operator who has seen it work and act up.

A common form of this informal mechanical knowledge involves the "redialling" or recalibration of machines. High-speed machinery breaks down quickly, even with proper treatment. Once this happens, the dials that tell an operator how to set the adjustments become useless. If a mechanic were called in each time to recalibrate the machine he would have trouble; but an operator who is always tinkering with it can use scratches, pen marks or fingernail polish. Felt-tip markers have wrought a revolution in the business of recalibrating. Other machine settings require wrenches, screwdrivers or allan keys, which most operators have illegally stashed away, ready at hand. If something unadjustable needs fixing, then a hammer may do the trick, or an iron bar, or a piece of pipe. In short, informal repair technology is condoned, even encouraged, by mechanics because it makes their work easier.

A discussion of all the tasks performed by an operator in the cone department is beyond the scope of this book. Readers who remain unconvinced that operating production machinery is a complex job are well advised to read Kusterer's text. One point bears stressing, however. The information that is obtained, assimilated and applied by production workers is absolutely essential to the efficient functioning of every industrial plant in the modern world. No industrial system could function without it.

The Shadow World of Paper Production

Most managers and engineers explicitly downplay the contribution made by production workers, but they rely on it nevertheless. Engineers reduce the work process to "ideal elements," which Braverman has called the "parallel activities" carried out by management. In other words, the manager controls production by having everything done twice, first on paper by engineers, and then again in reality by the production workers. Today the actual physical labour cannot proceed without first being described on paper. Herein lies the key to understanding how managers put cultural limitations on the evolution of technology. Most of the time a technical process cannot be adopted until the paper shufflers have defined it, which makes production control difficult. Managers, however, are willing to tolerate a technical irrationality to maintain their control and prerogatives.

Production engineers, who have an eye for the effective use of other people's labour, possess their own formalized knowledge, as the following story illustrates. According to Petersen, if an operator runs into a snag he tells his foreman, who then telephones the engineers. (Notice that the foreman is reduced to acting as a middleman between the real, working world and the engineers' paper world.) Eventually someone, usually a stylishly dressed engineer, drifts into the shop and makes the problem part of a bureaucratic game. Meanwhile, the operator sits idly by; this period of repose is probably why the operator reported the problem in the first place.

After a decision is reached and work resumes, the engineer will describe what happened, in theory, like this: "I put this part on the machine and used this tool, and this feed, and this speed. The metal came off like butter, and I took it off the machine ...." When operators overhear this they think engineers are crazy because they themselves actually do the work. The real world never functions according to engineers' simulations. However, their version is the one that counts for management.

The paper world acknowledges the contribution of labour negatively, looking for errors. Workers, on the other hand, consider the paper world as a source of irrelevant information. Both sides ignore the supervisory link.

Labourers cope with a million and one irrationalities in a crazy work environment by tuning out. They restrict their attention to what they must do, joining clubs that offer them social control. Jim Petersen reported the attitude of one coworker who told him, "I'll just pretend they (the managers) are not there. They're like a brick wall. You don't talk to it. If it's in the way you go around " (1).

Some tension between workers and management can be relieved by a tacit agreement not to interact. Workers cannot ignore their work, however, even if they do succeed in ignoring management. The peculiar nature of manual labour derives from the fact that it is the principal sphere of interaction with the material world. Manual work is thus less malleable than work in the paper world, where an eraser can be the final arbiter. Manual workers are locked into a work place in a way that those who work with papers are not. Paper can be shuffled aside, but a piece of hardware must be put to work.

When engineers think that conceptual work and dealings with the material world are the same, the difference of their understanding of reality with that of workers becomes obvious. An innovation designed by the paper world without the mediation of workers and users is often of little use. The Model T Ford, which, fortunately, benefited from worker input, exemplified "user friendliness." In other words, its owner or another mechanic could tune and maintain it easily; the Model T was made to be worked on. But owners of some automobiles, such as Chevrolet V6's of the 1950s, induced maintenance headaches: drivers had to jack up their cars and remove both front tires and lift the motor block to get to the spark plugs. Owners of the Ford Mustang V8 had to chain hoist the motor in order to get clearance for applying a wrench to the spark plugs. All these car owners paid through the nose for tuneups and repairs; they were forced to go to garages, or worse, pay higher costs at dealerships. Despite their user-friendly label, these cars were not made to be worked on. Clearly, their design engineers conceived them without mechanics or users in mind.

Time and Motion Studies

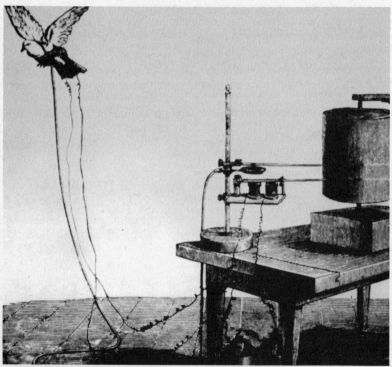

(From E.J. Marey, *La Machine Animale*, 1874: a bird transmitting the movement of its wings by an electro-mimetic signal to a myograph.) In the nineteenth century, experimental physiologists and psychologists started to study the movements of living creatures with the help of electrical devices and photography. This knowledge was then applied to human beings to divide up their work into simple homogeneous movements and measure the seconds required to perform each job so that workers would not waste any time.

Misconceptions often occur when the user's input is ignored. Ideally engineers should be forced to use whatever gadgets they conceive, but even then their products might not be user friendly. The ultimate users must thus be brought into the picture right from the start, since "one is never so well served as by oneself." Successful innovation demands interaction between supplier and user. For instance, if more female cooks were to design kitchens, these rooms might contain more counter space, and be easier to work in and clean.

In the work place, however, production workers are the first users. They make new processes workable by mediating between their design and application. Although engineers often see certain factors as "constraints" or "nonadjustable variables," practical workers transform them into "adjustable variables." Thus the workers' collective knowledge makes a company succeed in spite of itself.

How the Paper World Interacts with the Production World

In the study referred to earlier, Kusterer relates the following story to illustrate how harmony and mutual satisfaction were achieved in the factory where he worked. A welder in the radiator shop, paid by the piece on mostly short runs, served as the union's shop committeeman – he was in no sense a "company man." Time-study men were constantly arriving on the floor to figure out the necessary time to perform a job in order to determine the pay rate in advance. The welder developed an accommodating pattern of behaviour.

The welder had analyzed management behaviour. "We get along all right," he reported. "See, what they like about me is that I give them a good time. They always say, 'Jimmy, you gave us a good time'."

"What's a 'good time'?" Kusterer asked him.

"Even, like. That's what they need. Steady, so each job will take the same time. See, they come to me; they've only got to try it a couple of times, because I give them the same readings every time. That's the way they have to have it – so it's consistent," the welder replied (6).

Trained to believe that reliability indicates validity, the engineers reckoned they had obtained an accurate timing for a job if their readings showed the same results over and over. They could thus finish their timing job quickly, giving their superiors data to show that they had in fact developed a "good" rate. Understanding this, the welder met their demands without sacrificing his own working conditions. He simply developed his own internal timing mechanism, working at a steady, consistent speed. Like other workers in the same situation, he adopted different procedures during the timing session from those he regularly used to carry out production. Following all the approved methods and safety precautions to the letter, he appeared to work hard and relatively fast when being timed. Nevertheless he ended up working for a longer period than what he ordinarily needed when he used the common short-cuts in actual production.

The welder overcame the "natural" contradictions induced by the division of labour. Using his knowledge of the time-study engineers, he manipulated them without conflict and achieved his goal: a comfortable piece rate.

In Efficiency and the Fix Donald Roy has offered yet another example of how workers adjusted to their managers' guidelines in the same shop thirty years earlier (7). Periodically managers forbade workers from taking tools, jigs and fixtures out of the tool room before a job was issued. They demanded that tools be returned after use; that only the tool-crib man – not the set-up man – could go into the tool room; that triplicate forms be filled out, and so forth. Consequently, different departments of workers all decided to disobey these rules, with efficiency and logic; their cooperation was called the "fix." The fix also helped workers to "chisel time."

Consent in applying a technology is neither straightforward nor simple. If workers were to obey certain orders to the letter, nothing would get done. Intelligent consent requires both technical and social skills, in addition to judgment. Obtaining an informal consensus among workers keeps the system running smoothly.

In the following example, Jim Petersen relates how the work force in a Hamilton machine shop instituted its own informal pattern of job sequencing. It had alternative objectives and values. According to Petersen,

> The labour force picked up some elements of control that fell from the foreman's table and incorporated them into its working knowledge paradigm. Some control elements were acquired through game behaviour. The operators studied the scheduling system because it was an important element in the game of "making out." In shop C, where job cards were put on display boards at the beginning of a shift, operators quickly learned to shuffle the deck. They took responsibility for grouping and scheduling their work. Although this task could be easily and efficiently handled, it seldom was. In the Hamilton machine shop, scheduling was done mostly by a subforeman who put up the cards according to machine. In theory, the workers would take the cards as they received them. In actual practice, the operators often "jumped the board," passing over the jobs they disliked or taking the better paying jobs instead. Thus the scheduler, who was nominally in control of the job sequence, was reduced to being a clerk who distributed job cards. The foreman, who depended somewhat on the former, suffered a corresponding loss of control. The operators, on the other hand, exercised a surprising amount of constructive control over scheduling.

> An efficient production scheduler must realistically assess how long a given process will require. Unfortunately,the scheduler often falls victim to the heroic fantasies of the planning department, which is out to rob the operators of their bonuses if possible. The scheduling man at shop C once calculated the time needed to finish a large order of fish plates at 600-unit minutes per day. He decided that he could just squeeze them in ahead of an order of escalator sprockets desperately needed somewhere else. Had he succeeded, it would have rounded out production figures nicely for the week, but he did not know that the two operators seldom produced more than 400 to 450 minutes per day on plates. He would have known this fact had he noted down the actual production figures rather than ideal ones. The plates were simply too heavy to make a faster pace comfortable.

Consequently the time allotted for the job was about 20 percent short, and the sprockets, the last job on the line, collected dust and grease in front of the plate-producing machines. The scheduler complained, becoming belligerent when the operators told him they were unwilling to work any faster. The operators had withdrawn their consent and decided to take more time for the job, a strategy that is called "going in the hole" (1).

Going in the hole is used by operators to counter the deflated price strategy of the time-study man. As a result, both planners and schedulers are consistently behind schedule, even though their papers say they should be well ahead. Neither has the power to change anything, because their power has been stripped from them and transferred to a centralized corporate office in New Jersey or elsewhere. Thus they rationalize, saying that operators are inept or don't work hard enough – the old argument that "you can't get good help any more."

The operators, on their part, cannot understand why planners and schedulers are so stupid; they ask, "Why don't they pay attention to what is really happening?" Operators often intervene constructively by rescheduling their work intelligently. Of course their rescheduling is always done with enlightened self-interest in mind.

An experienced operator groups his work by carefully studying the board first thing every day. Here is Petersen's account:

> I often saw Bill, the man who broke me in on the vertical mill, standing in front of the job board staring out into space. In fact he was doing the planning department's work in his head without the aid of even a scrap of paper, let alone a computer. After scanning the cards he knew all the jobs by heart. He would take a handful of cards from the board and order them according to the setups required. All jobs needing a standard vise were sorted out, followed by jobs requiring a vise or a fixture, and so on. Two jobs using the same tool would be grouped together. In this way he made significant savings on setup and tool-changing times. This "grouping" operation was something no planner or scheduler could do (1).

Operators often smooth out scheduling inconsistencies when they can, but there are many times when they cannot intervene. Jobs are sometimes assigned to the wrong machine on the assumption that all machines of the same class are interchangeable. A further explanation by Petersen illustrates this fact:

> My good friend Larry worked on a small engine lathe in shop C, doing a job that required putting six inches of thread on a stainless steel rod with a threading device called a "chaser," because it pulls itself down the rod in much the same way a hand thread-cutting die moves down the work as it is turned. The chaser attachment is held by the tail stock, which can be moved in as the thread is being cut; but the tail stock on Larry's machine had only five inches of travel, something the scheduling man did not know when he asked for six. Larry did not feel like arguing about the scheduling, so he reverted to a "going-in-the hole strategy." He simply did the job the best he

could, knowing he could not meet the expected time. He let the tail stock feed out to its full five inches, after which the pressure on the chasers caused them to disengage automatically. Then he loosened the tail stock, slid it forward, and finished the thread. This method was exorbitantly expensive, but there seemed no alternatives. The fault lay in the scheduling, although it appeared on paper to be due to the operator's lack of skill.

Going in the hole gives an operator time to visit with friends. Larry discussed the problem with his friend Tom, also a lathe operator. Since they were both members of the informal coffee club, they often discussed job problems. Tom eventually announced his simple solution to his assembled friends: all Larry had to do was loosen the tail stock and let the chasers pull the entire tail stock along the way until they reached a predetermined point marked by a grease pencil mark. Then he had only to tighten the bolts on the tail stock; the chasers would complete their cut, disengaging automatically. Thus a going-in-the-hole-job was transformed into a 'gravy job,' and Larry even managed to wrangle an extra allowance out of the foreman on the grounds that it was impossible to do his job in the allotted time (1).

Sweat Shops and Supervisors

The supervisor, or foreman, standing up with the protruding jaw, oversees the workers and feeds them work.

In the last case it was impractical to change the job scheduling; instead, the combined ingenuity of the operator and his friend helped them bypass the machine's technical barriers and bring actual production time into line with the manager's paper time. Of course the company paid extra for this service.

We see that the informal technology of working knowledge is a vital aspect of production in our modern incentive system. But the planning and decision-making tasks that workers assume are inaccessible to those on the outside.

After a certain number of control factors are in the hands of the work force, their working knowledge becomes the only operational form of knowledge in the shop. Errors and inconsistencies accumulate in the engineers' plans as operators invent bypass procedures. More and more, planning and engineering departments work according to a model that is increasingly different from the realities of shop practice. This leads to shop crises such as penalties for late deliveries, sudden surges in defective parts, unexpectedly higher operating costs, and massive recalls in the automobile industry.

Donald Roy has established that incentive workers do not simply work to maximize their incomes (8, 9). Their response differs from that of the typical businessman. Roy set out to study the "goldbricking" of his colleagues, who withheld production in their shop even when they could make more money by working harder. In the minds of management, goldbricking was a strategy workers used to foul up production schedules. After six months Roy realized that making a full bonus was just a strategy in the workers' incentive game, and he soon began to use some nonproductive strategies himself. To his co-workers, money was not necessarily the ultimate goal. Fairness and job control were also important goals for them.

Production workers, furthermore, are not conditioned to hold the same money values as most businessmen. Fairness, on the other hand, is an important issue to them. Fairness is determined by a collective sense of how much work should be done in exchange for a given amount of money. A gravy job pays better than a fair wage; the usual strategy on a gravy job is to work as fast as possible and "bank" the time. Banking means to turn in only a portion of the work done on the day it is performed, saving the rest for later. Thus an incentive worker can cover up time lost on a job that pays less than a fair time. In Roy's day, management devoted a great deal of energy trying to keep the workers from banking time.

"Gravy," on the other hand, is an example of time that is regulated by an informal organization. The term refers to jobs which are so badly timed that an operator can actually make a bonus from them. Operators usually squeeze the last ounce of gravy out of these jobs to cover all the "garbage jobs" they must do. In other words, most operators run off gravy jobs as fast as possible, bank the time, and use it to cover time lost on jobs with impossible time requirements. Most job times are unrealistic, but floor supervisors usually manage to save some jobs from the time-study men, doling them out so that each machine routinely gets one or two a month.

Productivity Increases and Learning by Doing

The world's economy went into neutral in the thirties. Some firms, among them American auto manufacturers, undertook extensive technological changes, but others coasted along. One of the latter was the Horndall Steel Mill in Sweden, where nothing changed for almost 20 years (1932-52). Nevertheless, it produced steel continuously throughout this period. Absolutely no changes were made to the plant or equipment; yet strange to say, the output increased steadily at two percent a year. Economists during the 1950s were amazed. Finally they realized that the explanation lay with the labour force: it was becoming a little more efficient every year. In other words, the workers constantly learned little tricks and dodges that helped them work faster. The cumulative effect of their learning process was a long, slow but steady reduction in the time needed to make steel. This learning was as much a new technology as a new rolling mill or blast furnace was.

Graph 5 shows that the increase in production, or output, at the Horndall Mill exhibited the characteristics of what economists call a "learning curve." This curve falls off sharply at first and then flattens out to an almost straight line. The Horndall Mill was operating way down the curve where the change rate was very slight, but it was still measurable.

CHECKLIST
Checking Your On-the-Job Knowledge

The following checklist is designed to help you focus on how you acquired working knowledge, in formal instruction classes or through informal experience.

1. How did you learn the techniques you now use?

2. Were you given any formal instruction? If so, for how many hours?

3. Do you apply all the formal procedures suggested by management?

4. Do you use the manufacturer's manual? What formal instructions do you not follow? Can you efficiently follow all the formal instructions?

5. Do you remember how you acquired the basic procedures for working on the new equipment? What did you first concentrate on? When did you stop relying on the formal instructions?

6. How do you deal with the boring aspect of your work?

7. What are the main recurring problems at your work station? How have you solved them? Did you solve them according to formal rules?

8. How do you adjust to the formal rules – by avoiding them, acknowledging them, or by implementing them?

9. Has it ever happened that you solved problems created by management? If so, did you do so alone, with coworkers in your section, or with workers from several departments? Did lower- or high-level management have to recognize that it had created the problem and that you solved it?

10. Are there informal conventions, or rules, among the workers that make your place run? If so, what are they? What would happen if these informal worker-initiated rules ran the place?

After noting the Horndall case, economists discovered other industrial learning curves. In 1936 an engineer named T. P. Wright wrote about the factors affecting the cost of airplanes; he reported an unusual fall in the cost of aluminium frames which could not be explained by changes in equipment. He, too, concluded that the cost reduction had to be linked to the workers' growing familiarity with their jobs. In this case, however, the fall in costs was very steep because aircraft production was a new industry that was operating near the top of its learning curve (see Graph 5).

The learning curve results from several factors, such as the more intelligent use of the machinery, minor alterations of machinery, modifications of work procedures, the substitution of one material for another, and other incremental changes.

Kenneth Arrow, an economist, was awarded the Nobel Prize in Economics partly because of a well-known article highlighting this phenomenon, entitled "The Economic Implications of Learning by Doing "(10). Echoing what production workers know through common sense and practice, Arrow stated that learning is a product of experience. Learning can only take place through the attempt to solve a problem. It therefore takes place during activity. He then advanced the hypothesis that technical change in general can be ascribed to experience, that is, the very activity of production which gives rise to problems for which favourable responses are selected over time (10).

Many other economists have since seen that learning by doing and learning by using favour the growth of productivity. In particular this type of learning is the product of the time spent in production more than the absolute quantities produced.

Graph 5.1
Learning Curve

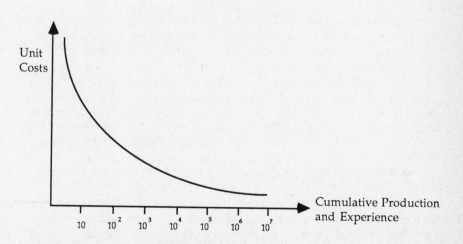

A learning curve: as the total cumulative production increases, the experience of the workforce also increases. Ways to save materials and energy and reduce down-time are found, thus increasing productivity.

But learning curves are disembodied, mathematical abstractions that are valued because they help in planning. Consulting firms such as the Boston Consulting Group have made both a name and a fortune by analyzing and applying them.

An interesting, logical consequence of the learning-curve theory is that the benefits of a curve accrue to the firm that controls the largest share of a market. This happens because learning results directly from the number of units produced, or what is called the **cumulative output** over time. The firm with the greatest market share obviously has made the most units; it thus progresses further down the learning curve than its rivals do. Operating with a lower cost structure, it makes more money too.

This theory is significant for the labour movement because it offers insight into the way management profits by orchestrating the worker's learning process. It does this by reducing the number of elements an individual learns to an absolute minimum. The repetition of the same task by manual workers has indeed led to spectacular successes by some giant firms during the last 80 years. But managers have never probed too deeply into the learning mechanisms of working people. Up to now they have treated labour like a natural resource, like timber to be harvested without thought for the future. Just recently, under pressure from Japanese industry, North American managers have begun to look seriously at the intelligence of the labour force as a production factor. It is open to question whether they will ever proceed very far in changing their attitude.

Henry Ford and Rouge River University

Long before learning curves were discovered, Henry Ford built a flourishing business based on their exploitation. It is important to recognize Ford's understanding of the existence of working knowledge, because most historians who specialize in technology attribute his success to innovative assembly-line procedures. What Ford really did was harness his workers' ability to generate highly efficient speed-skills in short periods of time, namely, when their attention was confined to a small number of operations. If Ford's assembly line was really an innovation, it was an innovation in social engineering, an unpleasant one at that.

The Model T Ford is a classic case of learning curves in the field of technological change. It is a more realistic model than that represented by the Horndall Steel Mill. Between 1909 and 1923 the Ford Motor Company produced only one Model T. Thus the Ford labour force made the same parts and built the same vehicle for 14 years. At the same time the car's prices in constant dollars fell from $5,000 to $900, while wages increased 300 percent. This proves that the work force can sometimes profit from a learning curve even when it exercises no official control over it.

The sharpest price decline occurred early, between 1909 and 1912, when, according to business historian W. J. Abernathy, Ford tapped the "innovative powers of the work force" (11). Much of the innovation must have consisted of the informal hammer and screwdriver type of changes. Machine operators probably made the jigs and fixtures suggested to them after producing certain parts for a long time. In time, these jigs and fixtures were probably pirated by company engineers. In 1915 Ford Motor formalized its dependence on / worker innovation by instituting a profit-sharing system.

Ford's lack of a firm base in patented invention made him more dependent on his labour force than a company with a solid technological monopoly. Thus he introduced some slick managerial subtleties. In 1914 he allied himself with John R. Lee, an industrial reformer; they agreed to make the Ford plant a model factory for industrial relations. Lee set up Ford's so-called Sociological Department.

One of Ford's biggest problems was the labour turnover. He needed a constant supply of 13,000 to 14,000 workers, yet went through 50,000 a year. Their cumulative experience was slipping through his fingers, costing him a reduction in profit.

The high turnover rate had several causes. Auto workers were hired and fired in the same way construction workers and longshoremen are now. Whenever Ford workers slowed down, made mistakes, or somehow vexed their foremen, they were fired. This alone accounted for the high turnover. By 1932 an estimated half of Detroit's male working population either worked for Ford or had done so in the past. Other reasons for the turnover included fatigue, alcoholism, indebtedness, malnutrition and simple alienation. As a result, Ford lost millions of hours of productivity increases based on working knowledge.

Lee decided to tackle the problem at its apparent source, the frustration and feelings of entrapment that inevitably accumulate after long hours of overspecialized, repetitive work. Lee's assessment was an early version of the attitudinal approach which is still popular today.

John Lee's Sociology Department proposed its famous $5.00 day. With characteristic cynicism, the Ford Motor Company tried to soothe the festering sore of industrial anaemia with the balm of greenbacks. It worked. In 1914 only 2,000 workers left. As the turnover decreased, the company kept the benefit of workers' accumulated experiences. Productivity increased.

CHECKLIST
On-the-Job Problem Solving

The following checklist will help you to identify the source of problems that must be solved on a job – the source of job know-how.

Suppose You Work at Word Processing

1. What have you learned about the work process since you started?

2. What are the possible variables in your work process? Consider factors such as the equipment, materials, end-product requirements, interactions with co-workers and superiors, sequence of operations, and so on.

3. How do these variables affect your work? What problems have they caused? How have you coped with the most recurring problems?

4. Is speed important at your work place? How is it measured? How do you cope? Is your speed advantageous for management, for you, or both of you? In what ways?

The source of increased productivity was simple: production workers make improvements as they continue to work. They fine tune, adjust, maintain, repair and improve a new technique. Eventually their persistence yields substantial results. There is no such thing as fixed capital stock; the stock is constantly improved, increased and modified. Fixed capital perhaps acts as an upper limit which can be approached during full employment and three-shift, full-capacity use. But with time, working knowledge in using this equipment extends the upper productive limit of this stock. Practical know-how increases the equipment's capacity.

Not all managers, however, are as intelligent as Henry Ford. Canadian management, for instance, pays very little attention to workers' experiences and learning curves. If Canadian management were more consistent about competing internationally, it would encourage on-the-job learning. It would both allow and pay for on-the-job training by having experienced workers teach new ones, instead of ranting about "malingering on the job" and the low "moral quality" of workers.

Production Experience: The Source of Invention

Learning by doing accomplishes more than increased productivity. Although production workers concentrate mostly on applying techniques, their improvements can lead to inventions. A worker adapts to a work environment which has recurrent problems. Eventually these adaptive efforts become second nature. Occasionally, however, workers perceive a way of transforming their work environment. Usually they are motivated by a desire to control better the rate at which their problems occur.

Invention may be an exceptional activity for most workers. Nevertheless, workers probably constitute a major source of all inventions, as the following story illustrates.

Joe Townsend, an ex-bus driver who became an historian of technology, researched the history of the most important coal mining machine in the United Kingdom after World War II (12). Called the Anderton Shearer Loader, it is an adaptation of the German Panzerfoederer conveyor, an armoured face conveyor of the late 1940s. The Loader involved no radically new engineering principle; its concepts and components had been used before in various machines. Its novelty instead lay in the new way it combined older devices for solving the peculiar problems of mechanizing British coal faces. The combination of disc (later drum) shearing and plough loading, with an armoured conveyor mounting and a propfree front working, proved effective. A typical innovation, it involved simply a new combination of existing techniques.

The Anderton Shearer Loader required a stream of follow-through improvements in order to adapt it to varied conditions and improve its reliability. The first breakthrough did not come from a professional Research and Development group but rather from a group of production and maintenance workers. Mr. Anderton, manager of the Number 3 Helene's pit in the Northwestern division of the National Coal Board, authorized Tommy Lester to lead a team of two fitters, a blacksmith and a draughtsman, who achieved the work.

Lester describes the first run of the disc shearer's operation on the number one face of the Rushy Park Seam at Ravenhead Colliery on June 23, 1952:

> It took the whole weekend to get it positioned on the 150-yard face; we had no idea how it would perform, so we switched on and hoped for the best, positioned as we were in the tailgate, we could not see what was happening because of the noise and dust, we knew it was advancing because the rope was winding, so we positioned ourselves in the goaf to see what was happening, and happening it was, spewing coal at a frantic rate, at least for them (sic) days, one of my apprentices remarked: "By gum, Mr. Lester, I could watch that bloody thing doing that all day!" And that is precisely what we did (12).

During the first few months of operation, some 50 modifications were made to the machine. The plough was redesigned, the angles were changed, and a new gearbox was fitted. In order to make the modifications, workers removed the machine from the face each Friday night, transported it to the Haydock workshop by truck – a distance of seven miles – and put it into production by the Monday morning shift.

When the decision to design a new plough was made, according to Lester, a discussion took place on the back of the truck transporting the machine to the workshop. The comment that no draughtsman was available brought this reply, "Oh! Damn the drawings. Let's make it first and see how it goes." After the plough was drawn in the dust of the workshop floor, the blacksmith produced a successful modification. So much for early planning and development! However, a more deliberate, accurate design was essential in the later stages.

The original conception of the Anderton Shearer Loader came from the pit. It was developed by two fitters, a blacksmith and a draughtsman. Most subsequent improvements were devised by the workers, as has established the records of the National Coal Board, which offers an awards scheme. Awards related to the Anderton Shearer Loader were given in 1955-56, 1967-68 and 1973-74. Townsend identified awards according to function, such as cutting, conveying, and transport, and to the occupational categories to which the recipients belonged. The innovators fell into two classes: qualified professionals and nonprofessionals, or workers. (See table for results.)

Table 5.1 shows that in every area of mining, nonprofessional workers consistently receive either an equal or higher number of awards for inventions than professionals do. Professionals sometimes win awards for their work, which consists of observing labourers at the work site. This table suggests that the workplace indeed figures as a major source of technical innovations.

Table 5.1
Share of Ideas and Inventions 1955-1974 of Professionals and Production Workers in Coal Mines

Technical Division	Colliery Professional	Production Workers
Coal-face winning	53%	47%
Conveying	40%	60%
Strata control	32%	68%
Transport underground	35%	65%
Tunnelling	52%	48%
Elsewhere underground	43%	57%
Winding and shaft	36%	64%
Transport surface	50%	50%
Maintenance	15%	85%
Coal preparation	52%	48%
Electronics	55%	45%
Other (safety etc.)	36%	64%

Source: Joe Townsend, *Innovation In Coal Mining Machinery*, Brighton: Science Policy Research Unit, pp.3.17-3.18.

The Anderton Shearer Loader case is not unique. In **The Wealth of Nations** Adam Smith told about a "lazy boy" who was supposed to pull a valve on a steam engine periodically to release excess pressure (13). With a rope he connected the valve to another moving engine part to release pressure automatically. As the rope did the boy's work, he was able to move more leisurely about the factory. The foreman saw him, checked his machine, laid him off – and made use of the worker's invention.

Such cases of industrial espionage by time men, supervisors and engineers are not uncommon. After all, an industrial engineer's job is to make others' work increasingly productive. But management is reluctant to permit workers to reduce their load and maintain the same jobs. Yet there are numerous examples of workers' innovations. Kusterer relates how a copy machine operator rigged a coat hanger between the copier and the automatic collator to regulate the collator. Similarly, a paper-cone machine operator used tap water to produce an improved cone edge. A miner once told the author that chemical "leaching" in mines, a revolutionary innovation, was first suggested by a miner.

There are few systematic, rigorous studies of this phenomenon, however, partly due to a scarcity of records. Companies rarely have idea boxes or incentive schemes; only a few companies, in fact, permit researchers to examine their records. Another reason for the scarcity of records probably lies in the professionals' bias against blue-collar workers, whose suggestions are considered less clever than those of engineers.

There are sound reasons to believe that the work process is the source of most inventions. Production workers focus on problems, especially on their identification. Various solutions, as well as their comparative advantages, must be weighed. The worker is the user who must focus on sequential acts when applying a technique. Production provides a rigorous test of experience. It offers the opportunity to make changes under controlled conditions and, more importantly, to reproduce the experiment. In contrast, modern science insists on empirical tests and the capacity for controlled reproduction of an experiment, paying little attention to the production work process. Although experiments in the work process are not measured, the systematic aspect seems an ideal medium for invention by workers.

Five Features of Acquiring On-the-Job Knowledge

Acquiring on-the-job knowledge encompasses five basic features. Many factors interact, multiplying the possible number of problems to be solved. In fact, the number of possible dimensions is so great that they cannot be represented graphically in traditional three-dimensional space. An immense number of possible operational sequences, as well as combinations of variables in each sequence, add to the complexity of acquiring job knowledge. The main problem areas are the following:

> 1) Knowing the routine procedure. Usually taught formally to a beginner, these routines soon become subconscious. Once the routine is set as a reference, the operator must cope with variations that are not explicitly recognized by management. Solving such problems determines the learning process as the workers focus attention on recurring obstacles.
> 2) Variations in the quality of materials.
> 3) Variations in the performance of equipment.
> 4) Variations between customer-client demands for products.
> 5) Social and human interaction in the work process
> – between foremen, workers, and engineers, for instance.

These problem areas set the stage for a worker's learning process. Every job combines numerous operations. Workers must adjust equipment in response to differing materials, clients' needs and the human environment.

Let us now look at a few examples of problems that broaden a worker's knowledge. For instance, paper-cone machine operators notice that the pa-

---

CHECKLIST
Evaluating Your Workplace

1. Have you been able to modify your work environment in any way? How?

2. Did any of your coworkers bring about improvements to their work processes?

3. Have these improvements been recognized by management? If so, who reaped the benefit?

4. Is there an idea box at work or an incentive scheme? If so, who uses them?

5. Does your union have an idea box? Is there an informal exchange of ideas about the work process?

6. Has the supervisory staff ever taken one of your ideas or procedures (or those of a coworker) and instituted it as a formal rule?

7. Where do ideas for new techniques come from in your firm – from suppliers, R & D department, clients, or workers?

per's moisture and wax content affect the performance of the machine. They must thus take corrective steps. It is essential that they understand how their machines work and how each part functions.

A machinist once provided me with a useful image for understanding this precept: when we ride a bicycle we have a pretty good sense of what the chain does, what the teeth on the gears do, and how the pedals turn the wheels. This knowledge actually helps us, for instance, to position our weight for climbing a hill. After a while machine operators reach a similar mastery of their machines. The instruments of production serve as part of a working system. For instance, bank tellers might use an adding machine as a means of keeping a running record of their operations, although it performs no addition when it just lists the teller's transactions.

Graph 5.2
Variables and Problems

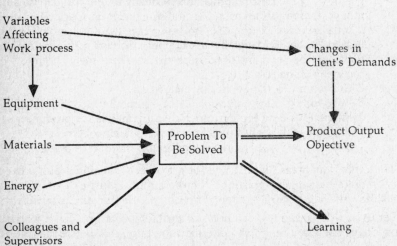

The worker at a station has a lot of variable factors changing the problems to be solved. This problem solving is the source of learning.

Workers solve most problems in isolation. If the machine breaks down, the mechanic is usually busy. Substandard paper may act up, but the material handler is seldom around. Few older workers are near to teach them. Few employers will pay for an older hand to teach a younger one. Supervisors often have more social skills than actual production experience.

Adjustment in Perceptions

Some barriers preventing the entry of an inexperienced worker into a machine shop are perceptual ones. The ordinary person is too sensitive to dirt and noise to become immediately an effective machinist, for instance. The new worker must thus undergo a desensitization period. The real parameters of the work are not obvious right away.

The desensitization process is aptly illustrated by this account related by Jim Petersen:

In shop D I had the experience of having to desensitize myself while learning how to cut very hard alloy steel on a vertical boring mill. The steel was so hard that it made a terrible squealing sound as it was being cut. Normally this sound indicates that the cut is being made too fast, but in this case we were using special steel tools, and I had to learn to ignore the sound and concentrate on watching the way in which the metal peeled off under the tool's pressure. This visual cue told me whether I was going too fast or slow and whether I was cutting too hard or softly. Many 'perceptual adjustments' must be made while learning a trade. This was one function of the long, traditional apprenticeship programs. Adjustments are part of a natural learning process and are within the reach of most normal people if they are given sufficient time and support (1).

Work-related perceptual changes are twofold. One type involves filtering out information that would normally be considered important, such as noise, dirt, the high speed of modern machinery, or the heat of a metal as it is being cut. These things alarm inexperienced operators because they are normally considered danger signals. The retrained mind filters them without conscious effort. On the other hand, a worker must learn to recognize and act upon other phenomena usually considered insignificant.

For example, a worker on a vertical boring machine trained himself in this manner. It is often necessary to barely touch the work with the tool in order to establish a zero point from which to begin cutting. One operator noticed that when the tool appeared to just touch its reflection in the metal, it was within a few thousandths of an inch from the beginning of a cut. He learned to use this visual cue. When he discussed this with another operator, he learned that the other had relied on this same cue for years.

The need to readjust one's perceptions is a barrier that requires a sort of training programme. It is perhaps the most important of all barriers. No one can begin machining without undergoing this adjustment period.

Everything in the machining process indeed constitutes a barrier to the entry of new workers. Learning to read blueprints – to decode their visual information – requires training. Working with specialized measuring instruments requires training also. The machines themselves throw up barriers. The controls are not always obvious; they differ from one another, depending on the make of machine. Standardized controls on machine tools do not exist, although the use of the console format for controls may eventually solve this problem. Consoles reduce machine operations to button-pushing operations. They help workers make links with common devices like typewriter keyboards and pushbutton telephones; they could make it easier to incorporate nonspecialized labourers, like office workers, into nontraditional careers.

Some of these barriers can be overcome in courses taught in community colleges. Future machine operators could learn math and how to read blueprints in such a setting; they might also learn to overcome their shyness about operating an engine lathe or milling machine. Workers, however, will not be able to fully understand these techniques until they actually work in a machine shop. Only then can the restructuring of perceptions and the painful mastering of multiple details begin in earnest.

Learning from Co-workers

Novices face other barriers created by coworkers when they first learn their trade. Experienced machinists often refuse to teach new employees. Instead they hide tools and fixtures; they set booby traps on a machine so the new operator will wreck it or have to scrap a job. Most new machinists in Canada must endure such kinds of initiations, surviving only if they are lucky enough to befriend an older machinist who is willing to act as teacher. Failing this, a newcomer's prospects are grim.

The rigours of learning the machinist's trade are illustrated in yet another account by Jim Petersen:

> When I began to work in shop C, I was painfully aware of some barriers to learning a trade on the job, although I did not yet realize the full extent to which industrial behavior had become pathological. I was therefore greatly relieved when I found out that Bill was willing to train me, and I had at least a few hours of vertical milling under my belt. My first job was a very simple one. I was given a casting, and I had to mill some flat spots on it. There was a fixture that made it even simpler. This was the first shop that I had ever worked in that had so many jigs and fixtures (1).

(A fixture is a device for holding a part on a machine while it is being worked on. Many parts have odd shapes and are difficult to hold down tightly. Much of the skill of the late nineteenth century machinist was invested in knowing how to hold down an odd shape so it could be machined safely.)

> It often happens that when technological changes are introduced, one problem is replaced by new ones. When old skill components are removed new ones are needed. Introducing jigs and fixtures into Shop C greatly accelerated the pace of work, but this increased speed made its own problems, as I discovered on my next job.
>
> I was given a hundred large steel plates to clamp into a vise and mill flat on one side. The pieces were flame cut, and the edges were ragged; it took me a while to learn how to hold them securely in the vise. Once I'd solved that problem I began to speed the machine up in order to make time on the job, but then I began to lose my finish. One of the technical specifications governing the machinist's work is the finish, or the kind of surface he leaves when he is through machining. A numerical scale has been devised for designating different types of finish; the machining drawings always specify when finish is important. There is a direct relationship between the quality of the finish and the speed at which a part can be made. In fact, all tolerances affect the speed that can be used. Higher tolerances mean slower work. As the machinist speeds up, the finish becomes progressively coarser. Milling machine operators are especially plagued by this.
>
> As I began to cut the plates at full speed, I found that I couldn't get the required finish by speeding up the cutter's RPM, but in doing this I also burned out the cutter's inserts after only a few passes, and

it took about thirty minutes to change all the inserts. Back to square one. Finally Bill showed me the way out of the dilemma. The trick was to make a couple of cuts with the spindle running at high speeds and then slow it was down to about 250 RPM. The problem then was that the cutters were so old, so banged up and worn out, that the inserts didn't all sit at the same level. A difference of a few thousandths of an inch in the height of one insert could leave a groove that ruined a finish. By making a few cuts at high RPMs, the high inserts were worn down to the level of the rest, resulting in a smooth finish. Bill had found a timesaving, efficient nontextbook solution, because it is laborious to set all the inserts so they run true (1).

The above example shows an informal work method that was not described in standard literature. Unknown to the supervision and engineering departments, it was essential for getting the work done during the given time. This story also illustrates the precise kind of situation in which knowledge can be transmitted orally; the problem must be one which an experienced worker has already encountered.

Technical literature, on the other hand, does not provide machinists with much information or advice about their trade. Jim Petersen made this criticism of the lack of written materials:

> The clampdown vise, for instance, is considered the embodiment of engineering technology. Is there a discussion of this device in engineering literature? No. It's too specialized a device to merit some mention even in a standard text on tool design. The only source of information is manufacturers' catalogues and instruction booklets, but these are seldom found on the shop floor.

> Neither engineering literature nor shop manuals written for the training of journeymen contain enough information to enable a worker to use the clampdown vise intelligently. Where does the information come from then? From the shop floor, where it's stored and passed on. Although it's part of one shop's working knowledge it's sufficiently general to be shared by more than one shop (1).

Speed-Skills: Learning to Make Money Fast

Workers and management share a common goal which motivates the mastery of a technique: speed. Increased speeds serve one purpose: making money. To workers, money is the reward. Speed skills give a special edge to workers' know-how. As Petersen states:

> In a production shop, men and machines operate at their limits. Problems are resolved both informally and pragmatically, often by overriding the decisions of the "hierarchy." Work pace is subject to a formal system of calculations. A fish plate, for instance, had to be milled in less than 1.35 minutes before a bonus could be made. This meant feeding the table past the cutter about 20 feet per minute. But to make any signifanct bonus the job had to go much faster. Besides bonus, there was also "fool around time" – time to perform bodily functions, drink coffee, talk to friends, or just sit and think. Although

these breaks are important for bodily wellbeing, they must be earned. Everything must run smoothly, and you must be well ahead or you can't even afford to take a piss (1).

Workers' speed-skills conceal the fact that production methods determined by production engineers have been bypassed. These hidden skills dominate the gray zone in which a tug of war between workers and management is waged. Here is another anecdote Jim Petersen provided to show how this tug of war occurs:

> My friend Butch was a lathe operator, proud of his high incentive earnings. He always earned 50 percent in bonuses. Suddenly the foreman set out to get him, perhaps because Butch had ideas about becoming a foreman. He hired Val, a young Quebecois from Noranda, to work with him. Butch responded by digging in his heels and treating Val as his enemy, although his partner possessed no malice whatsoever. With another man on the machine Butch naturally found it hard to make 50 percent bonus. Then, adding insult to injury, the methods department redesigned his biggest gravy job and cut its time (1).

The incentive game is not only as complicated as an electronic space war; it is much dirtier. The methods department can intervene at any point, to change the hardware, for instance, thus eliminating some tactical options for an operator. It is as though a service technician rushed in and added a new space vehicle having awesome powers and maneuverability, just as you were about to break the record on space invaders at the Pizza Palace.

> Butch's tactics were based on the deparment's plan to do the job in two steps, with two different setups. Butch's knowledge surpassed that of his planners. He had inherited some special tools from the man who had previously worked on his machine, enabling him to combine operations. This informal tooling and methodology belonged to the labour force, but management engaged in espionage. By watching Butch they discovered it was possible to eliminate one operation and one setup. They thus designed a fixture to combine operations. Actually their solution was less effective and more expensive than the informal one developed by the operators; yet they imposed it to cut down on the time (1).

Both management and workers look for ways to increase the speed of operators. They both try to control the processes that allow for increased speeds, since they are both aiming to make more money. But their solutions differ, as the foregoing anecdote indicates.

REFERENCES

1. PETERSEN, James Otto. (forthcoming) "More News from Nowhere: Utopian Notes from Hamilton Machine Shops." *Labour/Le Travailleur.*

2. ———. (1977) *The Origins of Canadian Gold Mining: The Part Played by Labor in the Transition from Tool Production to Machine* Production. PhD Thesis, University of Toronto.

3. BRAVERMAN, Harry. (1974) *Labor and Monopoly Capital: The Degradation of Work in the 20th Century.* New York: Monthly Review Press.

4. KOGON, Eugen. (1947) *Der SS-Staat; das System der deutschen Konzentrationslager.* Berlin: Verlag Des Druckhauses Tempelhof.

5. BURAWOY, Michael. (1979) *Manufacturing Consent.* Chicago: The University of Chicago Press.

6. KUSTERER, Ken. (1978) *Know-how on the Job: The Important Working Knowledge of "Unskilled" Workers.* Boulder: Westview Press.

7. ROY, Donald. (1954) "Efficiency and the Fix: Informal Intergroup Relations in a Piecework Machine Shop." *American Journal of Sociology,* 60, pp.255-266.

8. ———. (1952) "Quota Restriction and Goldbricking in a Machine Shop." *American Journal of Sociology,* 57, pp.427-442.

9. ———. (1958) "Banana Time: Job Satisfaction and Informal Interaction." *Human Organization,* 18, pp.158-168.

10. ARROW, Kenneth. (1962) "The Economic Implications of Learning by Doing." *Review of Economic Studies,* vol.XXIX, pp.155-173.

11. ABERNATHY, William J. (1978) *The Productivity Dilemna: Roadblock to Innovation in the Automobile Industry.* Baltimore: Johns Hopkins University Press

12. TOWNSEND, Joe. (no date) *Innovation in Coal Mining Machinery: The Anderton Shearer Loader-The Role of the NCB and the Supply Industry in its Development.* Brighton: Science Policy Research Unit, University of Sussex, p.2.9.

13. SMITH, Adam. (1909) *An Inquiry into the Nature and Causes of the Wealth of Nations.* London: Oxford University Press.

SUGGESTED READINGS

BURAWOY, Michael. (1979) *Manufacturing Consent.* Chicago: The University of Chicago Press.

KUSTERER, Ken. (1978) *Know-how on the Job: The Important Working Knowledge of "Unskilled" Workers.* Boulder: Westview Press.

TOWNSEND, Joe. (no date) *Innovation in Coal Mining Machinery: The Anderton Shearer Loader-The Role of the NCB and the Supply Industry in its Development.* Brighton: Science Policy Research Unit, University of Sussex.

CHAPTER 6

TECHNICAL CONSTRAINTS

Introduction

Technologies constrain the way we do things. Although there are always many alternative ways of performing a task, each technique nonetheless has its limitations. A number of them are common to all techniques, and we will examine them in this chapter.

Technical development is marked by general characteristics. The most important are the following:

1. Techniques vary greatly from one application to another.

2. They change slowly, undergoing a series of small modifications.

3. The new use of an old technique may appear to have created a totally new technique.

4. The accumulation of small changes sometimes results in technical revolution.

5. Once an invention is made, it is seldom lost. ("You don't have to reinvent the wheel.")

6. The process of trial and error, exploring dead ends, leads to crucial inventions.

7. Interdependent component techniques form constraining systems.

These characteristics are common to all lines of techniques. Let me illustrate them.

A given technique is used by many people in varying situations with different materials. Consequently, procedures and tools are adapted to suit specific tasks. The following illustrations show the varieties of sickles and hay knives used in the United States before the Civil War (1860-1865) and the types of axes employed both before and after the war. Such variations in design can be explained only in light of the conditions in which the tools were used.

Many factors, some of them irrational, affect changes in the design and production of implements. The traditions and habits of migrant workers may be responsible for promoting design modifications.

Instead of discussing all the possible factors, however, let us focus specifically on patterns of adaptation. Geography plays a role in determining which design is favoured. Water wheels, for instance, were adopted only from the 42th to the 15th parallel, that is, from the immediate north of the Tage River in Portugal and northern rivers of China, to the south of the Nile and Ganges rivers in India. In all these areas the inhabitants practised sedentary agriculture, using the water wheel. From this zone Arabs diffused oriental techniques to the West. An Arab traveller and historian, Ibn Batowtah, has related some of the efforts made before Marco Polo's travels.

Different Types of Ploughs

The different types of wooden ploughs which were used in the Spanish-Portuguese peninsula in different settings for different purposes, soils, under different land tenancy, etc. 1) rectangular, 1-2) radial, 2) dental, 3) curved. (From Julio Caro Baroja, *Tecnologia Popular Espanola*, p.510.)

Climatic and physical factors may directly influence how techniques are adapted in various regions. Inhabitants may also have divergent perceptions about technical opportunities. In the above examples of hydraulic societies near the Ganges and Nile rivers, the inhabitants – peasants, scribes, land surveyors, tax collectors and wealthy rulers – viewed the control of flood waters as a source of wealth.

Julio Caro Baroja, an historian who has specialized in technology, has quoted Oscar Wilde as saying, "It is not art which imitates nature, but the other way around: nature imitates art." Baroja suggests that this precept is even more true of techniques. Technical designs do not adapt to nature. Rather, nature is made to adapt to technical design.

Baroja has provided some of the best explanations of technical adaptation from the viewpoint of a regional history of technology. In **Tecnologia Popular Espanola**, he looked at windmills, water wheels and ploughs dating from antiquity to the Middle Ages.(1) These technologies appeared around the Mediterranean Sea and in western Europe, especially Spain and Portugal. In his text, Baroja suggests there are limits to explaining technical variations that occur because of the environment. Windmills were built, he claims, because fortified towns on hilltops found it difficult to protect water mills in the valley. (It is interesting to note that Don Quixote, the hero of Cervantes' **La Mancha**, attacked windmills as though they were fortresses.)

Let us look at what Baroja said about the wooden plough, which just scratches the soil without turning it over. Baroja examined many variations of ploughs, noting details such as the point (whether metal or rock), the link to the animals that pulled it, and the handle. He likewise examined the effects made by different types of wood and other materials, the traction animals, rainfall, soil, purposes of cultivation, number of crop rotations, and land occupancy. He then looked at the distribution of the various types of ploughs in relation to these factors, drawing maps for each type. He also noted the geographic origin of each type, concluding that "just as one can conclude that there is linguistic parochialism, one can identify ecological particularism" (1). Groups modify common tools just as they develop regional dialects. Progress, Baroja concludes, is linked to a society's ability to adapt tools and techniques to suit a variety of situations. For him technical progress requires technical pluralism. It has little to do with the replacement of one technique by a more efficient one.

For example, the rich agricultural region of Catologna is distinguished by a large variety of implements. Not only do Catalonians possess plenty of tools; they also have adapted them to perform numerous tasks.

Incremental Change

Techniques change by a succession of small adjustments. Because a technique is seldom lost, improvements relentlessly improve performance.

Persistence of techniques allows for cumulative improvement, not only in hand production – that is, **manufacturing** – but also in techniques based on scientific research. Petroleum refining is one such example. Fluid catalytic cracking, as originally produced in 1942, produced only 12,000 barrels of petroleum a day; but through minor changes, a total of 55,000 barrels a day, more than four times the original amount, was achieved after a few years. Fifteen years later, in 1957, a new plant at Tidewater's Delaware City produced 102,000 barrels a day, nine times the 1942 figure.

Petroleum cracking relies on catalysts. The process previously used was limited by a major problem: it was only semicontinuous. The catalyst had to be extracted from the tubes and reintroduced periodically. Production engineers overcame this constraint by recirculating the catalyst. They did this by changing the hydrostatic pressures in pipes and vessels. Another simple change was to withdraw the catalyst from the bottom of vessels instead of the top, a much easier operation.

CHECKLIST
Varieties of the Same Tool

Examine your kitchen knives and ask yourself these questions:

1. How many different knives do I have?
2. What explains their different shapes and functions: the different purposes, textures of the things they cut, different materials the blade and handle are made from, or the different movements needed when they are used?
3. Are some differences due to just style and fashion?

As a result, the petroleum plant layout could be simplified, resulting in greater flexibility. Maintenance costs were reduced by downflow designs. Cyclone separators were no longer needed for recovery of the catalyst, and their size was reduced. Catalyst hoppers were eliminated. The catalyst recovery procedure no longer restrained the scale of process and the variety of feed stocks which could be introduced. Such improvements increased the size of the Tidewater plant.

Varied Tools For Cutting Hay

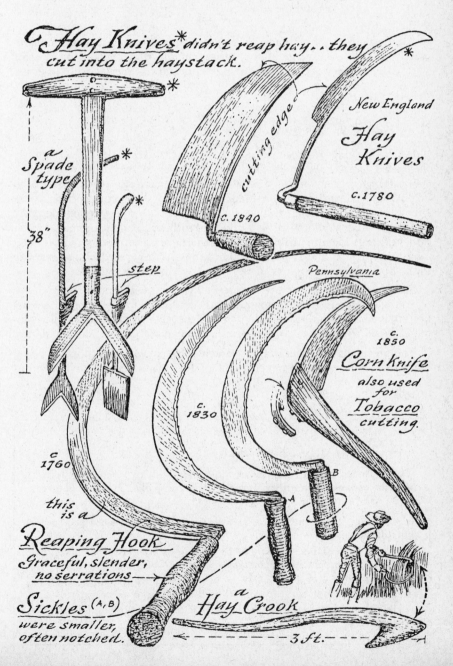

Hay Knives didn't reap hay.. they cut into the haystack.

a Spade type

38"

step

cutting edge

c. 1840

New England Hay Knives

c.1780

Pennsylvania

c. 1830

c. 1850

Corn Knife also used for Tobacco cutting.

c 1760

this is a

Reaping Hook Graceful, slender, no serrations

B

A

Sickles (A, B) were smaller, often notched.

a Hay Crook

3 ft.

Try the same questions out on other work tools. Some variations in design and use may not seem important, but they do show how we modify a tool to meet a variety of functions.

Many other improvements contributed to make the fluid catalytic cracking more economical: the reduction of erosion by using alloy steels, better designed transfer lines, and the replacement of natural catalysts with more fluid, synthetic ones.

Although the basic technical process may owe its existence to scientific researchers, most of the ideas for improvements which made the process economical came from production engineers and technicians who observed workers in operation (2).

New Use of an Existing Technique

Before logging was mechanized in British Columbia, "donkey" engines were used on rail cars, spars, chains and grapples to yard in the logs. Much later, after power chainsaws mechanized timber cutting, Crown Zellerbach asked Madill, a machine shop in Nanaimo, to adapt heavy construction trucks with a mobile spar and an engine in order to post them on top of a logging hill. Cut timber could then be yarded in with chains and grapples on the slopes of steep logging grounds. The technique was then combined with logging roads, trucks and radio communication systems in order to mechanize forest operations. Very little, if any, new technology was used.

Spars had been used before, and so had yarding with chains and grapples (on trains). But now these techniques were combined with a mobile construction truck and engine, along with power chainsaws, trucking and radio communications. This allowed the system to mechanize logging on steep slopes.

The president of Madill did not perceive that his machine shop was being innovative. Yet its equipment changed logging practice for the whole industry.

CHECKLIST
Adaptation – More Than Novelty

Major technical changes often occur without any striking novelty. The impact, nevertheless, can be enormous. Imagine you have worked in a sawmill for ten years. Ask yourself the following questions:

1. How many small improvements have been introduced since you started working there?
2. Who introduced these improvements – managers, equipment manufacturers, maintenance mechanics, or operators?
3. What did these changes involve – materials, control instruments, power tools, work environment, procedures, or the feeding of materials?
4. Did these changes increase productivity in terms of working hours? How many hours per person?

Very little technical adaptation was necessary to mechanize logging on flat grounds, a feature of timbered terrain in Ontario. The speed of the cutting and bucking phase reached a limit when logs could not be evacuated fast enough. Tractors were ill-adapted; four-wheel drive tractors could not easily manoeuvre in dense bush. Specific attention was given to adapting them to the local Ontario conditions. As a result, the Four-Wheel Articulated Skidder was developed. Its articulated frame gave it manoeuvrability; large tires gave it traction and flotation.

The 1956 prototype, however, had the disappointing habit of breaking down. The Clark Company in Michigan tried unsuccessfully to produce a reliable model. Timberjack Ltd. of Woodstock, Ontario, finally came out with one that sold in the thousands (3).

The difference between the 1956 prototype of the Woodlands section of the Pulp and Paper Research Institute of Canada (now called the Forest Engineering Research Institute of Canada) and Timberjack's model might have been simple mechanical techniques. Yet these small differences were enough to promote the use of the skidder thoughout the logging industry.

An incremental change can initiate a major change in technical practices. Some relatively minor adaptations of wheel and truck technologies, for instance, facilitated the movement of the transport industry to the far north. Several years before Imperial Oil requested Bruce Nodwell's help to design exploration vehicles, Nodwell had been working on off-road transport vehicles to provide year-round access to muskeg areas. He tried various unsuccessful applications of wheels before deciding that only a tracked vehicle would work. The largest tracked carrier in use was a tanklike vehicle made in Quebec by Bombardier Ltd. It could carry a 4,000-pound cargo.

Oil companies, however, needed a carrier with at least a six-ton capacity. In the 1960s, after five years of trial and error, Nodwell's firm developed a machine that could support ten tons. Although its total weight with cargo was in the neighbourhood of 25 tons, the carrier could skim over virtually any terrain at an average speed of 12 miles per hour, with a ground pressure of about two pounds per square inch.

The main problem encountered in designing the light treading carrier was how to give it enough track area to reduce ground pressure so the vehicle would not lose stability on uneven ground. Two solutions evolved, both of them in the track design. Nodwell used four-foot-wide tracks of rubber and steel mounted around seven rubber-tired wheels. This provided a cushioned track area, wide enough to distribute the vehicle's tonnage. About 40 feet long and nine feet wide, it weighed about 15 tons without cargo, and 25 tons when loaded.

Such a large machine, resting lightly, would topple over on uneven terrain if its tracks were inflexible, however. To solve this instability problem, each wheel inside the tracks was joined to an axle, and each axle was hooked separately to the drive shaft, the backbone of the vehicle. Since each wheel turned independently and was suspended, the tracks could walk over uneven terrain, wheel by wheel, thus minimizing the possibility of a spill.

Once the basic track design was adapted to a flat-topped carrier, other types of vehicles were created. Bunk houses, cook trailers and personnel carriers were attached to Nodwell tracked vehicles. An entire camp on tracks could be moved to a muskeg-covered drill site in winter or summer, and it could stay there year-round without bogging down.

The technical changes described above may seem relatively mundane. Yet they make all the difference between something that works and something that doesn't – pie in the sky or a concrete solution.

Dead Ends and Cumulative Synthesis

Sometimes technical change seems to make a huge advance all at one time. Nevertheless, even apparently sudden, sensational advances are often the last step in a gradual process of change. Many alternative solutions have been slowly and systematically eliminated. Thus technical and scientific development proceed hand in hand, by means of systematic exploration, deductive conclusions, and cumulative synthesis.

Let us look at an example of early technologies in nuclear physics. Before World War II a British nuclear physicist, Lord Rutherford, related his discovery of atomic structures. He attributed his major insight to a small segment of applied research performed by one of his students, a man called Geiger. The experiment, the first ever carried out by this student, confirmed the then-established theory that alpha particles are not scattered through a large angle. But something else occurred. As Rutherford put it:

> I remember two or three days later Geiger came to me in great excitement, saying, "We have been able to get some alpha particles to go backwards." It was quite the most incredible event that has ever happened to me in my life. It was almost as incredible as if you fired a 15-inch shell at a piece of tissue paper and it came back and hit you. On consideration I realized that this scattering backwards must be the result of a single collision, and when I made the calculations I saw that it was impossible to get anything of that order of magnitude unless you took a system in which the greater part of the mass of the atom was concentrated in a minute nucleus. It was then that I had the idea of an atom with a minute massive center carrying a charge (4).

Rutherford made this major scientific and technological discovery because of what seemed at first to be a mundane experiment to check an established theory. A revolution in nuclear physics was initiated partly as a result of just one more incremental step. No doubt thousands of such experiments had previously been made and would be made in the future. Such is the usual lacklustre work of research assistants and most scientists. Yet this is the truly proletarian work of scientific research – "normal science" – which rarely gains due recognition.

Many discoveries occur because of a previous researcher's rigorous determination that a set of phenomena cannot be explained by preceding theories. This negative finding forces scientific researchers to reach out further. When all incremental deductions have failed, they achieve a careful leap. This systematic approach has led to major technical developments as well. Recognition of the exact nature of an obstacle, as well as the reasons why previous attempted solutions have been unsatisfactory, brings thinkers to the edge of a potential invention.

Let us consider two major technical developments, the steam engine and the light bulb. When James Watt experimented with Newcomen's atmospheric engine, he recognized that the engine consumed excessive amounts of fuel; it lost much heat and it failed to utilize the expansive power of steam. This is Watt's account:

> I had gone to take a walk on a fine Sabbath afternoon. I had entered the Green and passed the old washing house. I was thinking of the engine at the time. I had gone as far as the Lord's house when the idea came into my mind that as steam was an elastic body it would rush into a vacuum; and if a connection were made between the cylinder and an exhausting vessel it would rush into it and might there be condensed without cooling the cylinder. I then saw that I must get rid of the condensed steam and injection water if I used a jet, as in Newcomen's engine. Two ways of doing this occurred to me: first, the water might be run off by a descending pipe, if an offlet could be got at a depth of 35 or 36 feet, and any air might be extracted by a small pump. The second was to make the pump large enough to extract both water and air.... I had not walked farther than the Gold house when the whole thing was arranged in my mind (4).

This modification appears small, yet it made the steam engine viable. A long, painstaking process – the elimination of false avenues – was a necessary prelude to new insights.

The case of the light bulb is similar. Edison and others working for, or in competition with, him – like Swan and Sawyer – examined many incandescent materials before choosing carbon fibre. During his search, Edison learned about vacuums and the performance requirements of the materials he was looking for, such as temperatures and melting points. Numerous experiments with other materials helped him narrow down both his options and the problems to be solved (5).

The New York Herald of December 21, 1879, described the legendary story of how Edison accidentally stumbled on the right material for his incandescent lamp. While sitting one night in his laboratory reflecting on some unfinished details, Edison began absent-mindedly to roll between his fingers a piece of compressed lampblack mixed with the tar used in his telephone. As he pondered several minutes, his fingers mechanically rolled out the little piece of tarred lampblack until it became a slender filament. Glancing at it, he wondered if it would produce good results as a burner if it were incandescent. We know the rest.

An Incremental Revolution: The Crankshaft

Many of the above examples of technological innovations relate to scientific fields and may appear atypical. Systematic experimentation in techniques, however, occurred long before the application of formal science to technology. Experiments resulted in important inventions, the most significant of which was the machine.

The core of the first machine system – the crankshaft – was born in the Middle Ages when mechanics found a reliable method to convert energy from one direction to another. With the crankshaft they were able to harness natural energy, which led the way to the development of other power systems, such as steam and internal combustion engines.

Probably evolving from the water mill, the crankshaft was about fifteen centuries in the making. Water that fell on paddles produced rotative energy. In Roman times simple gears had transferred this rotative power from the vertical plane to the horizontal. Since few work processes used rotative energy, however, mechanics were challenged to produce linear energy. They activated a hammer – a basic, universal tool – and put cams on a driveshaft. Much later they used the crankshaft to achieve a general solution to the problem of transforming rotative energy into linear power; eventually they accomplished the reverse transformation, in steam and internal combustion engines.

Although historians specializing in technology agree that many centuries passed before the crankshaft was developed, they disagree about its earliest date. Crankshafts probably existed in China before the Christian era, as the Chinese had water mills and advanced water-management techniques. Europeans used the crankshaft with a grindstone in the ninth century; but no society put it into general industrial use until the fifteenth century.

We can speculate how the crankshaft was invented. Someone probably transferred a carpenter's crank to a mechanical design, linking it with a connecting rod. Because it jammed, someone added a fly wheel to encourage the momentum and help it continue through dead spots. Although many such minor improvements would be necessary before the crankshaft became a reliable transmission system, the technique was revolutionary.

CHECKLIST
Problem Solving

Think of the hardest problem you have had to solve at work or at home and ask yourself the following questions:

1. How many different solutions did you try? List them with the dates. Try to remember why you tried each.

2. Why did you drop some solutions? If it was because you had a better solution, in what way was the new one better? How many solutions did not work at all?

3. Was the final and best solution a combination of various previous attempts?

In a way, the invention of the crankshaft ranks with the wheel in importance, although it is far less celebrated. The idea was around for a long time. Like the wheel, the crankshaft came about after many skilled mechanics had tinkered with earlier models – before mechanics were formalized tradesmen. Nobody can claim the invention because it took thousands of anonymous people to add incremental improvements. Different cranks and connecting rods were used for centuries. The crankshaft blossomed only when someone contributed the final adjustment that made the crankshaft generally reliable. At one point someone watching the shops near water mills must have perceived that the crankshaft was not simply a support technique used in milling.

It was a radical innovation. With it people could harnass and transmit power to a work operation.

As the concept of machine emerged, a change took place in the paradigm, or world views, of production. Machines – combining a natural source of power and a specific work task – were expected to do man's work. In the late Renaissance, when men's imaginations were fired by the idea of machine, views about production work changed. Not only did a new conception of the technical process appear, but new social organizations of work were promoted simultaneously. The workshop thus was born. New social forces became economically interested in the use of machines and workshops. The merchant capitalist changed into an industrialist.

This is how major technical revolutions happen: alternative changes are eliminated and steady improvements begin to occur. Cumulative results bring about astonishing innovations. Ultimately, credit must be given to the working people whose collective practical experience leads to systematic exploration and creative application.

Technique is Irreversible

Once an invention is made it is never really lost. The invention of the wheel, for instance, was followed by incremental improvements. Moreover, the irreversible character of technical development is general. As a result, technical advance appears to be relentless. Whereas individuals may choose to dispose of their wealth, they cannot get rid of their knowledge. If you "know too much," there is little you can do about it.

Just as learning has irreversible consequences, so does technical knowhow. The technical capacities of human beings are therefore best conceived as a stock to which we are always adding. As most older techniques are incorporated into new ones, we continuously improve our skills. Our stock of technical knowledge thus is not only maintained, but increased in the process.

Technical Constraints Within a System

Within a technical system, a technique acts as either a facilitator or an improvement. Support technologies are developed around a core technology.

We have defined a technical system as a group of interdependent techniques that serve the same general purpose or productive function. It is important to distinguish between different levels of systems: technical, industrial, transport, communications, trade, scientific, and thought systems. Here we are talking only about technical systems.

Within a system, constraints narrow the scope of possible technical solutions, dictating future developments. Steam engines, for example, must possess reliable valves and boilers with pressure-resistant chambers; they must be made of the proper iron and steel. In like manner, computer evolution depends on supporting technologies. Based on the core technology of semiconductor memory, it needs such technologies as card punchers, verifiers and readers, video display terminals, electronic magnetic disks and tapes, communication sytems, telecommunication lines, and printing machines. A system makes a technology more inflexible.

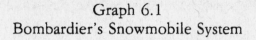

Graph 6.1
Bombardier's Snowmobile System

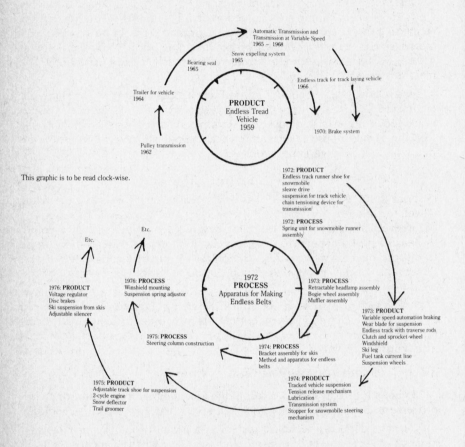

The technology described inside the circle represents the *core* technology: "a single endless tread with a sprocket motive wheel" for the snowmobile as a "product"; the "apparatus for making endless treads" for the production process. Around each of these *core* technologies, seven ancillary and support technologies are developed. This is represented by two "clocks": the "product clock" (above) and the "process clock" (below). Process innovation only starts in 1972 — once the North American market levels off. The arrows indicate how one technological development influences the direction of subsequent inventive or innovative activity by creating either an opportunity or a bottleneck. The two clocks and their arrows represent the *dynamics of technological constraints within the technological system* of the snowmobile and its assembly production:

(I have taken the earliest date of application or patent in the United States or Canada.)

We get the impression sometimes that, within a given technical system, a technology possesses its own momentum over which humans exercise little power. For example, in the years before internal combustion engines existed, the steam engines used on prairie farms often blew the threshing team to smithereens. Thus mechanics were forced to improve valve systems and the performance of boiler chambers under pressure. Short of abandoning the steam engine for harvesting – which they finally did – farmers had few technical options.

In a complex system like the automobile, any substantial change in a component technology calls for adaptation in other components. Such was the case with Bombardier's snowmobile. When Armand Bombardier's son Germain developed a single continuous tread with two sets of holes for motive sprocket wheels in 1959, he had developed a small motorcycle type of snowmobile. A whole series of ancillary inventions ensued. Graph 6.1 shows their

Graph 6.2
The Technical System of Early 19th Century

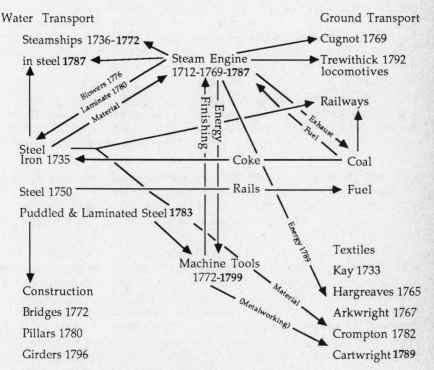

Steam engine technology was interdependent with coal, steel and, later, transport technologies. Each arrow indicates how one technical development facilitates another. The French historian of technology, Bertrand Gille, who devised this graph, suggests that in a system of inter-related techniques progress can be blocked by just one component. Source: Bertrand Gille, *Histoire des Techniques*, Paris: Gallimard, p.706.

sequence on two "clocks"; a product innovation clock is on top, and a process innovation clock is on the bottom. The graph shows how each innovation influenced the next.

For instance, the continuous wide tread tire accumulated snow beneath the vehicle, requiring the invention of a snow-expelling system (1965). Although a major obstacle to the vehicle's reliability was overcome, it could gather and maintain speed only after an automatic transmission was added in 1965, permitting variable speed in 1968. A safety problem plagued the rapid vehicle, however; it could not stop fast enough. A new brake system thus appeared in 1970. Later, the chain's tension was adjusted to allow maximum efficiency of the transmission, and the suspension was improved to enable the vehicle to go over rough terrain. Each performance improvement brought about a new problem on which to focus.

The same thing happens in production process technology (see Graph 6.1). Process techniques for the snowmobile started in 1972 with the key component, the apparatus for making endless belts, or treads. Year after year changes occurred, affecting most of the assembly process: the headlamps, bogie wheel, muffler, bracket for skies, steering column, windshield, and suspension spring were modified. Whenever a segment of the process was mechanized in the assembly line, bottlenecks then marked the less reliable spots. Production bottlenecks, which happened when a machine could not be fed fast enough, or when a machine's output was not processed efficiently, wasted time. Hence the next focus for technical change became a production bottleneck.

The direction of change appears to be predetermined by the logic of a system. Technology seems to have its own rationality, telling us where to look for technical improvements. But these strong constraints exist only within a given system and for a chosen purpose. If the use of a technical system is changed, the constraints may also be relaxed.

Even within a given system there are alternative solutions. For instance, the deadspots of a crankshaft can be overcome by using a fly wheel, or alternating two crankshafts slightly out of phase, or by coupling two power systems totally in reverse direction. In all cases the momentum will carry the crankshaft over the dead spots.

Another example is the internal combustion engine. Although today's engines are geared to petroleum, they can also be adapted to gas, oil, natural gas, alcohol, propane and so forth. Even the constraints within a technical system are flexible, because human beings create combinations of interrelated technical components. A technical system is not like a biological organism existing only as a whole, which dies if the weakest part fails to function. It is a constructed combination of component technologies, each of which may survive the demise of the system.

CHECKLIST
Identifying the Technical System

1. At your workplace what is the most important piece of equipment around which work is organized?
2. What techniques are related? Are they dependent on each other?
3. What technique is crucial? What are the support techniques? How are they related? How do they depend on each other? What is the function of each sub-technique?
4. What are the alternatives to the subsystems?
5. What global function does the general system fulfill? Can this function be socially avoided?
6. Are there alternative systems to the one you work with?
7. How does this system orient technical activity?
8. What are the dos and don'ts with this system?

REFERENCES

1. BAROJA, Julio Caro. (1983) *Tecnologia Popular Espanola*. Madrid: Editora Nacional.

2. ENOS, J.L. (1962) *Petroleum Progress and Profits: A History of Process Innovation*. Cambridge: MIT Press.

3. RADFORTH, IAN. (1982) "Woodworkers and the Mechanisation of the Pulpwood Logging Industry in Northern Ontario, 1950-1970." *Historical Papers*, pp.71-102.

4. USHER, Abbott P. (1954) *A History of Mechanical Inventions*. Cambridge: Harvard University Press.

5. HUGHES, Thomas. (1976) *Thomas Edison: Professional Inventor*. London: H.M.S.O.

SUGGESTED READINGS

BAROJA, Julio Caro. (1983) *Tecnologia Popular Espanola*. Madrid: Editora Nacional.

GILLE, Bertrand. (1978) *Histoire des techniques: techniques et civilisations, techniques et sciences*. Paris: Gallimard.

USHER, Abbott P. (1954) *A History of Mechanical Inventions*. Cambridge: Harvard University Press.

CHAPTER 7

THE DRIVING FORCE OF ECONOMIC NECESSITY

Economic forces are responsible for bringing about many technological changes. In this chapter we will look at the relationship between innovation and such factors as investments in equipment and machinery, effective demands, and relative abundance or scarcity of resources. The main economic factors which affect technological change will also be examined.

How Economic Needs Affect Technical Change

Most successful commercial innovations are first stimulated by the perception of a market need; only a third of them are initiated by a perception of technical opportunity. Although market needs and opportunity for development may coexist as causal factors, the major incentive for change is the identification of potential clients' needs. An analysis of the sequence of events leading to a commercialized invention – which I will call an **innovation** from now on – shows that the clear identification of potential users' needs is critical to the market success of a new product or process.

The production of scientific instruments is a case in point. Changes in scientific instruments come about mainly when a market survey shows they have sales potential. Some British instrument manufacturers, for example, elicit ideas from potential buyers by asking for their specifications and design performance requirements before they begin to develop new products.

Ordinarily a new scientific instrument is conceived in a research laboratory, where the scientist designs and builds an instrument for personal use. This makeshift prototype is assembled from spare parts and components of other existing instruments. If a manufacturer is convinced that a sufficient number of other scientists will buy this new model, he will conduct a survey to find out how many persons may buy it and how much they are prepared to pay. The exact design will then be adapted to meet these expressed needs, which may or may not be those of the original designer. In order to make a greater profit, therefore, the manufacturer will try to render the new model suitable for a maximum number of uses.

In all industries, the perceived market need is a more important stimulus to innovative development than the perception of a technical opportunity. This is true not only for successful new products but also for those that fail to make a dent in the market. Since technological innovations are commercialized inventions, one can expect that the market will be an overriding incentive. But the invention itself may have been developed much earlier because of technical opportunities, as in the case of the gas turbine, which grew out of a principle discovered by Leonardo da Vinci in the 1500s. Economic motivation did not motivate da Vinci's invention; it was applied only when power equipment manufacturers realized they could sell it at a profit.

Surprisingly, however, the above case is the exception rather than the rule. Even inventions seem to be spurred by economic demand. One often hears the saying," Necessity is the mother of invention." As this expresses common folk wisdom, can we assume it contains a kernel of truth? Others respond that leisure is the mother of all invention. The business of basic survival, this maxim implies, takes up too much time for the ordinary person, who can scarcely devote any free time to inventing a process that will probably fail nine times out of ten, and will certainly not work immediately. How then can these contradictory maxims be reconciled?

The words **necessity** and **needs** are vague. Whose needs are expressed, those of the indigent or those of the affluent? What products will satisfy these clients? Ultimately a need must be backed by money; it becomes an economic demand only when investment makes an innovation possible. For example, the existence of disease may be interpreted by a company as a social need for the development of drugs, but it could be seen alternately as a need to make improvements in diet, health education, exercise, housing, environment, water, or sanitation – all major factors that might well contribute to an illness.

A clearly perceived need, then, must motivate the innovator, since focussed activity is vital to success; but free time and adequate resources are equally necessary before an inventor can consider trying out various techniques. A perceived need and the enjoyment of leisure time nurture invention, but in a market economy the driving forces on innovation are product sales, profits and market power.

Economic priorities are also affected by social systems, property relations in production, and specific organizations of work. If there is such a thing as a rational economic human being – as economists claim – then he or she calculates anticipated returns by considering property laws and institutional constraints. Naturally the investor interprets material necessity and economic need according to personal interest, and operates within the constraints of a production organization.

Demands Orient Change

Jacob Schmookler, a hard-working intellectual who did not mind getting his hands dirty, spent the better part of his life looking at thousands of patented inventions (1). After reclassifying patents according to their potential users, Schmookler established that the number of inventions adopted by an industry correlated closely with the rate of production; in economic jargon, he assessed the "value added."

I have found similar conclusions; however, I was analyzing innovations – new Canadian products or processes which have been successfully commercialized – rather than patented inventions. After determining the name and industry of first user, I ranked 2,000 innovations made between 1945 and 1978 by 732 firms, in declining order according to user industry (see Table 7.1).

Table 7.1
Compared Ranking of First Users of Innovation and Main Purchasers of Domestic Goods and Services

Industry	Innovation	Goods & Services
Construction	3	4
Health & Welfare	4	7
Pulp & Paper	5	6
Motor Vehicles	9	17
Industrial Chemicals	14	35
Railway Transport	15	33
Smelting & Refining of Nonferrous Metals	19	13
Sawmills	21	21
Iron & Steel	23	23
Misc. Machinery & Equipment Mfgrs.	28	34

The comparison of the above rankings shows that some of the major users of Canadian innovation, which often define the technical requirements, are also the most important buyers of Canadian goods and services. Demand patterns do not, however, explain all cases: the industrial chemical industry, because it is linked to scientific research and development, uses more innovation than its demand ranking would lead us to expect.

Since the pulp and paper industry needs the logging industry, metallurgy draws on mining, and all these industries demand services from electric utilities and governments, one can see the correspondence between the demand for Canadian products (second column) and the principal innovators (first column). Exceptions occur, however. Domestic demand does not explain all innovations. It does not motivate the defense industry, whose exports supply the U.S. military system. Nor can domestic products satisfy Canadian firms

---

CHECKLIST
Identifying the Promoter of a New Technique

Imagine you are a pharmacist who must judge an innovation, then answer the following questions:

1. What social need is the production supposed to answer?
2. Who interpreted the need and economic demand?
3. Who will pay for satisfying this need?
4. Where is the financially solvent effective demand?
5. What other products or services could satisfy this need?
6. Who are the investors? What benefits do they derive from satisfying the demand?

who depend on imports. In general, economic demand nevertheless stimulates the creation of new products and production processes, especially in areas where abundant natural resources give Canadian industries comparative advantages over other nations.

The Abundance of Nature

The abundance or scarcity of resources clearly affects technical change. Many economists who examine product cost factors have noticed a bias in favour of changes on the part of industries which save labour, particularly skilled labour. This holds true especially in North America. The economic historian Habakkuk, writing in **American and British Technology in the 19th Century**, explains that the capital-intensive bias of American technology is related to the abundance of natural resources and the scarcity of skilled labour (3). This does make sense. Investors will choose technical innovations which make the best use of the available resources; the less costly the materials, the better. More precisely, investors will be influenced by the long-term availability and cost advantage of goods when they choose techniques.

In Canada, for example, the most innovative industries are nonferrous metal mining, wood industries, and electrical power generation. This is not surprising, since Canada's economy is resource-based. Given the Laurentian Shield and the Rocky Mountains, Canada boasts the largest amount of underground hard rock mining in the world. Since each ore – such as lime, copper, gold, silver, molybdenum, and cobalt – contains a different composition of nonferrous metals, smelting methods must be adapted innovatively. Abundant forests in a sparsely populated terrain have also permitted Canada to create a number of industries, such as sawmills, pulp and paper plants, which call for inventive techniques. But Canadians first had to exploit these natural opportunities by investing time in adapting new techniques.

Canada's large rivers and plentiful waterfalls offer many opportunities to transform the "white coal" into electricity, inducing a great deal of inventive activity. Since hydroelectric power is central to a network of technical exchanges between industries, Canada has introduced changes not only in industrial electric equipment and products, but also in power generation, electrical wire and cables, machines, ancillary instruments, and communication equipment. As labourers have developed hydroelectric installations, they have acquired technical skills which have subsequently permitted them to start innovating. Thus, in terms of engineering performance, Hydro-Québec

---

CHECKLIST
The Market Importance of a New Product

Identify the principal new product or service in your industry and ask the following questions:

1. What is the market?
2. What is its importance?
3. How many people or industries buy that service or product?
4. What is the total yearly value of the market in dollars?

now competes only with the U.S.S.R. in the long-distance high-tension transmission of electricity by cable.

Coupling its endowments of rich natural resources with technical competence in their recovery, Canada has acquired an international advantage. During recent decades, Canada's exports have changed from unprocessed primary materials to energy-intensive semiprocessed goods. Moreover, the Canadian pulp and paper and metallurgical industries are among the most energy-intensive in the world. Even when primary materials must be imported, Canada specializes in transforming them into energy-intensive products.

In summary, technical activities flow in the direction of abundant resources. The relative scarcity of labour and consumer demand has turned Canadian industry away from the manufacturing of end-product consumer products. The skills acquired by Canadians in managing their rich natural resources have been oriented instead toward the processing of hydroelectric power.

The Economics of Speed

Speed is crucial in a market economy, where the turnover rate affects technical endeavours and changes. Consider the economic motivations behind investments. An investor may provide $1,000 for the machinery to manufacture a snowmobile, another $1,000 for primary materials and energy, and another $1,000 in wages. Apparently it costs $3,000 to produce this snowmobile. But the investor must spend at least $9,000 on the snowmobile, because materials and parts must be stocked, and energy must be provided for before it can be built. Then it must go to a retail store where it will wait a few months before being sold. The time at both ends of its production is called "turnover time," or "capital rotation" time. In business, a rule of thumb is that the turnover times equal at least three times the direct costs of making a product.

Thus the rate of profit depends on the speed of turnover. Attempts must be made to shorten both the production time itself and the unproductive turnover times. This provides incentives for proposing new techniques.

Although an innovation may allow the industrialist to cut costs in half, that advantage will prevail only while the technique is confined to a few users. As soon as it becomes commonly used – thus lowering mean production costs – the market price of a product goes down. The person who initiates the change therefore hurries to take advantage of a temporary lead in order to make the most profit in the short time available.

Clearly, technical change accentuates the economic importance of speed. Examples are evident in Canada, where wheat hybrids developed by Agriculture Canada are used to increase the yield in the short northern growing season. One innovation aims to shorten the time required for maturation. Similar efforts occur in forestry, for example, with research to shorten the necessary growing life of a tree before it can be cut for second-generation timber.

Some techniques developed in these hybrids through bio-engineering closely resemble those used in chemistry. It is evident that the development of chemical substitutes must have been acquired, in part, because of the economic stimulus provided by speed. By overcoming natural reproduction cycles, the chemical industry dramatically reduced production turnover time, just as in the late 1800s, when dyes previously extracted from indigo – which took years to grow and dry – began to be produced from coal tars.

Range of Products and Scale of Production

In the preceding section, we have seen that economies can be reaped from speed and that this economic incentive orients technical change. Other economic incentives, however, affect the direction of technical change. Here we will examine two ways of reducing the costs of products which orient the search and choice of technical changes. The history of Bombardier's snowmobile will give us an illustration for both.

Bombardier's snowmobile technology was developed in the late 1920s. Its core is a doubled reinforced tread combined with a motive sprocket wheel. Since the technology had many applications, many different clients bought the vehicles in the 1930s. Hotel owners needed to get their clients in and out of snowbound towns at a time when there were no paved roads clear of snow; veterinarians had to make house calls; ambulances had to rush patients to the regional hospitals; Oblate missionaries travelled between Inuit villages in

---

CHECKLIST
Techniques to Save Time

Imagine you are a worker in the forest product industry, then ask yourself these questions:

1. What time passes between the ordering of components and their use?
2. How long do the components stay in stock before being used?
3. How long does production take?
4. How long does it take before a customer buys it?
5. What is the difference between the pre-production period and the time of sale?
6. How much longer is that than production time?
7. From beginning to end of the production process, how much time is required?
8. How much money is immobilized during the total turnover time? Is it always used productively?
9. Do stocks or equipment lay dormant part of the time? If so, what percentage of stocks?
10. How can the manager reduce the turnover time?
11. What technical changes would reduce production time?
12. What organizational changes would reduce nonproductive time?

Now ask the same questions with the manufacturing of an end-product, such as a word processor, in mind.

northern Québec; and the military needed to carry its troops. Each client needed slightly different versions of the vehicle. Doctors and vets could manage with two-passenger models; hotel managers needed station-wagon models for several passengers; ambulances required a similar model, but equipped with beds and good suspension; and the military needed to seat more than ten soldiers.

Basically, however, the technology of adapting road vehicles to the snow remained the same: front skies, treads, and sprocket motive wheels were used instead of tires. A similar core technique had to be adapted to meet the specific seating, capacity and performance requirements.

As a result, it was cheaper for Bombardier to build many different models. The cost per unit was lower because Bombardier Ltd. was building a "scope" of neighbouring products; some "inputs," such as equipment, know-how and components, were "shared." This also enabled the owner to keep his assets in use and his resources employed most of the time. When veterinarians were not giving him enough requests for vehicles, he could keep himself working at full capacity for hospitals, ambulance companies, post offices, and the military. To fill the order book Bombardier thus reaped economies of scope.

The Dis-assembly Line

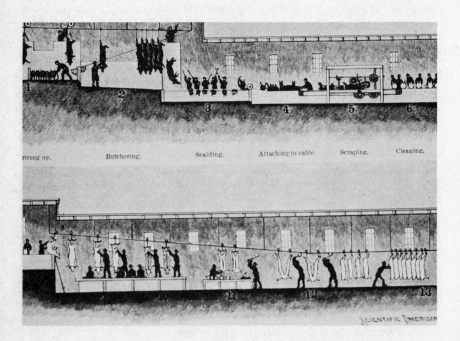

Line production in meat packing segments every stage of the work. The work, in this case a carcass, is brought to the work station either by conveyor belt or hanging on a line. At each instant, an animal is at each stage of processing, as the work flow is synchronized.

After World War II Bombardier Ltd. continued the product variation of its core technology to benefit from its basic experience. It then diversified the industrial applications, developing vehicles for such activities as forest management, petroleum exploration and snow clearing. But in the early 1960s Bombardier shifted its technical focus and started to produce, in great quantities, a recreational model called the Ski-Doo. Before this model could be mass-produced, however, the owner had to develop a simple, standard, reliable, user-friendly design. Thus in 1958 Joseph Armand Bombardier and his son Germain developed their prototype Ski-Doo. A few years later, Armand, the inventor and founder of the company, died, and the family could no longer rely on the inventive skills of the master mechanic. They thus decided to mass-produce their most popular model.

In the 1960s many competing firms were trying to make money in the snowmobile industry. There were, in North America alone, as many as 129 manufacturers of snowmobiles competing in the same market. They reduced the price tags of their brands to gain a greater share of the market. At one point Bombardier sold its "Elan" model for as little as $600. Reducing the unit price, however, was possible only because of certain technical changes. The technical design had to be standardized completely, and the parts made interchangeable, built to precise specifications and quality requirements. New production equipment, which was specifically developed to build a part, had to be used. For instance, special presses were first developed by J. Armand Bombardier and then built by Canadian Vickers just to mould the Ski-Doo's aluminium seat structure. Assembly line techniques were brought into their Valcourt factory: an overhead serpentine would bring the required parts for assembly at the right time. Line production required the synchronization of all the different stages of the production process. The coherence of these production components and the interdependent stages of the production process thus enabled companies to reduce unit costs.

This phenomenon is called **economies of scale**. By increasing the scale of production it is possible to reduce unit costs more than if fewer units are produced. This economic opportunity often encourages manufacturers to mass-produce and market their technologies. Of course, standardization of products and line production are necessary.

Potential economies of product scope – or variation – on the one hand, and opportunities for economies of scale, on the other, induce technical change in somewhat different directions. The first encourages product variation; the second, standardization. But, as we have seen with the case of Bombardier, the same company may develop the same basic technology in two directions at different times.

Innovation and Fixed Investments in Machines

Investors must interpret economic market signals. If sales, profits and market power are the driving forces behind innovation, investors are the agents who induce innovative activity.

Graph 7.1
Investment Cycles in Railroads —
How Do Patents Fit?

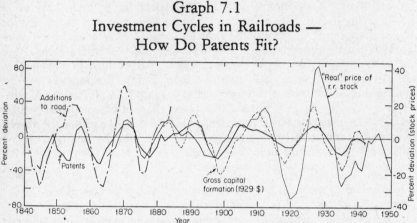

Railroad Patents and Railroad Investment, Deviations of Seven- or Nine-Year Moving Averages from Seventeen-Year Moving Averages. (1)

This graph shows how patented inventions in the railroad industry closely followed investments.

Economist Jacob Schmookler spent twenty years studying how industrial innovations followed investments. Patents are customarily registered in the Washington and Ottawa Patent Offices according to the main area of economic activity of the applicant firm. Engineers then reclassify inventions, such as hydraulic valves, according to techno-economic fields, in order to determine if a similar patent already exists.

Since neither of these classifications fully satisfied Schmookler, he reclassified patents for machines, instruments, transport equipment and all capital goods according to the industry most likely to use them. He patiently determined, for instance, whether a specific boiler technique was more liable to be adopted by the iron and steel industry or by the railroads. After twenty years he published two books, one containing his data and statistics. Although **Invention and Economic Growth** (1966) was recognized by Schmookler's peers as one of the best works on technical change, it received relatively little attention.(1) Now, some fifteen years later, Schmookler's ideas are being verified for all process inventions; only in science-related industries, such as the chemical industry, have his conclusions not been totally confirmed.

Having reclassified patented inventions according to the industry that would probably use them, Schmookler matched the time series of certain patents with investments.

The most significant finding of Schmookler's study concerns the relationship between the investment in capital goods, or equipment, and the number of capital goods inventions. The correspondence is most evident in a time series involving a single industry. One can see the similarities exhibited in long-term trends; the only notable difference is that lower turning points in major cycles generally occur in capital goods sales before appearing in capital goods patents.

Table 7.2
Compared Ranking Users of Innovation, Cumulative Investment and Growth of Investment between 1960 and 1977 in Fixed Capital

Industry	Innovation	Cumulative Investment	Growth of Investment
Government	1	1	29
Mining and Oil	2	3	2
Construction	3	8	12
Food and Beverages	4	10	20
Transportation Equip.	5	12	5
Hospitals	6	11	8
Paper Products	7	47	14
Utilities	8	2	3
Chemical Products	9	9	1
Electrical Products	10	19	18
Railway Transport	11	5	27
Forestry	12	17	15
Wood Products	13	16	6
Primary Metals	14	6	17
Telephone Systems	15	4	10
Machinery	16	21	10
Metal Fabricating	17	18	16
Textiles	18	20	23
Furniture and Fixtures	19	27	21
Universities	20	14	24
Non-Metallic Mineral Products	21	15	14
Scientific and Prof. Equipment	22	25	26
T.V. and Radio Broadcasting	22	24	4
Printing & Publishing	24	23	19
Rubber Product	25	22	9
Tobacco Products	26	28	22
Petroleum and Coal Products	26	13	7
Leather Tanneries	27	29	18
Clothing & Knitting Mills	27	26	25

Schmookler probably inferred too much from the sequence of events. We know that when one event precedes another it does not necessarily mean that the first caused the second; both may be the means or delayed results of human actions and plans. The most important notion to bear in mind is that inventive activity follows investments. If most investments during a decade are made in railroads, for instance, most machinery and equipment patents are destined for railroads.

I have established also in earlier research that a fixed investment in new machines is oriented not only by patented inventions, but by the innovation's first use (see Table 7.2). From what we have noted, we may conclude that if labour wants to influence technological change, it should try to redirect investment activity.

Table 7.2 shows that 13 of the first 15 users of innovations are also among the top 15 in either total cumulative investment or investment growth. But investment does not explain all innovations. Electrical products and forestry, which are not capital intensive or process oriented, are exceptions.

How does fixed investment bring about the development of new machinery or models? New investment offers a unique opportunity for the introduction of new techniques. It encourages innovative factories, techniques and machines. It also provides the occasion for getting rid of old equipment and practices.

New investment does not necessarily, however, bring about technical change; when order books are full and a factory is running close to capacity, an investor may not risk using the newest technique. In such a business climate, the investor will choose the most reliable, not the newest technique. But although technical changes can occur without fixed investments, Karl Marx and Jacob Schmookler believed that fixed investment plays the major role in orienting technical change.

REFERENCES

1. SCHMOOKLER, Jacob. (1966) *Invention and Economic Growth*. Cambridge: Harvard University Press.

2. DEBRESSON, Chris, and MURRAY, Brent. (1984) *Innovation in Canada* (2 vols.). New Westminster, B.C.: CRUST.

3. HABAKKUK, H. (1962) *American and British Technology in the 19th Century*. Cambridge: Cambridge University Press.

SUGGESTED READINGS

DAVID, Paul A. (1957) *Technical Choice Innovation and Economic Growth: Essays on American and British Experience in the Nineteenth Century*. New York: Cambridge University Press.

ROSENBERG, Nathan. (1976) *Perspectives on Technology*. Cambridge: Cambridge University Press.

——— . (1982) *Inside the Black Box: Technology and Economics*. Cambridge: Cambridge University Press.

SCHMOOKLER, Jacob. (1966) *Invention and Economic Growth*. Cambridge: Harvard University Press.

CHAPTER 8

TECHNIQUE ALLIED WITH SCIENCE

Dictionaries and encyclopedias define technology as the application of science to production. Since we have already noted some problems with this definition, we have reserved the word **technology** in this book for science-related techniques. Is technique really affected by science, however? If so, to what extent? Perhaps the converse is also true, since production techniques and industrial practice seem to influence scientific research. These questions will be explored in this chapter.

Science Enters Production

During the nineteenth century, scientists gradually expanded their laboratory experiments into full-fledged, industrial production processes. Leblanc, a surgeon for the French royal family, was the first to do so. Between 1764 and 1789 the French Academy of Sciences offered a prize for the production of alkali, a component of dye for textiles. Leblanc won this prize. After obtaining a patent in 1791, he set up a factory outside Paris to produce soda and sulphuric acid.

French revolutionaries, however, were suspicious of anyone supported by the royal family, and they forced Leblanc to publish his process. They also expropriated his factory, but returned it to him in 1801. By that time Leblanc was exhausted by both his work and the political turmoil, and he committed suicide. His process nevertheless continued, launching the alkali trades. Soon afterward, the alkali trade crossed the English Channel, where the English considerably improved on Leblanc's process.*

This process, in fact, gave birth to the chemical industry. It was a peculiar industry from the start, due to its links with science. The industry took from chemistry most of its knowledge about primary materials and their behaviours. Subsequently the road from the chemist's lab to the production plant would be taken often. As a result, the classification of industrial chemical products in Statistics Canada, "Standard Industrial Classification," resembles the classification of chemical compounds in a student's chemistry textbook.

The second major technological development in the chemical industry directly related to scientific research was Perkin's synthetic mauve, or aniline dye. W. H. Perkin was a 19-year-old chemistry student at Britain's Royal College in 1856 when he discovered synthetic mauve. Knowing that many compounds with the same formula as quinine existed, Perkin was challenged to synthesize them. First he obtained a useless reddish brown sustance. He then

---

*Alkalis are chemical substances that dissolve in water. Together with acids they form salts that destroy acids. Thus they change the tint of many colouring matters, turning the purple matter obtained from various lichens, for instance, from acid red into a blue base. Because of this property, alkalis are used in dyes.

obtained a black substance. Eventually he found a substance which could produce mauve dye in silk. Once he had received a patent, he quit college. A year later he opened a factory in which he manufactured mauve, thereby launching the aniline dye industry.

A Chemical Laboratory

Leibig, a 19th century German agricultural chemist, organized experiments systematically in his laboratory for the production of synthetic substances for agriculture. Later research and development laboratories would look even more businesslike.

The nascent chemical industry crossed the Channel again, moving this time to Germany, where chemists developed it systematically. One German chemist, Nikoden Caro, is credited with making the greatest contribution to his country's chemical industry after 1865. Caro had previously studied in England, where he had learned many dyestuff techniques. An early nationalist, he was concerned that so many young German scientists were forced to go abroad. Thus he devoted his life to organizing a systematic link between chemical science, engineering and industry. Caro founded the Institute of German Chemists (VDC) and Engineers (VDI). He helped found the famous Karlsruhe Technische Hochschule, the first technical school in a network of technical high schools, or polytechnics, to supply German industry with technicians. He also helped write a German patent law to enable scientists to obtain the rights to their inventions. The process established by this law is still reputed to be the world's most rigorous because of its stringent examination of novelty.

Caro's major contribution, however, was as chief chemist at Badische Aniline (BASF), which later formed the huge German chemical combine named I. G. Farben. Soon the German chemical industry became a powerhouse of scientific and technical knowledge. Among its first developments was aniline, a colourless, oily liquid, which is somewhat heavier than water. With its peculiar burning taste, somewhat like wine, aniline combines with acids to give bright, beautiful colours that dyes fabrics permanently.

The real economic advantage for BASF, however, was the production process it developed to make aniline cheaply out of coal tar. Before World War I, the German industry virtually monopolized all coal tar derivatives – aniline, alizarin and benzine – and continued to exploit related scientific research. BASF and Hoesch once spent 20 million marks on experimental research to develop an industrial process for producing synthetic indigo, a process derived from the patent of a Munich chemistry professor named Degussa. This new process finally cut the price of indigo by half.

By the 1920s the American chemical industry began to apply scientific research as systematically as the Germans. Other industries, such as electricity and electronics, drugs and nuclear power, followed suit. E. I. Dupont typified an American chemical company that operated on the basis of scientific research. Near its head office in Wilmington, Delaware, Dupont financed its own basic research. Inviting researchers to work in its laboratories, Dupont set them up with assistants and resources, permitting them to work independently. Dupont employees then noted whether the researchers had invented anything that could be marketed.

Among those invited to Dupont in the 1920s was a Harvard chemist named W. H. Carrothers, who was interested in polymerization research. (Polymers are chains of chemical compounds, some of which exist naturally. Wood fibre is a major source of "natural" polymers, and many other vegetable substances also contain it. The process of forming long chains with compound molecules is called polymerization.) Carrothers studied the conditions and causes of the formation of these chains. To Dupont's President Greenwalt, this was a promising area for the production of synthetic materials; he actually came into Carrothers' lab to observe the chemist's progress.

One day in 1928 when Carrothers and his associate were cleaning test reaction vessels, Carrothers noticed a long fibre which seemed fairly resistant and flexible. Greenwalt asked Carrothers to reproduce its synthesis, thus producing basic polymer 66, or nylon. Of course many more experiements were needed before the filament could be reproduced industrially: it is one thing to produce a polymer under controlled laboratory conditions, and quite another to scale up the experiment to produce large amounts of it economically. The controlled reproduction of a satisfactory material finally occurred on February 28, 1935. By 1939 Dupont was mass-producing nylon. A whole line of synthetic textiles resulted from this experiment, one that at first seemed incidental to basic research.

HOW SCIENCE DEPENDS ON INDUSTRY AND TECHNICAL KNOW-HOW

Scientific principles cannot be applied to production without the intervention of mechanical engineers and persons skilled in ordinary technical know-how, even in science-based industries. Earlier we saw how apparently minor mechanical improvements brought economic benefits to the petroleum refining industry. All science-based industries benefit from such incremental changes.

Once a science-based invention is developed into a workable prototype, only five to ten percent of the preliminary innovative work has been performed. Most of the cost for a technological change in a commercial product involves engineering, design, tooling up, production engineering, startup problems, debugging, adjustments, and so forth. All this occurs before operations become routine, engendering a simple learning-by-doing process.

Not all industries, however, are linked with a scientific discipline. Many important technical innovations, unrelated to scientific discoveries, make the headlines. For instance, Sadi Carnot's thermodynamics had little to do with the genesis of the steam engine. Nor did Newcomen's atmospheric engine, or Watt's steam engine. They were the fruit of guided trial and error. But the emerging science of thermodynamics did provide the rationale for understanding the natural forces at play in steam engines.

Often technical practice will define the agenda of scientific research. Thus the Bessemer steel-making process, the backbone of the iron and steel industry in the nineteenth century, was initiated without the preliminary scientific knowledge that would have given innovators insight into what was happening. Scientific understanding also followed, rather than preceded, the Gilchrist steel-making process. Decades after its inception questions arose from technical practices and experience, leading to scientific analyses.

Members of the metallurgical industry brought about technical changes through contact with users, relying little on science. Most industries today are still not directly related to scientific research activities. Few have research and

---

CHECKLIST
Determining Scientific Links

When technical innovators combine science with technique, science accommodates itself to industry. Workers can assess this relationship by asking the following questions:

1. Does the technology in your industry depend on a scientific field?

2. If so, which one – chemistry, nuclear physics, electricity, electronics, or biochemistry?

3. How are they linked – through scientic research results, scientific support in general, or through the use of scientific method in technical research?

4. Is the link direct with the company's own research and development department, or some other industrial research, or government and university research?

5. On what nonscientific basis does the technology depend?

6. How crucial to your understanding of the technology are the scientific and nonscientific sources?

7. Does the company use trade secrets or patents?

8. Does it draw on ideas from the work force, using an idea box, for instance?

9. What aspect of production depends on scientific knowledge? Which does not?

10. Could scientific research directly affect any technique you now use?

11. Do any science-related industries affect your own? If so, how?

development programmes. Modern industries still depend on mechanical trade, which borrows little from the science of mechanics.

The Effects of Technical Practice on Science

Just as modern technology is indebted to science, contemporary science owes it present character to the demands that production practices make on it. Technical practice focuses on what is to be explained by science. To a certain extent, science has always relied on technical activity, despite the aloof position of the privileged few who practised scientific inquiry without relating it explicitly to any productive activities.

Scientific activity depends on technique in two ways. It depends first on tools produced by technical activity: scientific instruments. In ancient Greece, for example, the level, square, rule and compass were instruments of both technicians and mathematicians; they were the tools of the masons, the architects and geometricians, such as Euclid. New measuring instruments in the seventeenth century played a part in the scientific revolution, just as the computer now serves university scientific researchers.

A Fluid Flow Process

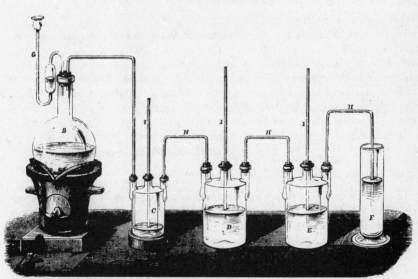

The fluid flow process of the experimental laboratory for production of sulfuric acid will be maintained, at a greater scale, in a chemical plant.

The second way science depends on technical activity is in terms of content. Technical practice not only gives scientists experiments to perform; it also poses questions. Thus technical activity in production orients the focus of scientific researchers.

When science does not take its cues from technical activity, it may go astray. For centuries, nonsensical scientific theories gave virtually no help to sound practitioners of chemistry and metallurgy. Fire, rather than science, proved the greater teacher. The Greeks who developed bronze casting and iron metallurgy simply had to vary their oven temperatures. That Greek science declined can be attributed in part to the aristocrats' unwillingness to direct scientific inquiry to understanding such phenomena. Since Greek aristocrats assigned a social stigma to someone who spent the whole day inside a forge near a fire, Greek scientists preferred to develop the pseudo-sciences of administration rather than the scientific principles of metallurgy.

The relative inactivity of scientists during the early Middle Ages can also be attributed to the distance between the cultures' elites, based on issues arising out of technique and productive practices. In the Renaissance, however, the demand for sound navigation practices allied science and technique once again. Much later, the Industrial Revolution in England gave scientists some stimulating new questions to explore. Mechanical engineers, looking to science for intellectual support, were instrumental in establishing science clubs – such as the famous Lunar Society – in the new industrial towns. Engineers and entrepreneurs were guided by demands of emerging mechanical and chemical fields to keep abreast with scientific methods and developments. In one respect, modern science was not so much the outgrowth of traditional scientific activity in academic establishments, like Oxford, Cambridge and the Royal Academy; rather it was the product of the activity in the science clubs, stimulated by the demands of engineers and entrepreneurs in new, growing industries.

Industry now seems to determine which fields of research will be developed. The computer industry, for instance, profoundly influences the direction of mathematical research. Because algorithms consititute the basis of the sequential logic of problem solving by computers, university mathematical research in algorithms has mushroomed. Since computers reduce all problems to yes-no questions, they solve complex questions at high speed. Other branches of mathematics are left dormant, especially those that do not accommodate themselves to the yes-no logic of algorithms. In this way the computer industry has transformed and oriented modern research.

The Industrial Approach of Modern Science

In general, society's economic needs direct scientific activity. A characteristic of modern intellectual science is the reduction of experience to a few simple, exclusive elements, thus neglecting interdependencies and ecological dynamics. The values of today's western industrial world, in which the domination of nature is a creed, may be seen in the objectification, quantification and reification of a scientific object of study. In other words, the application of scientific research is biased not only toward the content of certain domains; it is biased also in the form of its development. The nature of a dualist philosophy – mind/object, inert/live, and so forth – is related to the dominance-of-nature creed. The bias inherent in measurement and quantification is to master and reduce all phenomena to a few independent controlling factors. "Reductionism" in science brings about industrial transformation.

The utilitarian philosophy is also reflected in the organization of industrial research. Thomas Edison was a pioneer in what we call industrial research and development. He set out deliberately to "invent industrially," even setting himself a goal to develop a large number of inventions every week. By the end of his life he claimed over 2,500 patented inventions, and he probably produced many other inventions which were not registered. At his Menlo Park research lab in New Jersey, Edison systematically searched for technical solutions. We have described earlier how he examined in succession many possible materials for his incandescent lamp.

In a procedure typical of scientific research, he often examined parallel routes simultaneously. Since the results of one line of research feed into others, they both reveal common obstacles and help to specify requirements. If one line proved decisively unproductive and others seemed more promising to Edison, he abandoned the former early, without waiting for the results of all his experiments.

But Edison was not a scientist; he was a technician. He developed his knack for solving technical problems inventively while working for Western Union Telegraph Company as an operator. Drawing on the methods and findings of science, he said, "I know no genius but hard work."

Research and development, the buzz words of modern industry, represent the systematic application of scientific methods to technical development. Edison and his Menlo Park laboratories demonstrated the usefulness of a research department. Many other industries and corporations have followed Edison's lead. They screen scientific data with an eye for technical possibilities, and they pursue solutions to technical problems with systematic strategies. Evidence shows that this manner of industrial production is yielding revolutionary results.

The production of computers and transistors may be cited as an example. Alexander Graham Bell set up Bell Laboratories as the research arm of his telephone industrial empire. He saw it not only as a means of continuing his inventive activities but also as a corporation strategy for keeping abreast of scientific developments in the field of communications. He could thus plug into research and examine possible new materials. To accomplish this, Bell Labs had to hire some resident scientists to do basic research. Only by carrying out basic research could Bell Labs assimilate the results of other research scientists in centres and universities around the world.

William Schockley was a resident scientist in Bell Labs. Working in solid state physics, he examined the conductive characteristics of various materials. In particular he was determining which materials were semiconductive, showing curious behaviour patterns. By systematically studying semiconductive materials he devised a theory which described the controlled reproduction of semiconductive patterns.

The link between theory and practice, however, is indirect. Theories must be adjusted to pave the way for technical discoveries. Attempts to prove Schockley's theory experimentally opened up avenues for using certain new materials industrially. Before this could happen, however, sufficiently pure semiconductive materials, such as germanium or silicon, had to be produced. Mastering their production would prove important.

At the beginning of the twentieth century German researchers considered silicon as a possible medium in communications. They abandoned it when endless production problems plagued them. On the other hand, vacuum tubes required production technology that was less troublesome. As a result early radio technology relied primarily on vacuum tubes.

For example, Philips, the Dutch radio and communications corporation, established most of its technology on vacuum tubes. The United States Army developed the first ENIAC computer, intended for ordinance use, with vacuum tubes. But bulkiness proved to be a severe limitation. The ENIAC computer filled many rooms with vacuum tubes to attain a memory capacity which today can be lodged in a small box.

In 1951 Bell Laboratories marketed Schockley's revolutionary technology, inviting firms to attend a seminar in which it revealed the scientist's test results. The guests became licensors of Bell Lab technologies, henceforth paying royalties for the use of any Bell technology; this tactic would eventually bring in a multi-million-dollar profit. After signing the agreement, each corporation subsequently tried to develop a pure semiconductive material that could be mass-produced: germanium, then silicon.

At this time IBM was little more than a producer of traditional business machines. It had grown since the beginning of the century, when female typists began to replace clerks in large numbers. IBM's Watson saw the ENIAC computer and realized its potential for office use. Lyons Tea in England had already begun to process its accounts by computer, having set up a small subsidiary, Leo Computers, which it staffed with electronics engineers employed by the Royal Air Force. In 1951 Leo Computers brought out the first computer for civilian use in the United Kingdom. In the United States, Echert and Mauchly developed the first commercial computers but went bankrupt in the process.

IBM's advantage lay in its sales network and expertise in selling business machines. It did not concentrate its energies on basic computer technology nor try to monopolize the radical innovation. It focussed instead on fitting the computer into a specific market. It concentrated on applying and adapting the computer, as well as maximizing its technical possibilities, rather than doing more research. The concept of computers had been around for some time; IBM simply picked up the idea and made the new components work in the mid-1950s. Making no attempt to be first, IBM learned from others' mistakes. Using the military's experience and its own punch card techniques, it soon mastered the new technology.

Computers are now part of contemporary culture, having radically affected working conditions and living habits over a period of thirty years. Many of us now work with them. To be sure, the revolution has not yet ended. The point to remember, however, is that both computers and semiconductors originated in scientific research labs.

The Parallel Routes of Scientific Research

The scientific systematic method is best illustrated in the American development of the atomic bomb: the Manhattan Project. All possible technical routes to its development were examined simultaneously. As seen in the popular public television series, broadcast on PBS in 1985, Robert Oppenheimer insisted that this be carried out. Absolutely necessary sequences of experiments were examined. The time required for each experiment was reduced to a minumum by hiring a large staff. Whenever experiments could be conducted simultaneously rather than in sequential manner, this was done.

The Manhattan Project was a military scientific endeavour, military not only it its aims but in the organizational structure. Scientists marched to orders, their schedules and problems strictly defined. Communication among all the participants was minimized to avoid leaks. Only a small group of leading scientists knew the total game plan and understood how minor research data fit together, and how certain sequences would lead to the desired solution.

No economic motive existed for the Manhattan Project. If an avenue of research promised to yield useful results in the development, production and delivery of the atomic bomb, that avenue was pursued. The costs were not considered a problem to both military and scientific personnel. The military organization gave the project an industrial discipline.

Why do we discuss the atomic bomb in a book about technical change? Doesn't it represent destructive change? Perhaps the discussion is relevant here because nuclear reaction eventually led to the production of nuclear power for civilian use. This reason may be valid but it is not the only one.

In a later chapter we will discuss in greater detail how military expenditures affect technical change. In the present context we are concerned about the influence the military exerts on the organization of technical research. The militarization of both scientific and technical research has reorganized the industrial quest for technical changes. The Manhattan Project exemplifies a contemporary scientific and technological venture. It was a systematically planned discovery of a technical solution for the production of a specified result. Since World War II similar methods have been used in many other major programmes.

Scientific research not only contributes to technological development; it also provides a base and direction for productive experience. Both technical change and scientific inquiry are directed by industrial investment. Scientific activity no longer engages freelancers who are independently wealthy and educated. Instead, science is an industrially organized activity requiring capital investments and the use of sophisticated instruments, such as computers. Although scientific research originates outside the production sphere, it affects the technical changes forced on the work force. Thus workers must not consider it alien. Research activity today is similar to other wage-earning activities. As scientific research has become industrialized, researchers have become employees with little say about what they will investigate or how they will go about it. The labour movement has a direct interest in the orientation of scientific research and in organizing its salaried work force.

Human Knowledge and Social Productivity

The link between technique and science holds important implications for society's productivity. If controlled scientific experimentation with natural phenomena can be transformed into productive processes, society's knowledge of natural processes can improve our ways of producing goods. In other words, the accumulated understanding of humankind can increase the productivity of its work force.

Several sociologists and historians have perceived the importance of this change in the relationship between technique and science, among them Karl

Marx, Werner Sombart and J. D. Bernal. In drafts which Karl Marx did not publish (**Grundrisse**), but left for others to do in the 1930s, he showed visionary insight into today's alliance of science with production. In his time the chemical industry was just beginning, and he could see only the first signs of tendencies which he extrapolated.

Marx saw machines and tools as organs of the human brain, the power of objectified knowledge. Although he probably exaggerated, he saw capitalism as having started with the use of science in production. As a general system for exploiting nature's and humankind's capacities, capital uses science to its profit, thus starting a universal appropriation of nature.

The extreme tendency of a capitalist society is characterized by Marx in these words: "The entire process of production does not appear as part of the immediate activity of the worker but as a result of the technological employment of science" (1). Nevertheless the most advanced area of this growth requires a qualitatively new condition, which is attained "only when big industry has already attained a higher level and all the sciences are captured for the service of capital.... Now 'invention' becomes an economic activity and the application of science to immediate production a criterion determined and demanded by production itself" (1).

Marx discussed these ideas in early manuscripts – the **Grundrisse**, which later became **Capital** (1). In the final version he cautiously omitted these visionary forecasts. Elsewhere he specified that the direct relationship between science and production was just a tendency, one which the capitalist system of production, he thought, could not fully develop.

In general, science costs nothing to capitalists, but that does not stop them from exploiting it. Other people's science, as well as work and experiences, are used.

Personal and capitalist appropriation are two different things, however. Charles Babbage, a nineteenth-century promoter of industry, deplored the gross ignorance of mechanics that was displayed by manufacturers of sophisticated machines (2). Justus Von Liebig, a nineteenth-century German agricultural chemist, also tells hair-raising stories about the ignorance of chemistry displayed by manufacturers of chemical products.

Scientific knowledge is a socialized form of shared knowledge. Capitalist production requires, however, that this social knowledge be privately appropriated. Capitalist appropriation requires private, exclusive – quasi-monopolistic – appropriation beyond personal assimilation. Marx had no objection to the possession of personal property, as anticommunist propaganda leads us to believe, but he criticized the private appropriation of other people's personal work and know-how. The use of science for production, he claimed, therefore has its limits; they are imposed by exclusive private appropriation and the use of its results.

When Marx's closest friend, Engels, gave in to pressures which Marx had resisted during his lifetime – to legitimize the existence of a Marxist school and party – the philosophy quickly became an established, institutionalized tradition, even in some universities. Simultaneously, the chemical and electrical industries grew in Germany, along with a new nation, its educational and cultural institutions exploited the potential of applying science to production.

Werner Sombart, a nineteenth-century German sociologist, was such an academic Marxist (3). Influenced by liberals and socialists to oppose Bismarck and some large landowners in Prussia, he established an academic dogma based on Marxism.

A prolific writer, he clarified the relationship between science and technique, entrenching a school of thought which held that technology had been transformed by becoming scientific. Many of Sombart's books (most of them are published only in German), expound this idea, which is now commonplace even if partly erroneous. (Toward the end of his life, Sombart embraced the Nazi doctrine.)

J. D. Bernal, a scientist, illustrated the Marxist alliance of science and industry. A crystallographer, Bernal trained Rosalind Franklin, one of the three researchers who would help crack the structure of DNA in the early 1950s, thus explaining how macromolecules constitute the building blocks of life. Bernal had a prestigious scientific career of his own. And at the end, despite the loss of his sight in the 1950s, he wrote a four-volume work called **Science in History** (4). Along with many colleagues, Bernal had been shocked by the use of science for military purposes. World War II revived his concerns.

Bernal pinpointed the basis for the alliance of scientific activity with human industry, arguing that science is one form – but not the only form – of understanding nature. Human industry and technical knowledge are also forms of intelligence, or ways of understanding nature. Both forms of intelligence rely on human sensory experience. Both assist the physical activity of people, even if formalized science does so more remotely. Scientific knowledge, however, tends to be universal, whereas productive, technical knowledge is specific. Scientific knowledge emerges from previously accumulated human experience, whereas productive knowledge comes from experiences and trade skills. Scientific knowledge is communicated through the language of mathematics and logic, whereas technical know-how is communicated through direct practice and the rule of thumb. Both forms of knowledge rely on the contributions of human activities, but they do so differently.

In antiquity, scientific knowledge was classified differently from tools and technical, productive know-how. Geometry, for instance, was divorced from the builder's level. The elite who amassed surplus material goods and enjoyed leisure time controlled mental production as well. It was they who disseminated ideas, words and formal written language. Periodically through the centuries, scientific activity was so distant from productive human activities that it became useless. Fortunately, the Renaissance and Industrial Revolution upset old dogmas and inspired scientific ideas more relevant to human reality.

In the 1930s J. D. Bernal began to publicize his theories. Drawing on Marx, he noted that capitalism had developed science's relationship to production. Bernal believed that science was becoming what technique has always been, an indispensable part of the productive forces of society. Technical know-how needs to be backed everywhere by the scientific "know-why," in order to maintain the life and growth of a modern community. Science may have been developed partly for the wrong reasons and hoarded by a few, but, for Bernal, it was a treasure nonetheless. He wanted all people to reap its benefits.

Such a conclusion is obvious when one considers the issue of disposing of the waste made by nuclear power plants. Know-how is no longer sufficient – "know-why" is essential.

Bernal put his finger on the role reversal that has occurred since the nineteenth century. Science used to follow industry; now science is often leading industry in new directions. Science requires the free exchange of the ideas, information and experiences of researchers, however. Private industry, monopolistic capitalism and bureaucratic societies have trouble accepting this idea. The free exchange of information contradicts the appropriating tendencies of monopolists. And scientific researchers are strongly influenced by the values of industrialists who strive to dominate nature and people.

Scientific knowledge comes from the universal, collective production and sensory experiences of mankind. Bernal called science a "socialized form of productivity." Hence all people should contribute, control and gain from it by free access. Universal knowledge could become a means of improving human welfare if it is used by producers who consult each other.

Unfortunately, today's scientists appear foreign to the work force. Their discoveries often deprive workers rather than benefit them. Scientists seem part of the elite managerial class. This perception is due in part to the internal structure of contemporary science, especially its reductionist, dualist nature. But workers should understand that scientific endeavour is not inherently reductionist and dualist. Moreover, universal access to scientific knowledge can benefit most working people. Social pressure can also change the way scientists conduct research, thus transforming scientific activity. Since science (in both the West and Eastern Europe) is shaped and monopolized by a minority, however, it is not surprising that science protects and serves the interests of a small group.

CHECKLIST
How to Monitor Scientific Research

Workers should assess the relationship between their own productive activity and trends in scientific research. In making this assessment, ask yourself these questions:

1. How do universities, governments and industries perceive the needs of the work force?

2. Should more research be directed toward stress in the work place caused by noise levels, work stations, heat, or light?

3. What research would improve my own life: more knowledge about nutrition, the prevention of illness, education and training, leisure, urban housing?

4. What are the major subjects or fields of research funded now by government, industry, and universities?

5. What productive activities are related to their research? What industries are they linked to? What might be the social or political goals?

6. How do these compare to the research needs of our working or nonworking lives?

7. Who finances the research? Who performs it?

REFERENCES

1. MARX, Karl. (1973) *Grundrisse.* Harmondsworth: Penquin Books Ltd.

2. BABBAGE, Charles. (1970) *Reflections on the Decline of Science in England.* New York: Augustus Kelly.

3. BERNAL, J.D. (1971) *Science in History* (4 vols.). Cambridge: MIT Press.

4. SOMBART, Werner. (1919) *Der Moderne Kapitalismus.* Munchen: Duncker

SUGGESTED READINGS

BERNAL, J.D. (1971) *Science in History* (vols. 2 & 3). Cambridge: MIT Press.

FREEMAN, Christopher. (1982) *The Economics of Industrial Innovation.* London: Frances Pinter.

CHAPTER 9

THE PROJECTION OF VALUES

This chapter will explore the impact of cultural values on technical change. Our values bring about modifications in technologies simply because we must first imagine and project technical ideas before implementing them. Such ideas are coloured by our unique perceptions as well as our attitudes and world views.

Take the case of architecture, for example. Architecture is a projection of how we represent space. It directly affects our living and working environments and the relationships we maintain in those spaces. Good architects are aware of how a building's design affects those working in it, besides knowing what materials and builders are available for construction. They are aware that the space they imagine and create shapes our material culture – the way we live every day.

In this sense all technical artifacts have an "architecture" and "configuration," because they exist in space and time. They also order interpersonal relationships.

Lewis Mumford and Siegfried Giedion are worth citing here. In their studies of the history of building and architecture, they contributed important insights to our understanding of machines. In **Techniques and Civilization,** Mumford suggested that the concept of machine organization predates the era of mechanics and can be found in military discipline.

> The pattern of the new industrial order first appeared upon the parade ground and the battlefield before it entered, full fledged, into the factory. The regimentation and mass production of soldiers was the great contribution of the military mind to the machine process (1).

In **Mechanization Takes Command,** Siegfried Giedion showed how the idea of machine has affected all areas of human endeavour, especially home life.(2) Even when machine shapes were not necessary for home appliances, the designers adopted them nonetheless.

Technical artifacts represent ideas, and technical procedures enact imagined plans. When one person develops a new representation of space and time, this influences how another person imagines a technical application.

Ernst Cassirer, a German humanist who fled from Hitler in the 1930s, asserted that a hunting and gathering society considers space merely as a field for immediate action (3). It attaches the notion of space concretely to the fish to be caught or the elephant to be trapped. Contemporary society, on the other hand, views space as an abstract idea. We have divorced it from concrete activities that call upon the five senses. In order to draw maps we schematize space. Thus our concept of space has affected the way we visualize and has altered our technical creativity.

Cutting Up the Earth

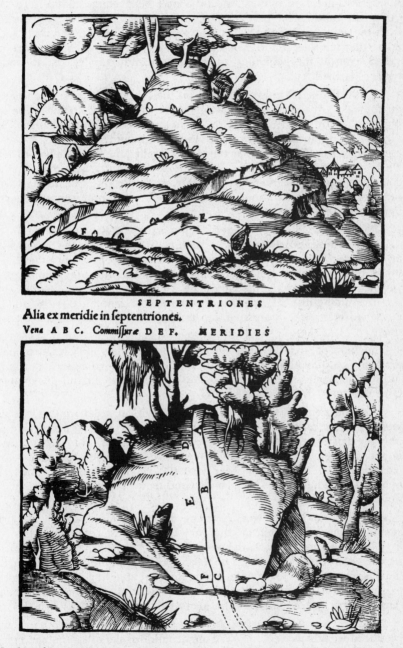

In the 16th century Georg Agricola published a mining manual entitled *De Re Metallurgica* in which he presented illustrations, such as this, showing how Mother Earth could be mined.

To illustrate the influence of attitudes on technical activities, let us consider their impact on mining. Ancient people believed that nature, especially the earth, was their mother. As animists they considered extracting minerals from the veins of the earth a crime against nature. Before committing such a crime they felt they had to appease the gods with offerings, a belief that prevailed even at the beginning of the seventeenth century, when modern science dawned.

By 400 B.C., Aristotle and Plato, on the other hand, were arguing that matter was inert and lifeless, a view that met with slow acceptance. The stoic philosophers of 200 B.C., however, called the world a living organism. Zeno argued, for instance, that nature experiences sensations and thoughts, and it generates creatures out of its images; Seneca called the wind the breath of the world which nourishes all life. In the fifteenth century Leonardo da Vinci compared the movement of water on earth with the flow of blood in a human organism. Other Renaissance thinkers likewise drew no distintion between living and inert objects.

The above world views affected mining activity in Antiquity and the Middle Ages. Some thinkers believed that precious metals were the earth's secretions under the sun's rays, and feared that mining would exhaust them. During the seventeenth century Henri More, a Cambridge philosopher, advanced such a view. At the same time Ablaro Barba argued just the opposite in a mining manual, asserting that the Potosi mines in Bolivia had been reopened because a "perpetual generation of silver" had regenerated the ore.

The views of Aristotle and Plato, modified by Judaic and Christian beliefs, gradually brought about a break with animism and polytheism. According to Judaic-Christian tradition, human beings are made by God in his own image. God also created nature for man.

A second step was taken with rationalism. Moses Maimonides, a seventeenth-century rationalist, argued against Moslem theologians, saying that only the existence of reason – not God's existence – could be proven. As an Egyptian physician, Maimonides believed that medicine's function was the emancipation of the spirit in order to cure the body. The effect of such a belief was to downgrade the body, nature and material things in relation to reason and the mind.

By 1700, rationalism was becoming more and more widely supported against religion. Descartes' rationalism was making the belief in God increasingly marginal to seventeenth century man: "I think, therefore I am," he stated as the cornerstone of his philosophy. Thought rather than God or action was considered the origin of everything. Feelings, intuition, and material existence, thus downgraded, were made subordinate to rational thought. Any material endeavour could be justified by rational calculation.

As for mining, Georg Agricola supported the view that Mother Nature produced wealth above and below the ground for the use of human beings. Francis Bacon claimed that humans should dominate nature. Once philosophers had deprived nature of a spirit, men could proceed to mine its resources. Nature had to be perceived as an impersonal entity before men could rape it.

The Protestant Ethic, Entrepreneurship, and Innovativeness

Just as philosophic theories abound, so do forms of social ethics. Each form manifests itself differently; yet people often confuse them. For instance, the spirit of initiative has been equated with private enterprise. The spirit of initiative refers to the spirited, or motivated, creation of a new social organization, whereas private enterprise refers to the ownership of property. As social ethics influence the human intiatives in historical periods, it is important to specify what values are the inspiration of which initiatives.

Many sociologists and economists believe there is something technically innovative in the cultural values of white Anglo-Saxon Protestants and in the institutions of private enterprise. Max Weber, a German sociologist, believed that private enterprise sprang from the Protestant ethic and the religious reformation movement of the late Middle Ages. Joseph Schumpeter, an Austrian economist – a favourite in management circles – spent most of his life analyzing how the entrepreneur gives shape to creations and inventions. Alfred Marshall, a British economist who contributed to the foundation of the dominant school of establishment economics, the neoclassical school, talked about economic chivalry. Finally, J. M. Keynes, the British economist who became a millionaire many times and went broke as often by speculating on the stock exchange, saw entrepreneurship as the "animal spirit of capitalism."

We have already noted that techniques reflect the values of a dominant social group. Institutions also reflect values. Social organizations and techniques share a common trait: they are both a means to an end. The end purpose of organizations and techniques reflects the values of the elites. Human production and distributive relationships are organized around techniques that in turn affect cultural and social designs.

Let's take the example of private enterprise. Max Weber, a nineteenth-century sociologist, spent most of his life comparing cultures and religions. In so doing, he traced capitalism's entrepreneurship to Protestant values. According to Weber, most seventeenth-century thinkers in Europe began to favour continuous physical and mental work. They extolled the human compulsion to earn, save, invest and reinvest. In their view, the accumulation of wealth was evidence of hard work. They encouraged others to strive for these goals – to develop their abilities and initiative, and to sharpen their wits in the pursuit of wealth. The middle-class self-made man was admired, whereas the hedonist who spent his money or flaunted his wealth was deplored. These values were widespread, Weber noted; they existed in varying degrees in most Protestant religions, such as Lutheranism, Calvinism and the Quaker persuasion.

Weber argued that the Protestant ethic – the spirit of capitalism – existed before capitalism became the dominant economic force in Western society. He suggested that Protestantism's material and behavioural values may have motivated the small entrepreneurial artisan as much as they affected the powerful merchant or banker.

Captains of Industry

The engineer, the industrialist and the banker are considered to be the captains of industry. Every culture and epoch has tended to believe that one profession is the source of more initiative and progress than another.

Benjamin Franklin is a famous embodiment of capitalist attitudes and lifestyle. He also promoted a lay version of these values. Franklin, invoked as an ideal in American schools, was not a practicing Protestant but rather a deist who adopted the moral values of the Protestant ethic. He was a utilitarian; that is, he justified honesty, punctuality, industry and frugality because they were useful in getting ahead. In his view neither God's call nor his moral sanction justified good behaviour. Personal well-being justifies the entrepreneurial behaviour.

The Protestant ethic is not just an historical relic; its influence still persists. Workers who analyze their work place can determine how much the Protestant ethic still influences managerial decisions.

Schumpeter's Contribution

Joseph Schumpeter translated Weber's views about the motivation of entrepreneurs into an economic theory. In 1907 his short book, **The Theory of Economic Development**, challenged most existing economic theories (4). Schumpeter believed that the motive power behind economic development and technical change resided in the entrepreneur. Real profits were generated only when they "innovated," by combining or using production factors for new purposes, organizing work in new ways, and creating new organizations.

The conception of new technology, he argued, was meaningless to society until it was commercialized by means of a new product or process. Schumpeter also drew a distinction between the entrepreneurial innovator and the inventor. To Schumpeter, the entrepreneur rather than the inventor was the agent of technical change. Schumpeter's analysis can be illustrated in the history of the steam engine. James Watt, who invented a construction mechanism to improve the steam engine, was not acually the most important figure in this story. His invention may simply have served to increase the efficiecy of Newcomen's atmospheric engine; it might well have gathered dust at Edinburgh University if an entrepreneur named James Boulton had not appeared on the scene. Boulton, who had made money in another industry, perceived the potential marketability of the steam engine and invited Watt to become his partner. According to Schumpeter, it was Boulton, not Watt or Newcomen, who was the true innovator here.

The validity of Schumpeter's analysis can be seen today. Our culture celebrates the individual who markets an invention. In North America especially, the hero is not the inventor who conceives of an idea but the innovator who materializes it. Schumpeter built his entire theory of economic development on this distinction. No wonder it is so popular with business people, for it projects them as heroes. Schumpeter also thought, however, that the motivation of the innovative entrepreneur was not only to obtain larger profits but to acquire monopolistic advantage; the prospect of a temporary monopoly in producing a new product was the entrepreneur's lure. Towards the end of his life, however, Schumpeter was led to believe that the progressive character of that impulse was disappearing.

Schumpeter's theories of economic development, despite the support they receive from business and in popular culture, nevertheless fail to explain the way many technical changes actually occur. Business traditions concerning productive endeavours vary in different periods and countries. Values as well as business practices change. Moreover, major technical changes often happen without the help of private entrepreneurs, who are often marginal in today's world. Indeed many changes have resulted from the efforts of such diverse innovators as public utilities, experimental farms, or state planning authorities. During the 1940s and early 1950s Schumpeter even recognized that monopolies and state planners were suffocating private enterprise.

CHECKLIST
Values Clarification

1. What values do managers promote in your work place?

2. Do they define any social responsibilities for the workers, or only for management? What values do they hold?

3. Do they make any value judgments about a proposed new technology? Do they use many loaded words, such as "superior" or better," to describe techniques? What values are implied in their ranking?

4. Can you get them to make their value judgments more explicit, if they have already expressed one? For example, do they compare the new technology with another one? If they consider it superior, can they specify why it is so?

5. Whom will the new technology benefit, and how?

Entrepreneurs of the eighteenth and nineteenth centuries, however, transformed society by using their unrestricted license to compete, often putting competitors out of business. It is true that the Industrial Revolution unleashed technological changes. For better or worse, private enterprise was responsible for developing most of our iron and steel mills, heavy transport equipment and petroleum refineries. But many recent technical achievements, such as power grids and telecommunication networks, were set up by monopolies.

The cultural values of entrepreneurship have blossomed with small private companies which were promoted during the Industrial Revolution. Although these values survive in some industries, they are not so central in the modern business world. Other institutional structures, such as oligopolies – a few large companies who control the bulk of production – and bureaucratic centres plan and dominate economic production.

Although entrepreneurship is still hailed today as the source of economic and technical progress, its role, compared to that played by state-regulated utilities and monopolies, is nevertheless limited.

Alternative Ethics

The Protestant work ethic and the spirit of entrepreneurship fostered by it are not essential to industrial and technological development. In fact, recent research into the Industrial Revolution has shown that family clans, not traditional, individual entrepreneurs, have played a pivotal role. An American anthropologist, Anthony Wallace, has described the achievements of the Darby clan, who developed the refractory oven used in iron refining. This improvement enabled steel processors to use the steam engine. Remarkably, the Darby family not only succeeded in improving on their original technological innovation; they also managed to keep it a secret for five generations. Other extended families, such as the Brownes, Dudleys, Foleys, Crowleys and Crawshays, likewise played an important role in developing technical changes during this period. The extended family was an ideal medium in which to communicate technical problems.

CHECKLIST
The Role of Entrepreneurship

1. Who founded the firm for which you work?
2. Who manages it? Who finances it? Who controls it?
3. How easy or hard is it to start up a firm in your industry?
4. What minimum investment is required to start production in that industry?
5. Is marketing of the products your company produces controlled by large companies?
6. Are primary source materials controlled by large or small producers? Are they concentrated in a few hands?
7. How many firms produce the same product? Are these firms independent or are they part of a monopoly?

In Canada, the most prominent innovative development was fostered not by white Anglo-Saxon Protestants but by a member of the minority culture. The company J. Armand Bombardier established in the 1920s became a leading innovator in a social climate deemed hostile to business because of its Catholic heritage.

Despite Bombardier's success, Norman Taylor, a Yale University student, attempted to demonstrate in 1957 that French Canadians could not become innovative entrepreneurs because their Catholic cultural values supposedly conflicted with business ethics. These excerpts from Taylor's doctoral thesis are worth citing:

> Self-made men on the grand scale are rare and are widely viewed with some distrust.... Schumpeterian innovations are for others to risk their capital on; when they are no longer innovations, they will bear looking at.... The bold and aggressive innovator is not prominent because society has not offered him the prestige it accords to achievement in occupations associated with non-material results and because such activity would not be consummate with the deep desire for security... preferring security as the tried way to innovation and risk (5).

Now, almost thirty years later, Bombardier Ltd. ranks prominently among innovators, disproving Taylor's analysis. It leads the world in off-road equipment manufacturing. Its founder, J. Armand Bombardier, was himself a devout Catholic, a family man, and a mechanic. Following the pattern of Quebec family enterprises, he initially put relatives in key company positions. As the company prospered, he put them in charge of the subsidiaries. With relatives controlling all component manufacturing, he soon developed the techniques appropriate for a snowmobile. In 1958 his son Germain contributed the single tread that facilitated the 1959 Ski-Doo design. By controlling all the components through relatives, J. Armand Bombardier was able to develop a coherent systems technology. The extended family links were ideal for rapid communication of technical problems and solutions. It would appear, then, that the small Protestant family is not the only institution to promote innovation.

Another interesting case of successful, alternative cultural values is that of Japan. Japanese entrepreneurs have shown extraordinary innovativeness, even though their culture is markedly different from that which fostered the Protestant ethic. Traditionally, the Japanese have valued the advancement of the family or group more highly than that of individudals. The group's well-being is considered more important than competition or individual achievement. A good student, for instance, earns approval by helping classmates who have academic problems. A similar group ethic is reflected by artisans and tradespeople: industrial enterprises use artisan groups to train workers, and they often make individuals responsible for the training of others.

In the 1970s Japan clearly surged ahead of the United States as a world economic leader. We can thus see that cultural values different from those of Western private enterprise do promote technological dynamism.

Alexander Geschenbron, who specializes in the history of the U.S.S.R., has concluded that entrepreneurship is simply one of several factors in the development of industries (6). Perhaps it is not a requisite after all. Innovative forces just as powerful as private entrepreneurship were at work in Russia, Japan and other countries. German and, to some extent, French, commercial and investment bankers are in the forefront of developing industrial technology.

The case of industrial development in Japan is especially interesting. Historically, Japanese culture has been used to assimilating other cultures. After assimilating elements of the Chinese culture, Japan then showed itself capable of using other cultures to advance technologically. What distinguishes Japan's economic and technical vitality from that of other, Western nations, however, is the part that originated in state initiatives. After the Mejii revolution in 1868, the government embarked on a deliberate policy to create new industries and import foreign technologies. They did so in a novel way, one that had no parallel in their history. The government imported not only new machinery and techniques from the West; it also encouraged foreign technicians, engineers, artisans and science professors to work in Japan. New techniques were likewise imported so the Japanese could improve upon them.

Japanese samurai, the country's future leaders, in turn, went abroad to study in England, France, Germany, the U.S.S.R., and the United States. Eventually these students became famous educators, bankers, industrialists and government leaders. The military elites, or at least the most important samurai, also redirected farm revenues to industrial investment. They adopted Western industrial methods and military organization.

Today Japan demonstrates a clear sense of entrepreneurship, perhaps better than most other cultures and countries. No other nation has embraced Schumpeter's theories about entrepreneurship with such eagerness and enthusiasm. Yet the Japanese have not accepted the Protestant ethic and Western individualism, values which are foreign to their culture. The Japanese spirit of enterprise is best defined as the spirit of collective endeavour, and it is widely promoted in the work place by Japanese management.

Yet another culture that has witnessed recent technological advances is China. The Chinese appear to draw less distinction between manual and intellectual labour, unlike Westerners. It is not uncommon for Chinese manual workers to be recruited to participate in scientific work, or for scientists to be assigned to do practical tasks. The Chinese also respect the strength and power of small, manageable group-consumer companies. Thus they deliberately avoid making huge, unwieldy production groups, and they spurn technologies associated with large organizations. They know from their historical experience with water control that big structures can get out of hand. (See the Appendix for other such examples of Chinese practice.)

Chinese cultural values – the belief in the unity of manual and mental labour and respect for the small group – have generated many unique technologies in biomass, where human and animal wastes are used for home heating as well as soil fertilization. Chinese communes, as well, demonstrate technical initiative.

Perhaps we should address again the confusion between entrepreneurship and the spirit of initiative. Entrepreneurship is commonly associated with individual initiative. Although the spirit of initiative is important in the advancement of technology, it is not confined to private enterprise in Western cultures.

Those who advocate entrepreneurship as the best means of realizing technical progress are making a value judgment which is invalid. There is no such thing as one superior organization or technology. Machines and techniques do not possess inherent, objective values. A harpoon fashioned from a piece of antler was as efficient to an Iron Age fisherman as the steam trawler is to today's fisherman. With the harpoon, small societies could bring in all the fish they needed. The large catch provided by a trawler, however, would create a problem; despite its admirable technological complexity, the steam trawler would have been inappropriate to a Magdalenian society. Yet it fulfills some present needs efficiently.

Whenever we discuss which technology is appropriate – a fashionable subject of debate these days – we must first specify the social group and cultural context that technology is supposed to accommodate. Judging from the examples examined in this chapter, cultural values are just as instrumental in promoting technological progress as politics, science, and techniques themselves.

CHECKLIST
Suggested Activities

To understand how an innovator's aims influenced the development of a machine, look up the history of a technique or machine that interests you. Then answer the following questions.

1. What was the vision of its innovators?
2. What architectural and spatial arrangements did the new technique or machine introduce?
3. What plans preceded the technical change?
4. What were their aims, or objectives?

REFERENCES

1. MUMFORD, Lewis. (1963) *Technics and Civilization*. New York: Harcourt, Brace & World, Inc.

2. GIEDION, Siegfried. (1984) *Mechanization Takes Command*. New York: W.W. Norton & Company.

3. CASSIRER, Ernst. (1944) *An Essay on Man*. New Haven: Yale University Press.

4. SCHUMPETER, Joseph. (1962) *The Theory of Economic Development: An Inquiry into Profits, Capital, Credit, Interest and the Business Cycle*. New York: Oxford University Press.

5. TAYLOR, Norman. (1957) *A Study of French Canadians as Industrial Entrepreneurs*. PhD Thesis, Yale University.

6. GERSCHENKRON, Alexander. (1962) *Economic Backwardness in Historical Perspective: A Book of Essays*. Cambridge: The Belknap Press of Harvard University Press.

SUGGESTED READINGS

BLISS, Michael. (1987) *Northern Enterprise: Five Centuries of Canadian Business*, Toronto: McClelland & Stewart.

GIEDION, Siegfried. (1984) *Mechanization Takes Command*. New York: W.W. Norton & Company.

MERCHANT, Carolyn. (1980) *The Death of Nature: Women, Ecology, and the Scientific Revolution*. San Francisco: Harper & Row.

NEEDHAM, Joseph. (1954 & following) *Science and Civilization in China* (13 vols.). Cambridge: Cambridge University Press.

WALLACE, Anthony. (1982) *The Social Context of Innovations: Bureaucrats, Families and Hereos in the Early Industrial Revolution, as Foreseen in Bacon's New Atlantis*. Princeton: Princeton University Press.

CHAPTER 10

SOCIAL CONTROL AND POLITICS

We have already noted that cultural values affect technological choices. Since values – adopted either willingly or unwillingly – are sometimes hard to discern, however, their impact is often subtle.

Politics, in the broadest sense of the word, exerts more obvious effects on the choice of techniques within a society. The term derives from Greek and means "the affairs of the city." In Athens "affairs" were settled by discussion in the agora, or the central meeting place, somewhat similar to a parliament. Although politics is distasteful to people who associate it with corruption, patronage, manipulation and coercion, it ideally refers to the democratic management of public affairs in a free society.

In practice, politics determines the right of people to choose certain techniques. Thus it sets standards for the most commonly used techniques and determines the ones which will dominate. (We should note, however, that some dominant techniques result chiefly from a generalized work discipline.)

Laws define, or limit, individual rights to certain technical operations, and these rights can be crucial to the diffusion of a technique. The struggle over who regulates society is a fundamental factor in the orientation of a technology. Rather than dwell on how politics orients technical development, however, we will focus on the impact of regulatory bodies. By way of illustration we will examine three ideas drawn primarily from hydraulic technology.

The Diffusion of Water Mills

The spread of water mills in the Middle Ages is one example of laws influencing the diffusion of techniques. Water mills have been important since early times, especially where the distribution and control of water was important. They probably originated in Greece. Their use around 100 B.C., and the conversion to a horizontal wheel from a vertical one, was recorded by a Latin writer. By 300 A.D. water mills appeared in the Mosel valley in Germany, moving then to England, Ireland, and Scandinavia. Mills were likewise built in the late Roman empire, as shown by the existence of a millers' corporation in fifth-century Rome. They multiplied in France from the tenth century on, spreading to more northern countries when settlers dispersed. Yet water mills did not become widespread in feudal Europe until the tenth century, or dominant until the thirteenth century.

In Chapter 3 we noted that between the eleventh and fourteenth centuries feudal lords struggled to abolish the use of hand querns, thus forcing peasants to bring their wheat to the water mills. The few peasants they exempted had to pay a monetary fine. Thus serfs not only had to use, but pay to use, the lords' mills. The lords were motivated by a desire to tax the peasants' wheat harvests. Monasteries likewise made use of water mills to meet their internal economic needs and release the monks for prayer and study.

Water Mills

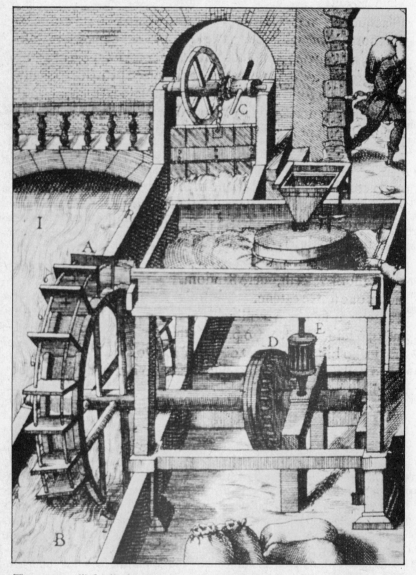

The water mill finally became dominant in 13th century Europe when lords were given monopoly rights over waterways and they forced peasants to bring the grain to their mills.

The lords issued many bans, or edicts, which formed the laws of the time: **banal laws.** Some bans specified, for example, the geographical areas in which certain rules applied. Bans could force peasants into military service, forbid them to sell wine on certain days, or confine the grazing of their live-stock to March and April in certain fields. One especially significant law gave feudal lords the exclusive right to build mills on water and to process the peasants' grain (1). According to the historian Marc Bloch, the spread of water mills was due largely to the institution of the legal monopoly giving feudal lords the right to control these mills. The triumph of water mills occurred at the same time as the spread of the banal laws, giving lords monopolistic water rights. Through banal laws, feudal lords gained monopolistic power over the use of almost everything – bulls, horses, ovens, grape presses, and, most of all, water mills.

Only repression made the implementation of such legal monopolies possible. The official attempt to destroy hand querns is well documented; it took place, for instance, in England (in Newcastle, Cardiff and outside of London) from the twelfth to the fourteenth century and in France (especially Normandy and Burgundy) from the thirteenth to the end of the eighteenth century. The best-known peasant struggle against the lords and monastic abbots who wanted to stamp out hand querns was the famous 1381 St. Alban's rebellion in England.

The imposition of the water-mill technology, including repressive efforts to destroy a preferred option, shows how laws affecting a technical choice can determine a technology. In this case the way the choice was made merely delayed the general acceptance and development of the water mill. Despite peasant resistance, the lords decreed its use. Thus, like it or not, the water mill became a key technology in medieval farming societies.

Several factors other than peasant resistance – such as technical reasons, geography, and, to some extent, slavery – also influenced the course of the development of water mills. Streams flowing to the Mediterranean Sea, for instance, fail to yield a regular flow of water throughout the year. Yet there are countries blessed with temperate climates and regular water flow where the water mill was not adopted. Hence we can see that geography alone does not account for its spread.

Agricultural expansion in the emerging feudal system, however, did favour the development of water mills. The absence of slaves to move the mills, together with a growing scarcity of labourers in the expanding farmlands, made the use of a powered mechanism attractive. This explanation, however, is not entirely satisfactory; if it were, water mills would have spread much faster.

Economics likewise played a central role. An economically feasible water mill, from the point of view of construction and maintenance, demanded large quantities of processed wheat. Hence they were best suited to densely populated regions, which could make them viable. Hand querns or animal-driven rotary querns were better suited to the needs of a scattered society. What made the mill finally flourish, then? Marc Bloch, in his study of feudalism entitled **Advent and Conquest of the Water Mill**, explains the major influential factors (1). But he concludes that these factors alone do not explain the spread of the water mill in Europe. Banal laws, in his opinion, were the most decisive element.

The forced use of water mills demonstrates the way in which laws can be employed to advance a group's power to make a technical choice. When certain techniques are imposed, alternative options are denied. In this circumstance, lawmakers are determining how an economic need will be met. They are imposing a common discipline, and their power becomes a technical force in society.

The Human Machine: The Raising of the Obelisk

When specialized tools are not available, like that above for the raising of the obelisk in Rome in 1586 or the building of the pyramids, many people are coordinated into a huge, well-disciplined "human machine."

The Human Machine

The second illustration of how regulatory bodies intervene in the matter of technical choice is the creation of work patterns. The following analogy will help explain this idea: whenever we cross a street we normally wait for the green light, or at least a letup in passing cars. Children acquire this habit early in life, just as new drivers must learn to obey traffic regulations. Without such restraints the safe circulation of pedestrians and vehicles would be almost impossible. The same principle applies to many work processes. Unwritten rules, obeyed by all workers, help organize the work place. As habits become second nature to people, they no longer notice they are following a protocol. Yet without them workers could not generate much concentrated technical activity.

Learning how to obey traffic rules and assimilate work procedures are just two examples of how individuals learn social discipline. Such discipline can be instrumental in bringing about vast technical changes, particularly if rulers know how to exploit it.

Consider the Egyptian pyramids, for example. These giant structures have a polygonal base with triangular sides which meet at the top. Egyptian architects had to design each pryamid separately. The Meodum pyramid, for instance, covers at least thirteen acres – 5,682 square feet – and reaches 3,619 feet high, about 150 feet higher than St. Peter's Cathedral in Rome. Not only is the size remarkable; so is the accuracy of construction: the four sides of the base measure exactly the same length, to six-tenths of an inch, and its four base angles measure exactly ninety degrees each, forming an almost perfect square. We may well ask how humans in the year 4750 B.C. could build monuments like this.

The second pyramid, called the Khafra, offers us some clues as to how such architectural feats were accomplished. The construction demanded a core work force of 4,000 workers, who were housed in barracks. We know only a little about the mechanical devices they used, and even less about how the workers transported the large, heavy stones (granite, diorite, and basalt). They apparently cut the rock with bronze saws set with diamonds, and made hollows with diamond rock drills; it seems they did not have sophisticated transport equipment to move the huge rocks. The workmen moved the rocks themselves, perhaps with the aid of crude devices.

To do so, they had to exert tremendous discipline. The minute organization and regimentation of thousands of disciplined workers may explain the construction of the pyramids; evidence shows that Eqyptian rulers could command and deploy such massive mobilization in other areas as well.

Autocratic rulers in many ancient states accomplished similar feats, such as the hydraulic technical systems built along the Nile, Tigris, Euphrates, Ganges and Yang Tse rivers. To become great builders of canals and dams, states had to draw on the organizational power of its citizens. (One Egyptian pharoah, for instance, annually counted people and measured land using precise census and mapping techniques.)

Egyptian scribes ruled from their offices; they were the first bureaucats to exist. (Our word **bureaucracy** comes from the French word for office, **bureau**.) Their responsibilities included overseeing water distribution, flood control and irrigation. Water-distribution officers, appointed by the state, cooperated with village leaders to irrigate fields. They all worked with clocklike precision. Peasants solemnly swore to obey the regulations while their fields were being flooded, and officers arbitrated the disputes that arose among the cultivators who lived along the river.

In ancient societies which developed such hydraulic systems, the bureaucracy was totally in charge. It maintained an information network, gathering intelligence and issuring orders to see that all regulations were obeyed. One Chinese society ensured fast lines of communications by using relay runners and horses. (In later hydraulic societies, the director of the postal system usually reported on water supply, as well as farming conditions, population, officials in charge, and so forth. This helped the government develop universal weights and measures to control people and the use of land.) In these activities, they acquired minute organization skills, such as those used to build the pyramids.

A hydraulic state like ancient Egypt exercised total control over its populace. Tapping a great organizational capacity, the pharoahs imposed the social discipline necessary to build the pyramids. These huge tombs displayed in pure form the ruler's organizational powers, since they served no other purpose than to celebrate the pharoahs' glory.

The pyramids may be an extreme example of how humans could be organized to generate the power of machines. Many technical achievements, however, have drawn on this social regimentation. Even technical activities which depend on sophisticated instruments often rely on it. This discipline may be voluntary and self-imposed, or it may be imposed by repressive regimes. Regardless of how it is attained, it is an important ingredient of technical change.

The Social Struggle to Regulate Technology

In contemporary Western society, investors have the power to determine which techniques will be promoted. This power does not extend to determining the overall direction of technical development, however. Technical and economic power are not synonymous. Even in a private society that champions enterprise, investors must interact with economic agents from the political arena.

There are basically three ways in which politics mediates investors' choices regarding a nation's dominant technologies. First, politics determines who has the prerogative to choose a technology for a given sector. Some firms, like Bell Telephone, are permitted to form monopolies. Others, such as Canadian National, are given charters. Still others, such as Ontario Hydro, are instituted by political movements with a techno-economic mission. Recent federal and provincial laws delineate management's rights in the area of technical change, in contrast to those of workers and users. Legislative action attributes economic, technical and organizational power to these firms.

The Treadmill

Industrialists and some social reformers used treadmills to generate power for industry and to punish or rehabilitate convicts.

Secondly, political regulations determine what technical choices will become dominant. Laws decide the performance characteristics a technique must have, for instance. Laws often set minumum or maximum sizes and weights, and they sometimes even decide what materials must be used. Thus standards favour certain techniques over others.

Thirdly, and perhaps most importantly, only regulations provide the broad social discipline needed to sustain a chosen system. Only a government, for instance, can set up a traffic or educational system to serve a large population.

The Canadian railway, energy and communications industries have shown how political actions shape technical orientation. Let us look at the case of electrical power in Ontario at the turn of the century, by way of illustration. In 1900, rival investors tried to control the distribution of hydroelectric power generated by Niagara Falls. Among them were Toronto bankers and industrialists. Hydro power at this stage could be exploited and transmitted either by private companies, municipalities or the province. The outcome, provincial ownership, was determined in the following manner.

Adam Beck, a cigar box manufacturer and Conservative member in the Ontario legislature, headed a public power movement. The purpose of this movement was to decentralize the distribution of electric power. Beck became chairman of a hydroelectric commission, which had the power to regulate private companies. Its purpose was to arbitrate between technical options suggested by private developers. This commission shaped Ontario's industrialization and technical development in far-reaching ways. It favoured decentralized access to electric power at fair prices. The electrical power system played a central role in orienting technical development in pulp and paper mills, mines and refineries towards energy-intensive techniques (2).

A 1984 Science Council survey about innovation in Canada shows that power utilities, especially the ones in Ontario and Quebec, have been the first users, clients and often initiators of technological innovation in 12 industries (3). They have stimulated the development and production not only of electric wire and cable, electric industrial equipment, other electric products and construction – the natural sources of technology for power; they have also fostered the development of new products in the machinery, control instruments, engineering, communications, aircraft, nonferrous metal smelting, metal fabricating, and paper industries. Today the power utilities look like the hub of an interindustrial complex of firms which supply technological innovations to industry. The hydropower complex forms the centre of gravity for the Canadian technical system.

Perhaps hydroelectricity gives Canada its only international comparative advantage: the energy-intensive processing of primary materials. Canada used to have a reputation for exporting mainly primary materials. In recent decades, however, Canada has specialized in the export of energy or energy-intensive products, limiting its other exports mostly to semimanufactured goods. This is probably due to the development of mammoth energy grids which have changed the environments of Canadian manufacturers.

The exponents of free enterprise claim that technological innovation in Canada is brought about by private entrepreneurs. This may well be the case for many new products; however, approximately one third of all Canadian innovations – new, commercially viable products – have been initiated or bought by either the government or industries regulated by it.

Governmental regulation is the ultimate factor in the direction of technical change. A democratic society develops a consensus, or majority decision, as to the direction of technical change, while an authoritarian government employs other measures for this task. Fortunately, the social direction of technical choice is not restricted to authoritarian political decisions.

CHECKLIST
Rules and Regulations

This checklist is designed to help you determine which body or bodies sets the rules and standards for your job.

1. **Technical Rights**

    Which institutions have the right to choose the technology at your job? Does any one firm have patent rights or inventions?

2. **Regulations**

    Is the work in your industry regulated by the industry itself, or by the government, or by both?
    What level of government establishes the standards?
    Can you specify what these standards are?
    How are they established or changed?
    For whose benefit are the standards designed?
    What do the regulations forbid?

3. **Technological Change**

    Can you define which changes are desirable to you?
    How would self-regulation or government regulation help attain such goals? What are the advantages and disadvantages of either forms of regulation?
    How do provincial or federal politics affect technological change in your activity?

REFERENCES

1. BLOCH, Marc. (1963) "Avènement et conquête du moulin à eau," in BLOCH, Marc., *Mélanges Historiques* (vol.2), pp.800-821. Paris: S.E.V.P.E.N.

2. NELLES, H.V. (1975) *The Politics of Development: Forests, Mines & Hydro-Electric Power in Ontario, 1849-1941.* Toronto: Macmillan of Canada.

3. DEBRESSON, Chris, and MURRAY, Brent. (1984) *Innovation in Canada* (2 vols.). New Westminster, B.C.: CRUST.

SUGGESTED READINGS

BLOCH, Marc. (1963) "Avènement et conquête du moulin à eau," in BLOCH, M., *Mélanges Historiques* (vol.2), pp.800-821. Paris: S.E.V.P.E.N.

MUMFORD, Lewis. (1963) *Technics and Civilization.* New York: Harcourt, Brace & World, Inc.

—— . (1970) *The Myth of the Machine: The Pentagon of Power*. New York: Harcourt Brace Jovanovich, Inc.

WITTFOGEL, Karl A. (1981) *Oriental Despotism: A Comparative Study of Total Power*. New York: Vintage Books.

CHAPTER 11
STATUS SEEKING

Up to now we have talked about functional techniques and rational motivations. Technical developments, however, are not always propelled by such factors as economics, science, and politics. Some technical activities acquire a logic and momentum of their own. Costly and seemingly nonfunctional, these techniques are the result of conspicuous consumption, showing the desire of the wealthy, and even the military, to raise their status and appear fashionable as well.

Montreal's Expo in 1967 and Vancouver's Expo in 1986 exemplify this search for status. One may well wonder why these two cities decided to organize their exhibitions despite the dire economic consequences that can ensue. Although the city fathers assure the citizens that such fairs make a profit, just the opposite usually occurs. The world fairs held by New York in 1964-65, San Antonio in 1968, Spokane in 1974, Knoxville in 1982, and New Orleans in 1984 all accumulated losses. New York's deficit was $71 million; Montreal's, $957 million and a debt of $2.4 billion; San Antonio's, $24 million; and Spokane's, $1.89 million. The fair in Knoxville precipitated the fall of the United American Bank, while the one in New Orleans made the city bankrupt. Seattle ended up in the black in 1962 only because it was given 74 acres of downtown property and attracted 25 percent more people than expected.

Will Vancouver's exhibition on world transportation accumulate a deficit or a profit? Whatever the case, the organizers of such fairs are not motivated by anticipated profits as much as they are motivated by the prospect of enhancing their status. World fairs do seem attractive: since the London Internatonal Exhibition in the 1884 Crystal Palace and the Paris Exhibition around the Eiffel Tower in 1889, numerous major cities have competed to host fairs at which countries can show off their latest technical achievements.

Technological exhibitions have an economic purpose: the exchange of technical information and demonstration of new techniques. Just as annual automobile and book fairs allow consumers to compare different products before making their purchases, technological exhibitions enable manufacturers and clients to inform themselves about new developments. Such markets have been organized to bring suppliers and potential clients under the same roof. This is also the case for new techniques.

New technical achievements, however, are not always commercially viable. As a result, fair displays of new technological artifacts are not a very secure financial investment. They involve some speculative risk, as manufacturers speculate on future sales. For instance, the Ontario Development Corporation, which built the Sky Train for the Advanced Light Rapid Transit System for Vancouver's Expo 86, hopes its demonstration will bring future

Boosting the Boss

Some techniques have no other purpose than to demonstrate the status of important people. But "status" is a double-edge sword. In the above drawing, the boss is being boosted up... but little does he notice that he is sitting on a catapult.

sales. The most likely prospect for the city hosting the display, however, is a deficit which will translate into higher taxes.

In this tradition, Vancouver's Expo 86 will showcase the city's new domed stadium, spherical theatre and driverless rapid transit system – the worker-less-automated-dream-come-true – mostly built with nonunion labour. Its purpose, then, is to show off the monumental symbols of a "great" city. The British Columbia government will probably argue that Expo 86 will attract new tourists and business to Vancouver in the future and put Vancouver on the map of the world's leading cities. But Expo 86 will also show off the wealth and power of the local establishment, just as a huge party would. Will Vancouver's pomp and ceremony be worth the cost to the ordinary citizens? There is room for skepticism.

If economic profits don't justify such technical expenses, what is the motivation for such endeavours? Veblen provides us with an explanation.

Veblen's Views on Status

The political economist Thorstein Veblen made some noteworthy studies on status seekers which are related to our discussion here. Veblen, who died in 1929, taught political economy in different universities, notably at the University of Chicago, where he influenced the Canadian historian Harold Innis, among many others. Veblen was the first political economist to analyze the expenditures of the rich. His first book, The Theory of the Leisure Class, published in 1899, analyzes this group's conduct (1). One chapter in particular, "The Conspicuous Consumption," explains how the rich spend what surplus remains after they have made investments.

Such conspicuous expenditures sustain many technical developments. They affect the choice and design of technology, especially the design of experimental techniques for demonstration purposes. We said earlier that leisure time, rather than necessity, may be the mother of invention. Since surplus time and income both feed investment, they motivate change. Investments may serve the purpose of demonstration – in order to prove that a technology does work and, more generally, to make a point.

Veblen claims that the wealthy spend their surplus income to distinguish themselves from workers. The wealthy think industrious people should consume only what is necessary for their subsistence. They do not apply the same restriction to themselves, however. The wealthy must consume goods wastefully to maintain their status, in the belief that this consumption gives them social dignity, or class.

Some of this behaviour tempts many people who are not wealthy, of course. We find it pleasant to interrupt work to enjoy friendly company, exchange ideas, play games, or listen to music. Most of us enjoy serving a good meal and hosting an enjoyable evening with friends; conviviality satisfies a social need. Wealthy "socialites," however, do these activities with an additional motive in mind: to prove their status. They buy certain objects, not because of their functional efficiency, but because they express social status. According to Veblen, hosting extravagant parties, giving expensive gifts, and hiring servants to run the house are signs of "invidious" ostentation.

Veblen observed that even working-class families spent some money ostentatiously to establish their social ranking. A farmer, for instance, would throw an extravagant wedding party for his daughter, while a worker would pay for a round of drinks. (Paying for a round of drinks or offering smokes not only promotes conviviality and sharing; these practices also help secure others' approval. They are a means to establish a form of social ranking within the group.)

Today we have various methods to win status among our peers. A common form of showing off at the work place is to waste time, either by going to the tavern after finishing a workload ahead of schedule, or by engaging in another activity at the work site. Yet another measure is to flaunt our possessions, such as our recently purchased car or computer, whether a Cadillac or a MacIntosh. One issue of **Business Week** reported that golfers may be overheard talking about their company's robots, for instance. Yet the journalist found that many robots lie idle in factories. Nevertheless the possession of one robot, even if it goes unused, proves that the owner is not only "in the swing of things" but in favour of "progress." In the early stages, a sophisticated machine may be only a conspicuous expenditure, having no functional use whatever.

Speculative ventures in real estate, commodities, precious metals and even frontier technology have almost replaced the frugality advanced by the Protestant ethic. Money can be made on the stock market or in real estate without putting a penny into production. The earnings, then, come from the expected future value of land, metal, currency, stock, or new technology. New technologies offer opportunities for speculation on future values. Patents given by government offices provide temporary property rights. Although innovators cannot easily gain exclusive property rights to new technological knowledge, patents theoretically give them exclusive rights in the area of application. In the development phase, a patentor may speculate on the potentially increased value of goods that will be processed by the new technology.

One way of selling holdings at an inflated price is to publicize them ostentatiously. In this scenario the wasteful individual replaces the productive individual as the model moneymaker. The technical artifact or commodity – whether a painting, a Rolls Royce, or a home computer – becomes an important status symbol. Individuals may buy Rolls Royces; cities organize international expositions; and governments display armaments which symbolize their power.

Military Expenditures and Arsenals

Military wares are bought by governments at public expense. They constitute a public form of conspicuous consumption equal to private consumerism. Both types of expenditures share common features: they are unproductive. They do not bring about the production of other goods, nor enter into the circulation of wealth. Proponents of military expenditures argue that useful technical spinoffs result from the development of sophisticated armaments. However, simple scientific experimental instruments, like nuclear accelerators, and monuments like the Eiffel Tower, have also motivated spinoffs.

The Military Arsenal

Much military hardware has no other purpose than to show off the awesome might of the military. (Drawing by R. Cobb)

Outside of war time, the production of defense equipment is motivated largely by the desire for prestige on the part of a nation and its military establishment. This applies to the United States and the U.S.S.R., as well as to small, isolated countries like Nicaragua. For instance, Nicaraguans recognize that their most efficient defense against potential attack by the United States or Honduras is a popular war, similar to the insurrection which toppled Somoza. Nicaragua's acquisition of sophisticated aircraft, and its heavy dependence on the Soviet Union for spare parts and skilled maintenance, can be explained only by the posturing of the Nicaraguan military before other Central American nations. Like generals who take power in coups in other countries, they need to have signs of their power.

Since 1935, when Western countries began to rearm, defense production has held the lion's share of industrial production. Industries in the United States never returned to a civilian regime after World War II, nor did they in the U.S.S.R. As Seymour Melman has described in **The Permanent War Economy: American Capitalism in Decline**, defense production became a permanent institution (2).

President Dwight D. Eisenhower, in his 1960 farewell address, warned Americans that the United States and western Europe were in danger of becoming prisoners to the unyielding power of the "military industrial complex." His warning went unheeded. After a temporary retreat in the late 1970s, the military complex has gained new strength. Canada, following its 1959 production-sharing agreement with the United States, has become a major subcontractor to the American military procurement system. A large share of Canada's limited manufacturing capacity is geared to making defense products, such as laser drives, radar units, and telecommunication equipment.

Seymour Melman describes this exercise of capitalism as production without profit. Cost-plus contracts from the Pentagon distract industrial enterprises from concerns about cost effectiveness, reliable products, and simple, functional designs. Since the military pays all increased costs and ensures profit margins, no wonder the U.S. defense system ends up with $200 hammers!

Mary Kaldor, an activist in the European Nuclear Disarmament (END) movement and a proponent of disarmament for the British Labour Party, discusses the weapons systems and defense industry in **The Baroque Arsenal** (3). She argues that the defense industry with its weaponry has spawned dysfunctional technology and a warped concept of technical achievement.

According to Kaldor, defense systems have become increasingly complex. The F-4 fighter plane, for instance, which served in Vietnam, had 70,000 components. The reliability level of a technical system depends, of course, on the less reliable subsystem, even when it has fallback subsystems. Operations and maintenance must also match new complexities. Some features of the F-14 and F-15 fighter planes, which succeeded the F-4, proved to be dysfunctional. Because these planes were too elaborate and complicated, they prevented the pilots from realizing the planes' supposed new performance features. Even if all the new features had been used, however, they would have caused astronomical increases in production and maintenance costs.

Then there is the question of design. In her book, Kaldor discusses how each new generation of weapons systems builds on previous ones without undergoing any basic redesigning. The goal is to make faster, bigger, heavier weapons without changing systems. Yet all these endless additions and auxiliary subsystems have made the overall systems ineffective, bulky and unmanagable.

The defense industry's perverted concept of functional efficiency infects the manufacturing industry as well. I have found, when studying innovations by Canadian defense contractors, that their complex, sophisticated processes are often custom tailored to military specifications. These needs bear little resemblance to the requirements of standardized nonmilitary products, which are made in series. Moreover, I found little evidence of technical spin-offs. In fact, the technical criteria for military and civilian products seem antithetical: the criterion for military products is that they should be sophisticated and complex, while the goal of nonmilitary products is that they should be simple, reliable and efficient. How can spinoffs develop under these circumstances?

The ostentatious waste of defense systems promotes technical developments that do not meet the needs of mass production. Worse, the development of military components, sustained at immense monetary and social cost, has left us a legacy of time bombs that will be hard to diffuse. The aphrodisiac of power, combined with excess surplus resources, has badly warped our sense of technical achievement. Technical performance is a goal in itself, whatever the use of the product.

CHECKLIST
The Status Seeking Value of Techniques

1. What technical objects in your home serve little purpose? Could you dispense with them? Are they a means of expression? In whose company do you exhibit these objects?

2. How do you mainly show your social status – in dressing, eating, drinking, or smoking?

3. Do you keep your front lawn attractive? Do you like to change cars every few years?

4. What expenditures or leisure activities do you like to boast about?

5. What proportion of consumer products in a Sears or Bay catalogue serve only to enhance status? In other words, which products are luxury goods that could be dispensed with?

REFERENCES

1. VEBLEN, Thorstein. (1953) *The Theory of the Leisure Class*. New York: Mentor.

2. MELMAN, Seymour. (1974) *The Permanent War Economy: American Capitalism in Decline*. New York: Simon and Schuster.

3. KALDOR, Mary. (1981) *The Baroque Arsenal*. New York: Hill and Wang.

SUGGESTED READINGS

KALDOR, Mary. (1981) *The Baroque Arsenal*. New York: Hill and Wang.

VEBLEN, Thorstein. (1953) *The Theory of the Leisure Class*. New York: Mentor.

CHAPTER 12

COMBINATION OF FACTORS

All the factors we have examined so far combine in various ways to effect technical opportunities. On the one hand, they can be restricted by the constraints within a system along with the fixed investment in machines. Norm-setting regulations and economies of scale likewise decrease technical activity, because they lead to standardized engineering designs and techniques. On the other hand, the combination of factors can have the reverse effect, leading to greater opportunities, as when incremental adaptations interact with economies of scope.

Graph 12.1
How Factors Combine

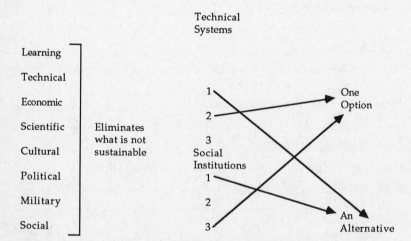

The interactive causation present in technical evolution is like ecological dynamics. The effects of the various factors combine either to restrict the focus of technical activity or to increase it. To assist your understanding, think of society as a field of various forces: some explain what does not occur and hence are called "negative constraints;" others supply incentives and are termed "positive constraints." When two different incentives motivate technological activity in opposing directions, they might cancel one another out. But if they converge in the same direction, they have a dynamic effect, which is called synergy.

Here are some possible combinations.

Example One
Investments and Systems Combined

As discussed in Chapter 7, Jacob Schmookler demonstrated that patented inventions increase after a surge of fixed investments in new machinery. Economic demands for techniques motivate investors to acquire new machines. Thus technical improvements and inventions increase.

Bertrand Gille has noted, however, that the grouping of techniques into interdependent systems reduces the options available to solve technical problems (1). Since all auxiliary techniques must be compatible within a system's core, the options are reduced, as we saw in Chapter 6.

These two factors – the increased demand for techniques and their organization into a system – point in the same direction: they restrict the field of technical research. A plant's productive system usually relies on machinery. Fixed investments in machine systems help narrow the range of technical solutions that engineers, technicians and workers can find.

Example Two
A Simple Design Combined with Government Standards

After trial and error, cumulative improvements in engineering designs lead to products that are simpler, more reliable, and easier to mass-produce, as we saw in Chapter 7. If the government sets legal standards, it influences the choice of technological designs, thus promoting standardized technical practices. Snowmobile manufacturers, for example, set noise and safety standards in the 1970s. In the late 1950s Bombardier had already come up with a simple, reliable design for the snowmobile: the Ski-Doo. The standards imposed two decades after the design was invented led to the adoption of a uniform standard in the industry. A technique becomes uniform due to the combination of converging factors.

So far, we have described how merely two negative contraints have interacted. When these factors represent positive incentives, however, the results are more difficult to discern.

Example Three
Adaptation with Economies of Scope

As discussed in Chapter 6, many conditions encourage variation in techniques: the raw materials, the material making up the machines, the uses for which the technique is intended, geographic conditions, and so forth. Economies of scope are made because the machinery can be used for products that are not basically all that different (see Chapter 7). Therefore the requirements of adaptation and reduced production costs combine to encourage product variation.

This combination of incentives leads to dynamic effects. Machines are shared for different products, which encourages the production of new products. Workers acquire new knowledge, which in turn may be applied to another set of products, and so the cycle continues. The impression is created that the technical opportunities are boundless.

Guideposts

In the second and third chapters, we saw how the social organization of work and new institutions were crucial in orienting technical activities. Social scientists call it a controlling factor. The social organization of work more or less controls which of the other factors will affect technical activity, as well as to what extent they will do so. Therefore, although the process of technical change is complex, social action does enable people to shape their own technological history through the shaping of organizations.

In the maze of factors affecting technical change, there are some guideposts that mark the path of technical evolution. The various factors we have examined contribute to polarizing technical developments around a certain technical system. The specific areas of technical and industrial activity around which many of the innovations occur are called "technical development poles," a concept developed by the French economist François Perroux. Once these development poles are identified, it is easier to predict where technical change is heading, as well as how one can affect it and what cannot be changed.

Take the example of Canada in the last few decades. Huge investments have been made in hydro dams and electric power networks. The James Bay project is the most recent example of these large investments. Gigantic hydraulic turbines and electric power generators have been combined with high-voltage transmission to produce and carry large quantities of electric

Graph 12.2
Main Technological Development Pole of Canada

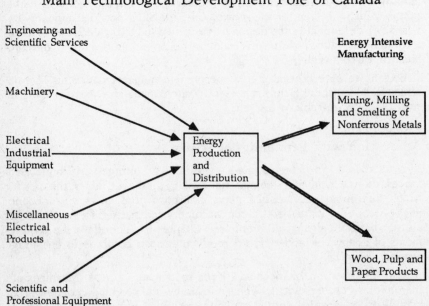

Source: DeBresson and Murray, *Innovation in Canada* (vol.1), New Westminster, B.C.: CRUST, pp.117-122.

power over a long distance. As a result of this available electricity, many industries in Canada have specialized in energy-intensive manufacturing processes: pulp and paper, mining of nonferrous metals, smelting and refining. A third of all the innovatons in Canada have been in this sector. Canada's exports have shifted in the last decade from raw materials to energy-intensive processed materials. The electric energy complex is the main pole of technological development in the country. This is its acquired comparative advantage in competing with other countries.

This development pole is the result of a combination of factors, in particular large fixed investments, electrical power systems, and diversifications in the application of electricity. Most countries and regions have similar strong points which polarize technical activity. They may choose to enhance the development of such poles of technological capabilities. But once they exist, they have a momentum of their own.

CHECKLIST
Review of Factors Affecting Technical Change

1. Which of the following factors orients the technology you use at work: human experience, working knowledge, accumulated experience, technical systems, availibility of natural resources, fixed investment in equipment, scientific discoveries, scientific instruments, research procedures, social discipline, regulations, a search for status?
2. Which of these factors do you consider the most important?
3. How do they increase or increase technical options?

REFERENCES

1. GILLE, Bertrand. (1978) *Histoire des techniques: techniques et civilisations, techniques et sciences.* Paris: Gallimard.

2. PERROUX, François. (1961) *L'Économie du XXième Siècle.* Paris: Presses Universitaires de France.

CHAPTER 13

LONG PERIODS OF TECHNICAL DIFFUSION

The last chapter looked at how evolutionary forces may converge to influence the direction of technological change. One of the implications is that a new technology takes a great deal of time to occur. This chapter will discuss why this is so, by focussing on the pattern in which innovations occur and then on the reasons they need time to spread throughout industry.

The Cluster Effect

Although scientific discoveries occur with relative frequency, they are not all equally important. One significant breakthrough in science usually precipitates many others, as was dramatically illustrated in the case of DNA. Biologists knew that chromosomes and genes transmit hereditary traits, but they didn't understand how. To unravel the mystery, researchers in separate branches of science adopted different approaches. Organic chemists studied the components of living bodies, looking at both their individual composition and their overall proportions to one another. Meanwhile structural chemists examined the shape of macromolecules, and crystallographers took photographs of them.

Once DNA was identified as a common component of genes, a biochemist named Loria suggested the answer to the riddle lay in DNA's molecular structure; this, he claimed, accounted for hereditary transmission. Francis Crick and James Watson then found that the complementary two-helicoidal structure of DNA allows a DNA molecule to automatically transfer its own traits to future structures through division and reproduction (1). As soon as the process of hereditary transmission could be tested empirically, biochemical discoveries multiplied. The structure of numerous other basic living materials, such as RNA, were then found.

The discovery of the periodic table of chemical elements evolved in a similar manner. After scientists established the table, they then synthesized numerous materials and compounds based on it. The latter were not found in nature.

It is worth noting that just one major discovery initiated each of these research booms. Collective research efforts narrowed the gap between neighbouring disciplines, enabling sicentists to fill in the remaining holes with greater ease.

In 1977, Gerhard Mensch, a German economic historian, proposed that basic discoveries occur in clusters at relatively long intervals (2). His hypothesis seems reasonable, since major discoveries do tend to generate other important ones. Whenever a new vision or new world view emerges, it initiates and accelerates scientific discoveries. What is relevant to us here, in our discussion of technological change, is the parallel that can be drawn between scientific discoveries and innovations. Mensch went on to argue that basic discoveries in turn cause basic innovations to occur, which set off long periods of economic growth.

Many historians of technology support the notion that important innovations occur in this manner. Because a major innovation is often a unique combination of techniques, it stimulates innovations in many other fields. The crankshaft, for instance, permitted the linking of horizontal and rotary movement, as well as the transmission of the direction of power. It thus led to the invention of many other machines.

Graph 13.1
The Inter-Industrial Sequence of Dissemination of Technological Change

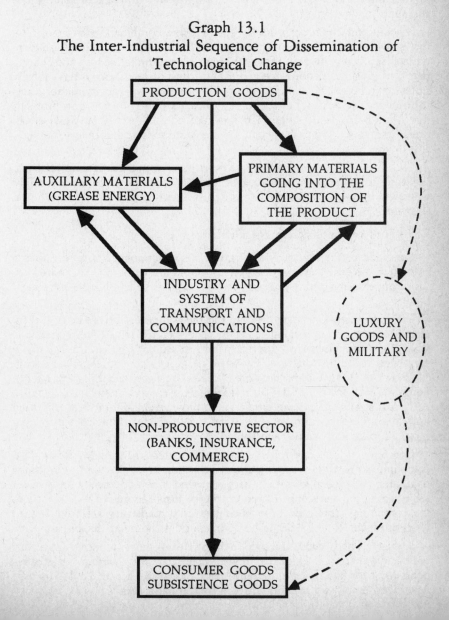

At this point it is necessary to clarify the difference between an innovation and an invention, a distinction initially spelled out by Joseph Schumpeter. In lay terms, they both refer to novelties, but according to Schumpeter they referred to distinct entities.

Inventions are specific new discoveries – processes, appliances, or machines – which may never leave the laboratories in which they are found. Indeed, they may never even leave the drawing board. Important inventions that do leave the laboratories and acquire a patent lead to the establishment of a technical system. Around it develops a cluster of different applications and support techniques.

Innovations, on the other hand, represent new combinations of productive forces, which may or may not make use of inventions. Innovations are commercialized, while inventions need not be. According to Mensch and Schumpeter, radical innovations occur during a time of recession, a time ideally suited for entrepreneurial risk-taking. New leaders emerge and either transform existing enterprises or set up new ones; they also invest in new products that offer more advantages than the current ones available. Such entrepreneurs reap a profit in the process, thereby attracting other investors to imitate them.

The cluster effect discussed above remains to be proved. It is not unusual, however, for theorists to advance or cling to an unproven idea, since it might well shed light on explaining interesting sequences in scientific or technical activities.

Sequence of Technological Diffusion

One idea that is supported by facts is that an important new technology will affect the entire production system – or at least a number of industries. This notion surfaces in the works of many economists and historians of technology.

Two examples – the steam engine and the computer – illustrate how technical diffusion occurs in a given society. Let us consider first the sequence in which the steam engine was used. Owing to a military decree, it was initially employed to pump waters in mines in 1716, and to houses in London in 1775. It then was used to drive waterwheels in furnaces and mills, and later to pump water out of dry docks. Next it served as a rotary engine in textile mills. After that application, it was employed to blow air first into iron works, then into mines. Finally it came to service transport vehicles. All in all, steam technology took over a century to spread.

Computer technology followed a similar pattern. During World War II, computers were employed for military purposes; in the postwar period, they continued to be used by the military, but were also adopted by universities for research purposes and by nuclear power firms. In microprocessor form, the computer's application has become widespread: they are found in all types of offices, family dens, and also in countless home appliances and cars.

Similarly, robots were first used in the nuclear industry to move dangerous radioactive materials. Later they helped make expensive high-grade components for both the aircraft and aerospace industries. Since the 1970s they have been employed in automotive plants to paint cars.

One given technique, therefore, has several applications, leading to its dissemination throughout the industrial system in a set order. The same can be said of most technologies, which appear to adhere to the following trajectory. In its nascent stage, the technology is simply an instrument. It leads to the development of equipment and capital goods, used by material processing, and then gets adopted by transport industries or by industries that produce durable or nondurable consumer goods. Typically the new technological product is first used by the wealthy – or the military. Next it spreads to lower-income groups as increased output and improved processes lead to cheaper production. This entire process takes so much time that it cannot occur within less than 30 years.

North American prosperity after the Second World War caused people to forget the Depression of the thirties. In the 1950s, however, computers and automation once again raised the spectre of widespread unemployment. One famous study, **Automation and Management**, written by James R. Bright, concluded that computers would reduce the overall proportion of skilled labour to unskilled labour but would not decrease overall unemployment levels (3). At the time Bright wrote his book, computer control techniques and automation were only just beginning to spread through industries, however; they had not yet reached the industries that produced consumer goods. Today they have. As a result, computers are now being used to reduce costs in industries marketing basic subsistence goods (food, retail, offices, banks, contruction, and so on). Their effects on unemployment are thus more tangible. They are easier to spot now that the computer technology has undergone a period of diffusion.

As Nathan Rosenberg has noted, a single innovation does not affect the economy; the ripple effect occurs when a combination of innovations occur (4)(5). The initial innovation undergoes countless design modifications to meet the needs of its specialized users. Each new application plays a part in the dissemination process. The overall effect is produced by a system of interrelated complementary innovations.

Some changes in a few industries, such as the chemical or computer industries, are pivotal in generating a vastly disproportionate number of changes that affect the entire economy; however, it is the spread of cost reductions, in such sectors as as transport, energy, services, and communications, that affects all the other industries. Since the transport and building sectors serve all the others, their capacity to use and spread new technologies to all industries gives them a special importance. The technological innovation that affects these two industries has an impact on the entire productive system.

Bottlenecks

A new technology expands through industry by creating bottlenecks. One typical example of a bottleneck is the compound steam engine.

The railways' demand for greater power generation created the need for cheap, high-quality steel in the form of strong alloys that were also heat-resistant. Such alloys were of little use to other industries until appropriate machine tool methods were developed. Accordingly, the compound steam engine had to wait until these alloys were developed. The railways had created a new demand which created a bottleneck in supply.

A bottleneck can be created by the lack of raw material. If the demand cannot be satisfied quickly, another bottleneck will be created earlier in the production chain. Design changes may be introduced to circumvent the problem. One change in the production chain thus will force the segment before and after it to change, too.

The Slow Diffusion of Steam Technology

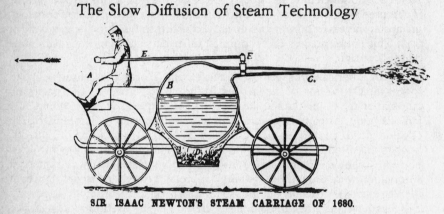

SIR ISAAC NEWTON'S STEAM CARRIAGE OF 1680.

In 1680, Sir Isaac Newton predicted that the steam engine would be used to run automobiles. (1) However, it was not until the late 19th century that some were built — not very successfully. The steam engine was first used to pump water for cities (2) (Chaillot water works) and then coal mines and then slowly spread throughout industry as in Graph 13.1.

This comparison between technological change and bottlenecks has important implications for labour. Workers should keep on the lookout for bottlenecks in the production system. This will ensure that unions are looking in the right direction, for wherever a bottleneck exists it is a sign of coming changes, posssibly technological ones. If the snag in the production system is not obvious, the next place to check is the segment of production marked by the highest labour costs, the greatest uncertainty, or the least reliability. That segment is a likely candidate for management initiative, reorganization, and technical change. A second area to check is the segment in which wages for skilled workers are highest. A third area is the segment of production which has the highest energy cost, since it may be in line for cost cutting measures. Finally, in times of prosperity and full-capacity production, business might look at cutting machinery replacement costs and improving the reliablity of production.

After a while, when a few industries have adopted the new technology, the demand for it will become substantial. A number of industries will combine to make greater demands for the new product. Economies of scale then become possible. Often the transportation and construction industries play a key role in the dramatic increase of demand for a new technology.

Development economists call this "complementarity effects." Several techniques combine their effects and reinforce one another's advantages. This can open up new opportunities: for example, the combination of rail transport, ocean transport, and refrigeration allowed Australia to export its meat.

The Buildup of Systems

Once a new technology has diffused through most industries, new technical systems are built up. After a while, the established system generates its own momentum, thereby orienting subsequent technical developments. It will tend to block the emergence of a new one. (Steam power was blocked by water mills; turbines were partially blocked by steam engines.) Investors, engineers and technicians acquire vested interests in the current system; their resistance in turn slows down the pace of change. When the pace of innovation slows down, according to Mensch and Schumpeter, stagnation and depression will settle in.

Feedback Effects

As a result of this sequence in technological innovations, investments seem to occur all at once but in irregular cycles. For instance, new fixed investments occur much more rarely in the transport industry than in other industries because the whole transport industry has to be changed each time an investment is made. When such investments do transpire, they tend to be quite large. As a general rule, the length of investment cycles in different sectors of the economy differs because the machinery is not replaced at the same intervals.

Graph 13.2
Feedback Effects

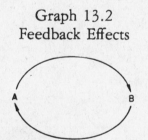

The Combination of Different Cycles

Investment cycles have different lengths. When cycles with different lengths combine, they may cancel each other out, or have the opposite effect – amplify one another.

The training of engineers should illustrate this notion for us. Generally undergraduates decide to pursue graduate work during their third year. Their decision will be influenced by the current economic outlook. In a given year, therefore, the supply of master's degrees and doctorates in engineering or science will depend on the business climate four or five years before. Normal business cycles last three to four years; inventory cycles, on the other hand, are thought to last seven years. The educational cycle for training graduate engineers does not correspond to the two previous cycles. The discrepancies may amplify or cancel one another out.

The Early Steam Engine

One of the first steam engines used in France to pump water from the River Seine at Chaillot just outside Paris.

The simple combination of cycles of different lengths can coincidentally produce the appearance of a much longer cycle and a greater crisis of adjustment. In simpler terms, many things can go right at one time; however, everything can't go right all the time. But when everything starts going wrong at the same time, the result is disastrous.

In addition, there are other factors that create upswings and downswings in the economy. Technological change is certainly not the only factor, or even the main factor.

First, the context in which change occurs affects the pace of diffusion, as well as the extent of the influences that accompany the change. The culture supporting a technology takes a generation to spread. For example, training courses in computers and word processors took a long time to set up, delaying the effect of computers.

Secondly, a period of high wages or low interest rates may accelerate the development of labour-saving innovations, while a period of low wages or high interest rates may retard them. Thirdly, rapid population growth and territorial expansion, as witnessed in North America during the nineteenth century, might also accelerate the pace of change. Similarly, wars and revolutions may expand or restrict the size of the market. Institutional change will affect the speed of diffusion, while social actions may reorient techniques in another direction entirely. A final factor to consider is public policy.

Given all these factors which influence the pace of technical diffusion, can one possibly blame technological change alone for causing major dislocations and crises?

A new technology, however, will follow a sequence that is affected by the divisions of industries. Periodically, the equipment sector has to purchase some of its own production. Similarly, the maker of producer goods has to occasionally absorb some of its own production because the consumer goods sector cannot absorb it all. As a result, technological innovation will tend to first revolutionize the producer goods sector before it is able to transform the consumer goods sector. This tends to be the case whatever the socio-economic system.

Technological change, then, has a much longer sequence to follow than, say, a business cycle. Transforming several industries may in fact take at least half a century.

In an earlier chapter we looked at the reasons why entrepreneurs invest in technical change. The prospect of making extra profits entices investors, which in turn accelerates the change. As all firms adopt the new technology, the costs and prices of products are lowered. Once one segment of production is revolutionized, the neighbouring segments will be the object of change. Capital will leave the industry where the extra profits are disappearing and go to the industries where the new technology enables new profits to be incurred.

During the whole periods, more capital will flow to those industries that are supplying the technological change than to all the others. They are called the growth industries because their rate of growth is higher than that of the others. The computer industry is our latest growth industry.

The cycles of booms and busts are generated by the private accumulation system itself, not by technological change. The booms and busts are simply multiplied by the number of industries they encompass. Moreover, the bust is amplified when the new technology finally affects the basic subsistence industries and subsistence sectors. But one cannot blame technology as such.

New technologies in biochemical engineering are just starting to come on the market in the 1980s. These commercial technologies are the first practical translation of the discovery of DNA, on the part of Watson, Crick and Rosalyn Franklin, between 1951 and 1953. In all likelihood, the wide-ranging economic effects of these innovations will not occur for at least 30 more years. Diffusion needs time.

By the same token, industrial countries are now experiencing the economic impact of a variety of radical innovations that occurred during the 1950s – transistors, computers, and television.

REFERENCES

1. WATSON, James D. (1968) *The Double Helix: A Personal Account of the Discovery of the Structure of DNA.* New York: Atheneum.

2. MENSCH, Gerhard. (1979) *Stalement in Technology.* Cambridge: Ballinger.

3. BRIGHT, James R. (1958) *Automation and Management.* Boston: Division of Research, Graduate School of Business Administration, Harvard University.

4. ROSENBERG, Nathan. (1963) "Capital Goods, Technology and Economic Growth." *Oxford Economic Papers,* vol. 15, pp.217-227.

5. ———. (1968) "Economic Development and the Transfer of Technology: Some Historical Perspectives." *Technology & Culture,* vol. 11, pp. 550-575.

SUGGESTED READINGS

ROSENBERG, Nathan, and FRISCHTAK, Claudio R. (1983) "Long Waves and Economic Growth: A Critical Appraisal." *American Economic Association, Papers and Proceedings,* vol.73, no.2, pp.146-151.

SCHUMPETER, Joseph. (1939) *Business Cycles* (2 vols.). New York: McGraw-Hill Book Company, Inc.

III
CRITICISM AND PROPOSALS
FOR CHANGE

In the final two chapters we will examine some of the criticism of the ways in which technical changes have been described by social scientists and historians and then move on to suggest alternative strategies. Understanding the factors that promote technical change is not enough to pave the way for action. We must first look at the deep-rooted beliefs that have made us so fatalistic about controlling our techniques.

CHAPTER 14

THE WAY WE THINK

What we know and understand about technical change has been largely conditioned by how we think about other subjects and by what we have learned about scientific advances in other fields. The dominant analogy found in most of the writings about technical change is that of evolution.

The publication of Charles Darwin's **The Origin of Species** in 1858 sparked a scientific revolution, as well as an upheaval in religious beliefs (1). Darwin's theories, however, were not only used to explain zoological differences and biological changes; they were also used to explain social and cultural changes. Herbert Spencer is perhaps the the most famous proponent of this approach, now termed social darwinism. The same biological analogy has been applied to the history of technology.

Basically Darwin's theories can be broken down into three tenets for the purposes of our discussion:

1. A species' adaptation to local and specific needs provides a genetic pool from which evolution takes place.

2. Some acquired traits are inherited.

3. A selective death rate favours the fittest species to the detriment of the weaker ones, which become gradually extinct.

Why have Darwin's theories been promoted to explain technological change? First of all, if we assume that animals and humans share a number of common traits and that humans in fact have gradually evolved from animals, it is logical to then assume that we are biologically determined. Many of our traits, according to this point of view, are inherited, just as our evolution is an extension of that of animals. A belief in biological determinism leads to a belief in technological determinism, as we shall see shortly.

Secondly, technological traits have many of the same traits as other evolutionary processes. The events of technical history appear to be ordered; time points its arrow in one direction only so that many events seem to be irreversible. Many historians who have specialized in technology have asserted that technical invention proceeds in a one-way, cumulative direction. You don't have to reinvent the wheel, as the saying goes. Once an invention has been made and its usefulness demonstrated, it is not likely to be lost. Furthermore, many technical changes are interrelated; it is impossible, according to A.P. Usher, author of A History of Mechanical Inventions, to study merely one invention or change; one has to study each invention within a given system, along with other changes (2).

As we saw earlier in the second part of the book, technological change is subject to many diverse forces. The evolutionary approach likewise tends to explain occurrences in terms of constraining forces. Within this framework, why something occurs is perhaps less important than why something else didn't happen. Indeed many technical choices are clarified by such an approach, since many technical options are incompatible.

Thirdly, a popular way of interpreting history is to view events as a chronicle. According to this approach, the outcome is basically inherent in the beginning. One event is also assumed to cause the subsequent event.

Fourthly, the evolutionary approach to the study of technologies has been widely promoted in academic circles. On the whole, paleontologists, archeologists, and anthropologists have worked to promote this theory; paleontologists, in fact, classify animal and human artifacts using the same system as the evolutionists. Such scientists are especially interested in finding human implements and evidence of techniques to explain how humans existed. The evolutionary theory can indeed explain many early technical changes – at least until humans started to keep their tools and formally communicate with one another by means of language.

The following quotes indicate to what extent historians have adopted the evolutionary theory to explain technolgical advances.

"Technological history must be considered as a genetic sequence of events. Technology is a central core in the evolutionary process (2)."

"Technical stalemates have to have only causes internal to technique itself (3)."

"All technical problems have solutions....The hand-held silex must acquire handles and the dragged bundle will acquire a wheel (4)."

Weaknesses of the Zoological Analogy

One main weakness of this approach has been to reduce the history of technology to a simple chronicle of events. The course of these events is not determined by their beginning. In contrast, there is another approach that we can adopt, one that assumes that humans do have a role in shaping events. Although the material conditions within a given social context restrict the options, it is assumed that humans do choose from among these options. In addition, there are shifts and ruptures in the course of history that change the direction of technical development. Such ruptures usually occur during a time of crisis. They occur, furthermore, at various levels: there emerge radical breaks in social relations, new institutions, new ways of doing things, new forms of knowledge, and new world views. Such ruptures are important in influencing technical development.

Again, according to Darwin's theory, the overspecialization of a species inhibits its ability to adapt to abrupt changes. The more specialized the species, the more difficulties it has to adapt. This principle has been applied by the Nobel Prize-winning economist, Simon Kuznets, to explain the decline of traditional industries. When their instruments become excessively specialized, especially in large technical systems with many interdependent parts, they are difficult to adapt. This leads to declining returns of improvements, stagnation and disappearance. This lack of adaptability, or rigidity, Kuznets termed the "dinosaur effect" (5).

The analogy may be useful in elucidating why established industries find it hard to adapt to technological change, but it shouldn't be applied to all techniques. After all, humans, unlike animals, possess one valuable trait that enables them to revert to previously abandoned techniques: memory. The memory of past experiences and techniques is preserved in our language and culture. For example, games, sports and rituals keep past ways of doing things alive. Institutions – museums, archives – and all our books and records likewise conserve our collective memory. New techniques incorporate the old, but we can always revert to the old version.

If, over several generations, an animal species has evolved a specialized organ, it cannot suddenly discard that organ when the conditions suddenly change. Humans likewise cannot suddenly abandon certain biological features, but they can abandon unworkable technical systems, replacing them with simpler ones and keeping some of their components.

Our ability to preserve and transmit techniques has four important consequences:

1. They allow the rapid diffusion of techniques. We don't have to wait an entire generation to acquire certain techniques if we teach ourselves new ones.

2. Techniques can spread much more rapidly than biologicial traits.

3. As a result, techniques can be rediscovered, overspecialized techniques can be broken down and simplified, and technical "evolutions" can be reversed. For instance, alcohol was the first fuel used for internal combustion engines in the late nineteenth century; it was replaced by petroleum in the twentieth century. Now that petroleum is considered too costly, we are experimenting with ways to once again make use of alcohol.

4. Techniques have an extraordinary persistence through the ages, as we have seen thoughout this book. The selection of a new technique doesn't necessarily mean that a former technique is totally abandoned. Even when a technique is partly abandoned, as in the case of the water wheel, it can reappear in combination with another technique, as in electric turbines and hydraulic dams. This very malleability seems to attack the notion that only the fittest techniques can survive.

Many old techniques may in fact continue to evolve alongside the new ones rather than stagnating at all. For example, the horseshoe industry, which originated in the second century, witnessed an increased number of patented inventions up to the First World War in the United States. As long as people needed to use horses, but in new conditions, the technology continued to develop; the horseshoe had to adapt to meet the demands of the western frontier, urban life, and finally the trenches.

Quite clearly, then, we are not stuck with a particular technique because we have inherited it from the past. In accordance with diverse social and economic goals, we choose different techniques to suit our particular aims. The scope of opportunities will be constrained by various factors, which we have already reviewed in Part II. Nevertheless the intended effect of the technical change is due to its promoter.

Technological Determinism

"Our daily habits and actions...are dominated by an implicit faith in perpetual progress," Lynn White, an historian of medieval technology, has
noted (6). This belief is all pervasive, underpinning our current religious and
political doctrines. Yet it was unknown to Greco-Roman antiquity or to the
Orient, Lynn added. It is a recent faith that was rooted in Judeo-Christian
teleology.

Graph 14.1
Diversity and Progress Among Major Lineages of Animal Life

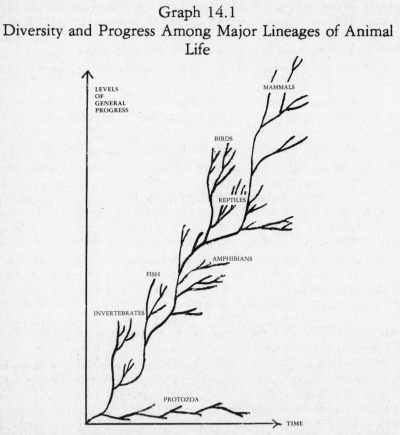

Teleology is the belief that all phenomena are determined by an overall
design or purpose. Both Judaism and Christianity believe in the messiah, although they disagree on when that messiah will appear. They also believe
that the world has an end, a destiny, overseen by the hand of Providence. Humans are the chosen instruments of this destiny.

When Darwin's scientific ideas about evolution spread in the second half
of the nineteenth century, a curious blend was forged between his ideas and
Judeo-Christian teleology. Rigid cultural evolutionists foresaw a predetermined historical destiny. Many determinists then blended this idea with
Marxism, espousing the notion of "the direction of history," which would be
brought about by communism. Communism was seen both as a reality and a
vision of a future utopia.

Graph 14.2
Social Evolution

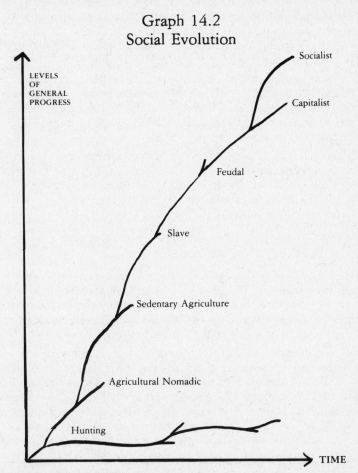

Americans have developed another image of the ultimate destiny, calling it an "advanced" or "developed" economy. Regardless of the final version of the new faith, the ideas of social and cultural evolution have reinforced people's belief in a one-directional, convergent destiny for mankind. And central to this determinism is the belief in progress. The instrument to bring about such progress is technology.

Technical progress plays the same role in the twentieth century that gold played in the fifteenth and sixteenth centuries. During the rise of mercantile capitalism, gold was considered to be the source of all wealth, especially in Spain and Portugal. Later, with the rise of industrial capitalism, Adam Smith publicized the idea that free trade and the unrestricted production of goods were an even greater source of well-being. "Laissez-faire" became the dominant creed. Today it is "laissez-inventer." We are all convinced that invention should proceed indiscriminately, because we believe it is intrinsically good. What is novel is always better, never worse.

The reality, of course, is quite different: investors do not exploit all inventions, but select the ones that suit them best. Nevertheless we are urged to surrender to the ethos that presents technological and scientific progress as a phenomenon beyond our control. We are assured by such technological determinists as Bertrand Gille that "all technical problems ultimately have a solution." (3) Powerful scientific institutions and influential periodicals likewise promote the idea that science can solve any problem.

"If religion was formally the opiate of the masses, then surely technology is the opiate of educated people," J. McDermott remarked in an article he wrote on the subject entitled "Technology: the Opiate of the Intellectual." (7) The belief in technology's benefits is our new lay religion, and it is powerfully endorsed by all governments.

Each nation has made of progress the cross it carries. America sees itself as a carrier of progress, its Manifest Destiny. The U.S.S.R. regards itself as the carrier of the direction of history. Progress has become a state affair. In every election, all political parties refer to progress as their goal.

How the Illusion is Maintained

People often believe that the objects they revere possess powers that are associated with their use. They make the objects into fetishes. Today we tend to display the same behaviour towards technical artifacts that primitive people displayed towards their statues. We are inordinately attached to technology – we revere it – just as the ancients revered their gods.

Gold used to exert this same fascination on people, who considered it sacred. Gold, like a machine, is a commodity, and it was considered the source of wealth. Technological hardware also seems to incarnate the blood, sweat and tears of human efforts to improve the way we live. Although technologies are the result of multiple social efforts, the hardware appears to rise above work, to lead an independent life of its own. This is an illusion, of course; the hardware without any instructions or humans would be useless.

Curiously, hardware also tends to obscure the social background from which it comes. It becomes a hieroglyphic that needs to be deciphered. Mechanics have to figure out a new engine; until recently, one had to have had a great deal of training to be able to programme a computer. The hardware, then, appears, to be greater than the people who created it, exercising its own strange, mystical power.

Techniques were not always exchanged the way technological hardware is now. Even today, many of our techniques have no hardware and cannot be sold as commodities. But when the techniques become incorporated into objects and are sold as commodities, we then attribute the effects of the techniques to the objects themselves. We bequeath the objects with power. Accordingly, when a new technical system is introduced, such as an assembly line, it appears to personify the new technology itself. The system and its hardware appear to have transcended their creators; "it" has dramatically reorganized the production process.

Similarly, novices often blame the computer for failing to process instructions or for simply "bombing," forgetting that any computer has to be programmed. Intimidated by this new machine, they assume it knows what it is supposed to do, and fault it when it doesn't. Computers become invested

Graph 14.3
The Computer Tree

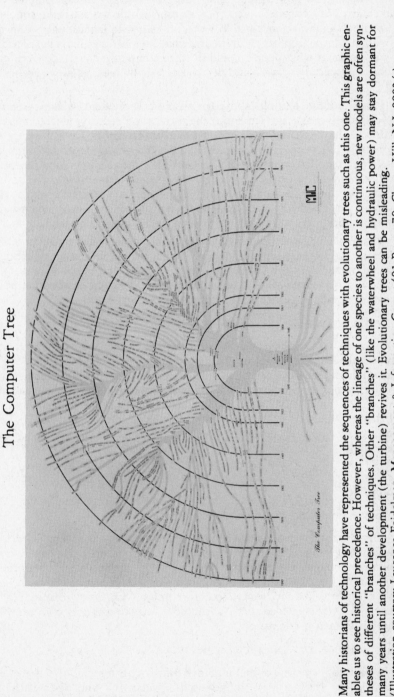

The Computer Tree

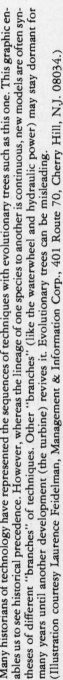

Many historians of technology have represented the sequences of techniques with evolutionary trees such as this one. This graphic enables us to see historical precedence. However, whereas the lineage of one species to another is continuous, new models are often syntheses of different "branches" of techniques. Other "branches" (like the waterwheel and hydraulic power) may stay dormant for many years until another development (the turbine) revives it. Evolutionary trees can be misleading. (Illustration courtesy Laurence Feidelman, Management & Information Corp., 401 Route 70, Cherry Hill, N.J. 08034.)

with strange new powers seemingly beyond our grasp or control. Five-year-old children are enrolled in computer classes; adults flock to take courses in computer literacy; science-fiction writers invent wild fantasies about a world dominated by computers. Admittedly, what computers are capable of achieving is amazing; what people could do with computers would be even more amazing, especially if we could become as socially creative as we are technically.

In addition, technological expertise is rare. Individuals who possess such expertise sell it as a service. Since the turn of the century, all the industrial countries have passed laws to ensure that inventors have a temporary monopoly (17 years) over their inventions. The right to produce someone else's patented invention has to be obtained; the licensee pays the patent holder a royalty to do so. Hence, inventions and technical knowledge have become valuable commodities. When an invention is new, its practical value is unknown. Therefore people speculate on the expected economic value of its application, like they speculate on the value of gold or land.

The social forms technical changes take in economic exchanges create the illusion that technological hardware and knowledge are powerful. But we can rid ourselves of this notion. We have long abandoned the idea that gold bullion is the source of all wealth. Hasn't the time come to shed the notion that a technology transcends its creators and overpowers them?

The Language of Mystification

How do magazine writers perpetuate some of the common myths about technology? An analysis of five American magazines, which count among the most influential of the periodicals dealing with technological change, show these common stylistic devices. (The magazines surveyed include **Business Week** (8), which deals with the concrete and political interests of business; **Fortune** (9), a glossy business periodical devoted to trends; MIT's **Technology Review** (10), which publishes well-established authors for engineers, high-tech business managers and policy makers; **Science** (11), which publishes articles by authors published in more specialized fields; and **The Scientific American** (12), which popularizes science for the nonacademic public.)

1. Excessive Use of the Passive Voice

The most conspicuous grammatical form common to the feature articles in these magazines was the passive voice. A sentence in the passive shifts attention to the object of an action by placing it as the subject. The doer of the action can be omitted altogether, as in this example: "System A was chosen." Empty subjects like "it" were also quite common. Excessive repetition of the passive conveys the idea that "Technology" is imposing its own rationale, without human participation.

2. Fondness for Abstract Subjects

A passive form was often combined with an abstract subject, such as "a drive," "the interface," "competition," "patterns," and "performance." While articles in **Business Week** tended to be specific about which firms introduced particular techniques, writers occasionally referred vaguely to industry as a whole. Vague concepts were in abundance in many of the articles.

3. Personification of Technology

Technology was personified in the feature articles of all five magazines. The feature article in **Fortune**, for example, avoided using the passive by making technologies the personified subjects of active sentences (9). Technical hardware thus becomes the doer of the action: "the sliding forms cantilivers outward" or "long span bridges...will be opening up vast territories" (11).

In the literature about technological change in general, animating new techniques is a common stylistic device. Such personification attributes to the hardware the actual powers and aims of the inventors and users. It negates the idea that people are always acting through a technical means. It also suggests that they have relinquished all responsibility over the technique's social effects.

4. The Vocabulary of Evolution

Teleology is the belief that all phenomena are determined by an overall final design and purpose. From a teleological point of view, the world is predestined – predestined for progress, for example. This notion is usually coupled with the idea that technology evolves as part of an overall evolutionary pattern. In a feature article in **Science**, for example, the direction of technological evolution is simply postulated without question (11). The careful case history of the telephone in **Scientific American** implied that the "emergence of the telephone" was a foregone development (12).

While historians are trained to never explain the past by referring to the future result, writers who focus on technology – popular writers and academics – seem to believe that the outcome of technological evolution is implicitly or explicitly preordained. Readers of popular articles on technological change can therefore expect to find many images and comparisons that announce technological revolution, describe the different stages of evolution, or resort to jargon designed to confuse rather than simplify the issues.

5. The Use of Vague Tenses, Locations and Settings

In four of the five feature articles in these magazines, the notion of time is limited to an indefinite past and a future with no duration. Definite past tenses were rare. Locations where technological change has occurred were not always specified, although **Business Week**'s article did mention the names of the firms.

In short, such stylistic forms end up attributing to technologies the intentions of businesses. No specific social group is held to be responsible for technological change, since technologies are themselves personified as actors. The technological hardware holds a promise of future wealth and has a power of its own. We are emphatically enjoined to let "technology" proceed unchecked because we can't stop progress.

CHECKLIST
How to Evaluate Articles on Technology

When you read articles on technology or technical change in newspapers or magazines, ask yourself these questions.

1. What particular technology (or change) is being discussed?
2. Where is it situated?
3. Who is in favour of the change? Who stands to benefit?
4. How often is the passive used? What effect does this have?
5. What adjectives are employed to describe the technology or change? What does this indicate about the author's viewpoint?

REFERENCES

1. DARWIN, Charles. (1974) *The Origin of Species.* Harmondsworth: Penquin Books Inc.

2. USHER, A.P. (1954) *A History of Mechanical Inventions.* Cambridge: Harvard University Press.

3. GILLE, Bertrand. (1978) *Histoire des techniques: techniques et civilisations, techniques et sciences.* Paris: Gallimard.

4. LEROI-GOURHAM, André. (1971) *L'homme et la matière.* Paris: Éditions Albin Michel, p.27.

5. KUZNETS, Simon. (1967) *Secular Movements in Production and Prices.* New York: Augustus M. Kelley.

6. WHITE, Lynn. (1962) *Medieval Technology and Social Change.* Oxford: Clarendon Press.

7. MCDERMOTT, J. (1969) "Technology: The Opiate of the Intellectual." *New York Review of Books.*

8. *BUSINESS WEEK.* (1981) "Steel Jacks Up Its Productivity." October 12, pp.84-87.

9. BYLINSKY, G. (1981) "A New Industrial Revolution Is On The Way." *Fortune,* vol.104, October, pp.106-114.

10. ABERNATHY, William J., and UTTERBACK, James M. (1978) "Patterns in Industrial Innovation." *Technology Review,* June-July, pp.40-47.

11. *SCIENCE.* "Bridges Past and Future."

12. HOUNSHELL, David A. (1981) "Two Paths to the Telephone." *Scientific American,* vol.244, no.1, pp.134-141.

SUGGESTED READINGS

CHILDE, V. Gordon. (1951) *Social Evolution.* Cleveland: World Publishing

WHITE, Lynn. (1962) *Medieval Technology and Social Change.* Oxford: Clarendon Press.

WHITE, Lynn. (1967) "The Historical Roots of Our Ecological Crisis." *Science*, vol.155, no.3767, pp.1203-1207.

DEBRESSON, Chris (1987) "The Evolutionary Paradigm and the Economics of Technological Change" in the *Journal of Economic Issues*, June 1987.

LOWE BENSTON, Margaret, and DEBRESSON, Chris, eds. (1987) *Work and New Technologies: Other Perspectives*, Toronto: Between the Lines.

CHAPTER 15

CHOOSING TECHNICAL DIRECTIONS FOR SOCIETY

The thrust of the earlier chapters has been to show how a social organization, particularly the organization of production, acts as a controlling factor on all facets of a new technology, including its initial selection, design, and diffusion. The resulting technical system in turn maintains the social organization that fostered it. The social fabric and the technical system thus mutually reinforce each other, serving common goals. Herein lies the clue to controlling the impact of technological change.

Yet the most prevalent attitude towards technical problems is that of the "technological fix." If a new technique has an undesired impact, we try to

Graph 15.1
Dynamics of Choice and Change

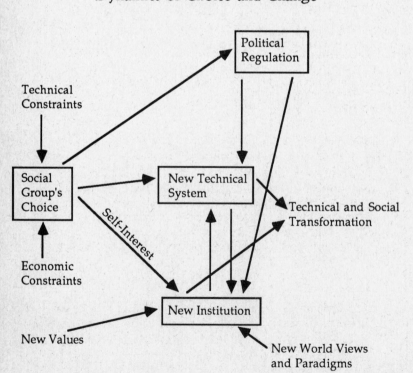

Graph 12.1 illustrated how different constraints combined to restrict possible choices. This graph illustrates how a social group will promote a social institution and a chosen technical system which is compatible with the former, for its self-interest.

"fix it" by other technical means. This has been the typical reaction to the social problems resulting from technical change, problems which we have inherited from past centuries. In the 1980s we are still reacting like the medieval peasant who gave up a scratch plough in favour of a metal plough. Our eyes are still riveted on the tool's performance.

This narrow focus is no longer sufficient; indeed it may become dangerous to society. Technological changes today affect far more people than ever before. They also affect our whole ecological system. For instance, industrial production and nuclear technologies may be affecting the ozone layer in the atmosphere, endangering the condition of life on earth. Although, in the past, human beings have shown a great capacity to adapt, we cannot assume that we will have all the time we need to adapt to some of the environmental changes we are triggering.

Eventually, six conditions are necessary to affect the future direction of technological change in a meaningful way. Perhaps they are not sufficient, but they are all necessary. They include the following: (1) bringing about social innovations; (2) enshrining technical rights in our democracies; (3) focusing attention on the design of technical systems; (4) promoting new technical and social systems on the part of new social groups; (5) encouraging new values which will shape future technical designs; and (6) shaping a new view of technology.

Social Innovations

The first condition for orienting the direction of technological change is to focus on the controlling factors. If I am right in my conclusion that social organizations play a pivotal role in shaping technological change, we should then attempt to create new social institutions which shape technical designs.

Melvin Kranzberg, an historian of technology, suggests there is a lag in our perception of a work organization's importance.

> What at long last broke the interminable human routine was the invention of the division of labor, or the organization of work. From the simple beginnings, "the partition of tasks between men and women or between old and young," the organization of work developed complexity with an astonishing speed. In a few thousand years, a mere few dozen generations, it ramified into modern industrial society, with its 25,000 different full-time occupations, each of which defines its practitioner in terms of income, education, social status, living standard, life style.

> The dynamism of the history of work organization, especially in the Western countries, has had a ceaseless impact on the whole of society, repeatedly shaking it to its foundations. Yet intellectual perception lagged behind, and only very slowly did thinkers awaken to the immense significance of how the work force is organized to perform its tasks (1).

Whereas our social consciousness should always remain a jump ahead of technical inventors and their promoters, it trails them. This slow reaction is due to our belief in technological determinism, the notion that technology evolves independently of human actions and imposes its consequences on society. This belief is all-pervasive; it has become the universal religion of our times. Yet analysts of divergent social leanings have reached the same conclusion: in general, human beings falsely hold technical means responsible for the end results.

BLAMING TECHNOLOGIES

Two researchers with different backgrounds and ideologies both agree. David Noble speaks to labour with a declared labour bias. John Child is a management scientist who addresses himself to managers. They have nevertheless reached the same conclusion. Noble writes:

> Technology does not have a unilinear development; it consists of a range of possibilities, alternatives, which are delimited over time – as some are selected and others denied – by the social choices of those with the power to choose, choices which reflect their intentions, ideology, social position and relations with other people in society. In short, technology bears the social imprint of its authors.... Social impacts come about not so much from the technology of production itself as from the social choices which the technology embodies. Technology, then, is not the irreducible first cause; its social effects in reality follow from the social causes that brought the technology itself into being: behind the technology that affects the social relations lie the very same social relations. Little wonder, therefore, that the technology always tends to reinforce rather than subvert these relations (2).

The management scientist John Child agrees:

> A given technological configuration (equipment, knowledge of techniques, etc.) may exhibit certain short-term rigidities and perhaps indivisibilities and will to that extent act as a constraint upon the adoption of new work plans. However, rather than the technology possessing "implications" of effective modes of organizational structure, any association between the two may be more accurately viewed as a derivative of decisions by those in control of the organization regarding the tasks to be carried out in relation to the resources available to perform them (3).

In order to monitor and possibly reorient technology, we should direct our attention towards social relations, especially in production, at the shop floor level. This, of course, implies going beyond the property relations in production in order to examine the hierarchies in the overall organization of production, because social relations condition technological designs.

Until very recently, the choice of a technological design depended on who owned the technology. In the twentieth century, however, public corporations and state governments own some of the new technologies. Concerning state corporations in the West and state-level companies in Eastern Europe, it is unclear exactly who is making decisions in the name of the public. Slowly, in countries as different as the United Kingdom and Poland, the idea is emerging that state or public ownership is not synonymous with social ownership or control. The Polish Solidarity movement proposed socially owned, self-managed factories as an alternative to state corporations (see end of Appendix).

Unfortunately, very little research has been done on precisely how the different types of social organizations influence technologies. The literature on technology is replete with studies about how a technology affects a social organization, but the reverse research has not been done. Clearly, it must be, if we want to gain social control over the direction of technological change.

This book has focussed mostly on the major ways in which work can be organized, from sedentary agriculture, slavery and feudalism to the more modern forms of organization found in factories, such as batch and line production. Yet there is a whole gamut of other organizational structures that researchers can examine, from partnerships to corporations and guilds. In a study of guilds, for example, one can look at how the apprenticeship-journeyman system affects the design of techniques.

The twentieth century has witnessed still other organizational innovations worthy of our attention. They include public corporations and utilities, such as the Tennessee Valley Authority in the United States and Ontario Hydro in Canada, federally sponsored experimental farms in both countries, and self-managed factories owned by the workers in the United States. How do these publicly operated corporations influence major technical decisions? In the private sphere, pilot experimental plants have been set up in the petroleum and agriculture industries. Have these experiments changed the design of their respective technologies? Have self-managed factories done so? Such questions, and many others, should be asked also about another, lesser-known area, state planning in the Soviet bloc. What influence does a totalitarian, centrally-planned economy, like that of the U.S.S.R., have on technical choices? How do these influences differ from those attributed to a decentralized planning system like that found in Yugoslavia?

A New Institution: Self-Managed Firms

In the last decade, self-managed firms have yielded very interesting research data. Researchers from industrially advanced, capitalist countries who have studied self-managed firms have collaborated with exiled researchers from totalitarian regimes of Eastern Europe, where the state makes centralized decisions about all investments, to find alternatives. Socially owned, self-managed firms are an innovative form of organization which seems to have many advantages.

Small, self-managed cooperatives are often more productive than large state-owned or public firms, for obvious reasons. First, if the workers receive financial benefits from a company's increased productivity, they will contribute more effort to make the increase occur. Also, useless overheads and management functions can be eliminated. The shadow world of paper production can be reduced to a bare minimum. Perhaps the computer can be designed to assist such self-managed production systems.

Another advantage of such firms is to draw upon the working experience of the work force. In an earlier chapter, we saw that working knowledge is a source of invention which is left largely untapped in the capitalist or bureaucratic systems. Self-managed firms could make workers' participation in the design of technical changes an integral part of work.

One can speculate about other advantages of self-managed firms. By the closer integration of decision-making and production functions, instant feedback on the process of production becomes possible. The system can be constantly altered to compensate for errors and omissions in planning. Self-management could act just like an interactive computer programme that stops at frequent intervals, informs the operator of its current state of activity, and asks for more input.

Much research still needs to be done, however, on self-managed production systems. Probably reliance on work force skills and creativity would encourage the design of less capital-intensive techniques, and less complex and inflexible technical systems. This may help promote greater technical autonomy and less dependence on rigid interdependence systems, thus increasing society's capacity to adapt itself to various economic shocks. Additional research and social experiments are needed to confirm these assumptions.

Such institutional innovation, however, is limited. Self-managed production units.may help resolve some problems at the level of factories, but they do not enable society to control global technical systems.

Establishing Technical Rights

In today's world, not a single country has a political forum in which to discuss crucial issues related to technologies. During an election voters are not asked to decide on the nature of a technology they would like to see developed in their communities. Nor do many of us exercise any authority in these matters at work, unless we move within top management circles. Nonetheless, technical rights are now being apportioned to different social groups in industrialized countries.

CHECKLIST
Social and Technical Designs

Technologies do not exist in the abstract; they bear the imprint of the society in which they are embedded. In turn, technical systems reinforce social systems. Here are some questions that need to be asked.

1. What is the most suitable social organization to advance certain goals?
2. Which technical systems would best sustain this organization?
3. Which features should the systems have?
4. Would the technical systems promote or subvert these goals?

Presently we are witnessing struggles over technical power in North America and Europe. Management is now asserting its right to make technical choices. In fact, several clauses concerning technological change have been added to the Canadian Labour Code, clauses which give management these very rights. Municipalities have passed bylaws which regulate techniques. Environmental laws and occupational health legislation also regulate the choice of techniqes. Even governments which criticize state interventionism regulate technical rights. For instance, soon after President Reagan was elected, his administraton offered firms specializing in the design of computer chips new property rights in the form of "masks." These new property rights, which are neither copyrights nor patents, are being given without adequate public discussion.

Sooner or later, principles will have to be established as to how technical rights and prerogatives should be apportioned. The U.S. Congress, for instance, has established an Office of Technology Assessment to guide their members, who must make decisions about different technologies. This Office allows for some evaluation of technical alternatives, but it does not yet enable the average citizen to do so. More importantly, citizens have to participate in setting the criteria for choosing technical alternatives.

We should ensure that technical rights be apportioned democratically. Since technical choices affect other people's lives, a political mechanism must be set up to enable a community to choose the technology best suited to serve its interests. Establishing such mechanisms will necessarily entail a discussion of alternative technical designs and the values which will guide our choice of technologies. Technical assessment is a new field of research developed for that purpose. In order to make an assessment of technical alternatives in relation to social goals, researchers must compare performance, costs, benefits and social impact. Perhaps a public process of technical assessment complicates the democratic process, but it also makes democratic choices very concrete.

Our present democracies have failed to define technical rights. What rights we now seem to have were established on the principles of eighteenth-century enlightenment, based on small, uninfluential technical systems. Constitutions in liberal democracies have only recently established property rights, and have assumed that technical rights were incorporated in the investor's rights. As Thorstein Veblen pointed out at the beginning of the twentieth century, technical prerogatives have been left to private investors since the eighteenth century.

Let us clarify this concept. Technical power is related to investment power, but it is distinct from it. The following theoretical example should point out this difference. Suppose a group of individuals has a million dollars to invest. They can choose among three sets of producion systems. The first includes multipurpose and flexible types of machines, which rely on human skills and experience, but also allow for maximum adaptibility to shifting product needs. The second system is an assembly line combined with highly specialized machines where skills and varieties of productive experiences are limited. The third option, the middle ground between the others, is the semiautomatic process. In each case, let us suppose that the million dollars will suffice as initial investment. No matter which system the investors choose, they will determine the interpersonal relations of production workers, the scope and variety of possible working experiences, the number of products which can be made, and so forth. In so doing, they exercise technical power.

Because technical power is often exercised at the same time as investment power, it has been largely ignored. By using this technical power, the investor confines, or limits, future social organizations and interpersonal relationships.

The social criticism of the nineteenth century focussed essentially on economics and the accumulation process. For instance, Marx demystified the existence of some "natural" economic laws, or general economic interest. But much of this social criticism did not specifically consider technology. At most, Marx considered the use of the technical capabilities as biased in favour of the investors. (He thought that another social system would make better use of the same technical design.) Quite obviously, applications of certain techniques are socially biased; but so are technical designs. It is not certain that one could use the same technical design for alternative social goals in a different social system. Technical systems designs, especially, are intimately related to the social goals of organizations.

The criticism of economics and property rights, therefore, must broaden its focus to include technological and social designs. Analysts should understand the mechanisms of technical power.

Just as there are no natural property rights for any social group, there are no eternal technical rights for any group. Rights and prerogatives concerning the design, choice and implementation of technologies are established by law and conventions. They are the outcome of a consensus made by a majority. Thorstein Veblen thought that industrialists, who seldom knew much about techniques, should not be responsible for society's technical choices. In 1919, in **The Vested Interests and the Common Man**, Veblen drew attention to this discrepancy between Western laws and customs, on the one hand, and the exercise of technical power on the other (4). Investors ignorant of technology were given sole technological prerogatives.

I am not advocating that a monopoly be taken away from one group and given to another. The monopolistic control of technical choices must be replaced by a more democratic apportionment. When the choice of a technical system orients everyone's relationships, it should not be left in the hands of the few. The greater the variety of institutions and technical proposals, the more alternatives society will have from which to choose. Technical pluralism is our insurance for the future.

In such a pluralistic setting, self-managed cooperatives should be entitled to propose their solutions. Technical initiative is not the exclusive province of private enterprise. Forms of entrepreneurship have been varied in the past, and new ones are likely to emerge in the future. While several sources should be encouraged to take technical initiatives, however, some political mechanism must exist for society to choose among the technical options.

Choosing Technical Systems

The mechanisms of regulating technical choices also have to be invented. In Chapter 10, we saw how regulation was the key to orienting technology and deciding which technical systems would be dominant. Until now, this has been done through the imposition of one group's will over another's. More democratic processes for choosing the socially dominant technical systems are desirable. Society's choices should reflect a consensus or majority opinion.

The advantage of building a consensus, when it comes to making technical choices, is to reduce government's discretionary powers to a minimum. The experience of workers in Poland demonstrates that there is no worse combination than that of political and economic power in a state-owned and -operated enterprise. Bureaucratic decisions become totally arbitrary and subordinate to the bureaucrats' own interests (luxury appliances, cars and holiday resorts are maintained for the privileged few, for instance). Moreover, without the sanction of a market, bureaucratic costing and pricing procedures are purely arbitrary and militaristic. Although market prices may be unfair to some, at least they are predictable to all, whereas the bureaucrats' commands are arbitrary, unpredictable, and known to just a restricted few.

The market mechanism we examined in Chapter 7, however, requires several conditions in order to function; it requires many different actors as well as equal access to information. I will deal briefly with the second condition, information. Technical information, however, is very unevenly distributed. New developments need time to be publicized. Furthermore, the promoters of new techniques want to keep them secret in order to reap extra profits from them. Without taking away the motivation of creative innovators, it is possible, however, to make all the different advantages and disadvantages of alterate techniques known in the marketplace.

Governments play a role in enabling the market for new technologies to function. By financing technological assessment, it can help generate the information necessary for the market mechanisms to function. The second function of government is to assist in the regulatory process.

Implicitly or explicitly, governments always regulate technical choices. By setting the rules of the production game, governments decide the direction of technical change. For instance, construction norms and standards and food regulations orient the development of technology. Even when governments do not set any norms, they are regulatory by default. It is not unusual for the more powerful to impose their norms on the governmental regulatory bodies. The regulatory process itself must be made more democratic.

By the same token, many of the regulatory functions can be minimized by the development of a broad consensus in society as to the desirable social goals. This is very important for technical development. Every culture is full of self-imposed social disciplines which are not even written into law. For instance, the development of ecological consciousness has already incited many people to separate their garbage. Minneapolis and Saint Paul, Minnesota, have experimented with a plan which grants tax exemptions to those residents who sort out their waste into three categories, thus enabling the cities to remanufacture the paper, metal and aluminium components. Since the amount of material and energy required to produce one ton of paper from the recycled paper is much less than the amount required to produce it from wood fibres, the advantages are considerable; they may well outweigh the costs.

Technical experimentation of this nature is a desirable means of exploring concretely the costs and benefits of a new technique. Advantages or disadvantages of new techniques cannot always be foreseen until implementation has started. Fears about new technologies may disappear after the trial, while others may surface. An assessment of the new technology must be repeated after the trial. Majorities of workers and those directly involved in implementing the new technology must be given veto or moratorium rights, in order to stop the implementation of a new technology until it is made appropriate.

Regulation can be implemented in two ways: by means of an authoritarian decree or through a self-imposed social discipline. Even in the second case, moderate self-censorship, which tolerates some deviant behaviour, is always preferable to the imposition of a technology.

Social Groups to Promote New Technical Direction

Realistically, new social institutions, such as self-managed cooperatives and new technical systems, will be promoted and diffused only it they serve the interests of a particular social group. At the turn of the twentieth century, Thorstein Veblen suggested that engineers were better suited than investors to make technical decisions. At that time, engineers were skilled tradespeople and technicians. Since Veblen's time, the definition of engineer has changed dramatically, however. An engineer in North America is now a university-educated technician with little or no productive experience.

Working people are probably better suited to direct technical change than any other group in society. (My definition of working people includes those working in factories or at home, not merely paid employees in industrial settings.) My reason is mostly negative: the present elites are now too divorced from concrete work processes to concern themselves with the effects and potential impacts of different technologies. In Chapter 5, I gave some positive reasons. Working people's accumulated know-how is an insurance against future shocks and disasters. Although their working ethic is not so austere as the penny-pinching Protestant capitalist described by Max Weber, it is a sound ethic whereby earning a livelihood is more important than immoderate habits of overworking or overspending.

It is unlikely that the elites will redirect their efforts and allow ordinary people to regain control over technical development. By elimination, therefore, we are left with working people to do this task.

An historical paradox remains. Since the Russian Revolution of 1917, movements which have taken power in the name of the working class have ended up building a totalitarian government which controls all areas of social life. In December 1981, when General Jaruzelski called for martial law in Poland to destroy Solidarity, it was clear to everyone that the Polish state opposed all direct worker participation in political affairs. Out of the working classes, oppressive political movements can emerge, as has happened in the U.S.S.R. New elites draw recruits from the working classes until a group reproduces itself directly. Today bureaucrats have special schools for their children. With an ensured university education, the children of bureaucrats can become bureaucrats also.

The idea of a state wich does not oppress a social group appears to be impossible. If there is a state bureaucracy, some social group will seize it, or use it to its own ends. Some social contract between various groups, therefore, seems better than embarking on the quasi-irreversible course of authoritarian rule.

Labour movements have had other limitations, besides the dead-end, totalitarian experiments of Eastern Europe. Much of the organized labour movement has limited itself it its own immediate interests. Although such an approach is a valid starting point, the absence of social vision has limited labour's contribution to society.

The starting point of resisting the imposition of technical designs is obvious. In the work place, workers experience new techniques. As workers use them, the techniques quickly reveal defects. For example, when word processing technology forced women to stare at screens at a distance of one foot for four hours, it did not take them long to experience the eyestrain, headaches and high incidence of birth defects. Scientific studies are now documenting and formalizing this information. Besides the narrow ergonomic and health examination – dealing with relationships between workers and machines – the criteria and processes of the choice of techniques should be questioned by the labour movement.

David Noble has argued in three articles entitled "Present Tense Technology" (**Democracy**) that all alternative technical projects are worthless unless existing management technical designs can be resisted (5). The forms of resistance are numerous. In the extreme, the best way to make a technique inoperative is to follow, letter for letter, all the rules and procedures invented by engineers and managers who do not do the work themselves, and thus do not know how things work. This was the last resort of some German workers against the Nazis and, more recently, by Polish Solidarnosc workers resisting the junta. Withdrawing intelligent consent and "working to rule" can stall a production system. The key power of working people lies in the fact that employers require their intelligent consent. Its withdrawal is a powerful tool to force a reconsideration of technical designs.

Formal **veto** and **moratorium** rights concerning technical changes make a lot of sense. Those who work a technique should have the right to veto its use. In fact, such a principle should be extended to the community, to all those affected by a technology. Communities should have the right to veto the construction of a nuclear power plant in their community, for instance. The Yellowhead Ecological Society, which formed around Clearwater in the North Thompson Valley of British Columbia, acted on that belief: they did not want nuclear mining in their valley, and they stopped it. In the late seventies, Bill Bennett, seeing his own constituency in a turmoil over the prospect of nuclear mining in the Okanagan, decreed a 7-year moratorium, which Bill Van Der Zalm ended in 1987. In Denmark, veto rights have been obtained by municipal workers in one community in Denmark, setting a precedent.

Moratoriums of technical developments or their diffusion can enable us to regain control of technical choice, providing the moratorium period is properly used. David Noble has made another useful suggestion: that the introduction of a new technology be accompanied by mandated social assessments. Further, it would seem that the principle of justice which states that a person is innocent until proven guilty implies that technical artifacts which are contested by a community should be considered guilty until proven innocent.

Discussion of the assessment of social impacts should occur not only in union halls but in communities at large, with families and friends. We cannot permit the isolated work force of a specific work site to make all the decisions about the acceptability of a new technology. Although the work force itself should have veto power, acceptance by the workers should not mean automatic acceptance by the community. To preserve jobs in the past, workers have often accepted dangerous techniques, like nuclear plants, which their community might have contested. Such suggestions point to the social need of establishing a political space for the deliberation of technical choices, citizens' rights to participate in the choices which affect their lives, and a democratic political process concerning technological choices. The idea of a Bill of Rights concerning technology has been raised by the International Association of Machinists. The time has arrived for democracies to include this dimension of power in their processes.

Even if a democratic process were established, however, it would be worth something only if it were used. Working people must exercise their technical rights and make proposals to the larger society. Work-oriented research and development, directed to the needs of working people, must be conducted to enable unions and community organizations to advance feasible technical alternatives to management proposals. Michael Cooley and several shop steward organizations in the United Kingdom have promoted such research and development in a group caled CAITS, the Centre for Alternative Industrial Technical Systems (see the Appendix). This institutional innovation looks promising. Unless working people present social alternatives, the image of the egotistical high-wage, "damn-the-unemployed," organized labour will impede the labour movement from participating in the reorientation and control of technological change.

And there lies the crux of the matter. At present the labour movement has no alternative set of values, or social vision, to propose to society. No redirection of technology will ever occur without action motivated by a social vision. Some social visions may reveal themselves utopian; time will tell. But every technical design has an intent. As we saw in Chapter 9, technical choices express cultural values. When the values are made explicit, the social choices are easier to make.

New Values

The following proposals sound utopian, a characteristic of most books about technology today. However, instead of describing the beauties of an ideal society fashioned by Technology with a capital T, I have tried to suggest alternative values that may guide the choice and design of new technologies.

The Democratization of Technical Knowledge

On the one hand, science has become exclusive, proprietary, and speculative. On the other hand, there is shop floor culture, which is rooted in the productive experience. C. P. Snow, Kenneth Boulding and Lynn White have analyzed the tension that exists between different cultures – the scientific and the technical.

One way of bridging the gulf between them and making science truly universal, as it purports to be, is by improving the manner in which research is done. Working people should have an opportunity to determine which issues will be studied, including those which are relevant to them; they should also share the research results. At the same time, academic researchers must accept that the problems of working life are as important as those defined by industry, the military, government agencies and academic elites. In this respect, the field of productive practices offers a broad scope for interested parties. If many users could decide which studies are relevant, society would be one step closer to filling the gap between the so-called experts and nonexperts.

It is not just a question of widening our research horizons and publishing the results, however. It is important for workers to acquire scientific and technical literacy. Jonathan Benthall explains the reason for this need in **The Body Electric:**

> In our society, manual labour has been largely drained of its intellectual or managerial or technocratic class. Control of social production cannot lie with the workers so long as such control necessitates intellectual work beyond their scope.... The workers must gradually reappropriate the intellectual ingredients of labour. In its further stages the process entails the absorpton of technology and science by the workers (6).

To continue in the present course will lead to only a greater sense of powerlessness, frustration and alienation on the part of outsiders. They will continue to escape by practising hobbies that perpetuate past technical knowledge, such as gardening, fishing, and hunting, or indulging in the latest technological fads, like computer games. But the trend must be reversed.

Conserving Technical Skills

As we saw in earlier chapters, many ancient and outdated techniques are still practised in some form today, despite new developments in another part of the world. Society should continue to preserve our technical skills, which would ensure that we keep our technical options open. To preserve past skills, they can be transmitted to the young in apprenticeship programmes. If children, for example, were taught how to use different knives, saws, and tools for cultivation, the gulf between theory and practice in our culture would be narrowed.

Specialized skills have been restricted to dangerously few workers. As a consequence, in the future, when managers will want to reprogramme a robot by recording a skilled worker's procedures, skilled workers still able to serve as a model for robots will be scarce. Melvin Kranzberg expresses similar preoccupations:

The worker of the 1970s, seated at the console of an automated factory, seems to have risen from his old status as slave to become instead an overseer of slave machinery. Perhaps the oncoming army of robots will eventually reverse the condition man dwelt in throughout the long dawn of prehistory, when he had no word for work because work was synonymous with living. Perhaps in the future he will have no word for work because he no long needs to do any.

More precisely, he will no longer need to do work in its pejorative sense, the unending, bone-wearying, soul-starving toil of plowing and planting, of lifting and dragging, of digging in the mines, of feeding machinery, of fighting the moving assembly line. Instead, he will be free to do the work that a robot cannot do, and which expreses his own humaneness, to build, carve, paint, write, act, design, to recover the charm of craftsmanship in an atmosphere of freedom. Is this prospect so alarming (2)?

To these hopes, however, Kranzberg added the following condition, that humans develop their own skills as quickly as the machines they build.

Developing an Ecological Awareness

In 1967 Lynn White, a prominent historian of technology, wrote this about the emerging ecological movement:

Science was traditionally aristocratic, speculative, intellectual in intent; technology was lower class, empirical, action oriented. The quite sudden fusion of these two, toward the middle of the nineteenth century, is surely related to the slightly prior and contemporary democratic revolutions which, by reducing social barriers, tended to assert a functional unity of brain and hand. Our ecological aim is the product of an emerging, slightly novel, democratic structure. The issue is whether a democratized world can survive its own implications. Presumably we cannot unless we rethink our axioms (7).

One way of rethinking our axioms is by cultivating a respect for nature's ecological balance. An ecological awareness means being aware of technology's overall impact on biological systems, not only on our own region but in all other regions as well. Today proponents of ecological values assert that production for production's sake is not a sufficient criterion for progress. Ecologists understand that any progress has to be sustainable.

On the subject, Nicholas Gorgescu-Roegen, an economist, has made a radical departure from dominant economic theories. He has contested the widely-held view propagated by economists (who influence government policy makers) that the economic process is a completley circular and self-sustaining affair, with a self-stabilizing circular flow, isolated from the physical world. Instead, he starts from this premise: that all production uses matter and energy. Matter and energy, he explains, enter the economic process in a state of low entropy; they reemerge in a state of high entropy. (Webster defines **entropy** as a measure of disorder in a substance or system, adding that energy diminishes in a closed system.)

Each production process increases entropy, or the disorganization of matter, and reduces the available energy. Planners should keep this in mind. Rather than choosing techniques according to how much energy they generate, planners should select them according to another criterion, the energy balance, or the ratio of energy they will use in relation to the one it provides. This would also demand that a product's durability be considered when it is still in the design stage.

During the 1973 energy crisis, the American government initiated studies that took these problems into consideration, but nothing much was done about the results of the studies. China, on the other hand, has adopted an ecological approach and adopted some practical options to ensure energy conservation. The Chinese have built small decentralized hydro mills instead of large centralized ones. They have developed biological pest control techniques to replace chemically-based ones. They use enhanced biomass heating techniques to manage human and animal wastes.

Communications for Social Interaction or Propaganda

Communication technologies today tend to isolate individuals rather than bring them together. The flow of information is one-way, especially with television viewing. Yet interactive television technology is possible. In his book, entitled **Ecotopia**, Ernst Callenbach describes the social interaction that could take place on the basis of this interactive technology (8). People could finally talk back to their television sets, hold public meetings, and so forth.

The use of videos in telephone conferences provides a glimmer of what is possible: people seeing and hearing each other despite a separation of hundreds of miles. Should not a new principle be established in the communication industries, a principle that favours interactive technology over those that alienate, those that are unidirectional? The network linkage of home computers makes this value choice concrete.

Re-evaluation of Gender Roles

As we saw in Chapter 3, industrial society has given rise to a rigid sexual division of labour. Technical designs could aim at desegregating the child-raising and educative responsibilities of women, as well as enabling women to have access to any type of work, if they so wish. Techniques for reproductive control could also be redesigned to force males to assume some of the responsibility. The women's movement has done much to question inherited values. What new forms the family will take in the future, however, and what technical systems will be best suited to it remain unclear.

A New View of Technology

Throughout history, there have been few radical redirections of technology. We can easily enumerate them: sedentary agriculture (6000 B.C.), hydraulic societies and technology, extensive agriculture (Middle Ages), machines and workshops (15th-18th centuries.) Today, the computer may be the means of such a radical departure, redefining work and society. Perhaps.

But if that were to happen, new institutions, values and social fabric would have to emerge. In the previous experiences of redirection of technology in human history, new "world views" and ethics were also necessary for the change. In Chapter 9, for instance, we described how the animist view of the earth had to be destroyed before people started to mine underground ores. Similarly, for an historic redirection of technological change to occur, a new world view might be necessary. Since the start of the Machine Age, society's belief in unavoidable Technical Progress has become universal. Perhaps the start of a radical redirection may be assisted by ridding ourselves of this modern religion of technical fatality and regaining control of our technical designs.

REFERENCES

1. KRANZBERG, Melvin, and GIES, Joseph. (1975) *By the Sweat of Thy Brow.* New York: G.P. Putnam's Sons.

2. NOBLE, David. (1984) *Forces of Production: A Social History of Industrial Automation.* New York: Knopf.

3. CHILD, John. (1972) "Organization Structure, Environment, and Performance: The Role of Strategic Choice." *Sociology,* pp.1-22.

4. VEBLEN, Thorstein. (1969) *The Vested Interests and The Common Man.* New York: Capricorn Books.

5. NOBLE, David. (1983) "Present Tense Technology I, II, III." *Democracy,* Spring, pp.8-24; Summer, pp.70-82; Fall, pp.71-93.

6. BENTHALL, Jonathan. (1976) *The Body Electric: Patterns of Western Industrial Culture.* London: Thames & Hudson.

7. WHITE, Lynn. (1967) "The Historical Roots of Our Ecological Crisis." *Science,* vol.155, no.3767, pp.1203-1207.

8. CALLENBACH, Ernst. (1977) *Ecotopia: The Notebooks and Reports of William Westion.* Toronto: Bantam Books.

SUGGESTED READINGS

MCGARRY, M.G., and STAINFORTH, J. (1978) *Compost, Fertilizer, Biogas Production from Human and Farm Wastes in the People's Republic of China.* Ottawa: I.D.R.C.

NOBLE, David. (1983) "Present Tense Technology I, II, III." *Democracy,* Spring, pp.8-24; Summer, pp.70-82; Fall, pp.71-93.

SNOW, C.P. (1984) *The Two Cultures: And A Second Look.* Cambridge: Cambridge University Press.

VEBLEN, Thorstein. (1969) *The Vested Interests and the Common Man.* New York: Capricorn Books.

APPENDIX: THE BEST LABOUR INITIATIVES

Since technical rights have not been defined in contemporary democracies, they are the object of legal guerrilla warfare at all levels of daily life: in the work place, in municipal and federal regulatory bodies, and in the courts. Thus political institutions – a polity – and a process by which to settle matters relating to technical change become more and more imperative.

In the following pages we present examples of concrete initiatives taken by the labour movement in response to specific problems brought about by technical change.

Workers' concern about occupational health and safety was the primary reason why labour entered the arena. Sometimes labour limited itself to discussing only health and safety problems, ignoring the nature of a specific change. At other times their preoccupations included a wide variety of issues. Because of workers' growing concern in the last ten years, more and more groups of workers have begun to negotiate clauses on technological change. A few union locals have participated in the choice and design of a technology, and some have challenged the technical division of labour and hierarchy, or management. Others have initiated their own research into technologies, proposing alternatives to the ones being suggested. In the following section I will quote extracts from documents which illustrate these efforts.

I. Occupational Health and Safety

The Canadian Federal Labour Code allows workers on the floor to refuse work if there are reasonable grounds to believe that there is immediate danger. Provincial codes, however, have different phrasing. Depending on whether workers are under federal or provincial jurisdiction, the situation might change. This legislation raises certain questions, such as in the interpretation of the phrase **immediate danger**. Obviously a leak in a nuclear or chemical plant constitutes an immediate danger. But what about the cumulative effects of doing the same operation under radiation? (It is worth noting that workers have no legal coverage for delayed damages, such as the effects of radiation 15 to 20 years after exposure.) Another case is when an emergency causes a work stoppage and inspectors arrive on the scene. Of equal importance is union presence. Local representatives must be on hand to document the affair properly. This points out the need for a union to have its own medical and research personnel.

Sad to say, many industrialists have been cavalier with public safety. Even though our society usually punishes those who endanger the lives of others – giving a ticket for a traffic violation although the driver may be ignorant of a particular law – some industrialists not only endanger the public but plead innocence because of ignorance. For instance, they market DES, a drug mistakenly intended to prevent miscarriages, which causes cancer in children, and take if off only after it is proven harmful, in this case many years after it has been proven harmful.

Courts will exonerate an industrialist whose product or work place causes injury because of cumulative effect or repetition. The "vibration white finger disease," for instance, is due to the endless drilling of a jackhammer, yet it will not be held responsible, nor will the back fusion that is attributed to the work station of cashiers. Since the work place is considered private, employers are not legally assigned social responsibility.

The great problem with standards is their variability. In the United States, for instance, the maximum exposure to lead is defined by the Environmental Protection Agency (EPA) as 1.5 micrograms per cubic metre in **constant** exposure, while the Occupational Safety and Health Agency (OSHA) puts it at 50 micrograms per cubic metre of **intermittent** exposure. Not only do the figures differ; the measurement concepts are not comparable. The way standards are measured also poses questions. In one test, only one out of 20,000 IBM computer terminals was tested for radiation emission. (Workers, however, do not have the option of using only a tested machine.) Moreover, levels tested at a distance of three feet don't apply, since their work requires them to be two feet closer. And although workers suffer the compound effects of several sources of radiation, their machines were tested for radiation in isolation. It is obvious that workers must take whatever steps they can to protect their health. It is sometimes useful for them to work with management on a health committee.

What is DES?

DES is short for diethylstibestrol, a synthetic female estrogen, or hormone, which was designed to prevent miscarriages. It is estimated that between 1941 and 1971, several million women took the drug during pregnancy, especially if they had a history of previous bleeding, miscarriages, premature births, or diabetes. At least one million males were born from these women. These DES sons face a greater chance of developing fertility problems and testicular abnormalities than do their peers. The testicular changes seen in some of them may mean an increased risk of testicular cancer, as well.

Fertility Problems

Studies show that DES sons, as a group, have more sperm and semen abnormalities than men not exposed to DES.

Testicular Abnormalities

About 30 percent of DES sons have some type of testicular abnormality. The most common cysts in the epididymis are benign, or not cancerous. The epididymis is the collecting structure on the back of each testicle where mature sperm are stored. Cysts are painless growths that feel like small lumps. They may disappear and then recur later. Extremely small testes and undescended testes are other common DES-related changes.

How to Find Out If You Are a DES Son

Many DES mothers and sons do not know they were exposed. Your mother may not remember taking DES or any other medication during pregnancy. Ask her if she took DES. Ask if she had any of the following problems during pregnancy: bleeding, miscarriage, premature birth, or diabetes. Did she take any hormones during the first five months of pregnancy? Can her medical records (doctor, hospital, pharmacist) be checked to see if she took DES?

II. LABOUR CODES

Extract from the Canada Labour Code – PART V: **Technological Change.**

(1) In this section and sections 150 to 153, the technological change means (a) the introduction by an employer into his business, equipment or material of a different nature than previously utilized by him (b) a change in the manner in which the employer carries on the work that is directly related to the introduction of that equipment or material....

Notice of Technological Change

An employer who is bound by a collective agreement and who proposes to effect a technological change that is likely to affect the terms and conditions or security of employment of a significant number of his employees to whom the collective agreement applies shall give notice of the technological change to the bargaining agent bound by the collective agreement at least ninety days prior to the date on which the technological change is to be effected.

Contents of Notice

The notice referred to in subsection (1) shall be in writing and shall state (a) the nature of the technological change; (b) the date upon which the employer proposes to effect the technological change; (c) the approximate number and type of employees likely to be affected by the technological change; (d) such other information as is required by the regulations made pursuant to subsection (3).

Regulations of Governor in Council

... (3) The Governor in Council, on the recommendation of the Board, may make regulations (a) specifying the number of employees or the method of determining the number of employees that shall, in respect of any federal work, undertaking or business or any type of federal work, undertaking or business, be deemed to be significant for the purposes of subsection (1) and subsection (b) requiring any information in addition to the information required by subsection (2) to be included in a notice of technological change....

Extract from the **Labour Code of British Columbia:** Agreement Respecting Technological Change

A collective agreement entered after this Act comes into force shall contain provisions for final and conclusive settlement without stoppage of work, by arbitration or another method agreed to by the parties, of all disputes relating to adjustment to technological change, which may include provisions for (a) notice by an employer of intention to introduce technological change; (b) opportunities for retraining or transfer of employees; and (c) severance wages of employees displaced by the technological change.

Provisions Ordered by Minister

Where a collective agreement does not contain provisions for adjustment to technological change, the minister may, after considering the report of a person appointed by him to investigate the matter, prescribe by order provisions for that purpose. They shall be deemed terms of the collective agreement and binding on all persons bound by the agreement.

Introduction of Technological Change

(1) Where an employer introduces or intends to introduce a technological change that (a) affects the terms, conditions or security of employment of a significant number of employees to whom a collective agreement applies and (b) alters significantly the basis on which a collective agreement was negotiated, either party may refer the matter to an arbitration board under the collective agreement or pursuant to Part 6.... Technological change means (a) the introduction by an employer of a change in his work, undertaking or business, or a change in his equipment or material from the equipment or material previously used by the employer in his work, undertaking or business; or (b) a change in the manner an employer carries on his work, undertaking or business related to the introduction of that equipment or material. *(end of excerpt)*

Canadian Labour Codes are vague. What, for instance, does a **significant number of employees** mean? The B.C. Labour Board ruled that, for Eurocan Workers organized with the Canadian Paperworkers Union, **significant** means approximately 50 workers. When a pilot project is underway, however, does that project become significant? Interpretations vary according to the court or arbitrating body. In general, items not obtained in negotiations cannot be awarded in arbitration. Moreover, the union – never the employer – is charged with the burden of proof concerning technological change. Thus the union must be ready with facts and research information, even though technological knowledge is often proprietary.

On the whole, the Labour Codes seem to avoid discussing job actions affected by technological change. The following extract refers to the use of the Labour Code regarding technological changes in microelectronics.

III. The Issue of Rights and VDTs

Federal Microelectronics Task Force – A Comment

In the Chips: Opportunities, People, Partnerships, report of the Labour Canada Task Force on Micro-Electronics and Employment by Ken Hansen.

In March 1982, federal Labour Minister Charles Ciaccia appointed a six-member task force to examine the impact of the "new technology" on industrial relations in Canada. The task force's report, released in early November, is the result of staff research, a review of the literature, and submissions presented at hearings the task force held across the country. The task force heard from business, government agencies, labour unions and women's groups.

Its report is based on the assumption that the microelectronic revolution will benefit all sectors of society. The concerns that have been raised about health and safety, greater management control, permanent job loss, invasion of privacy, and in particular, the negative consequences for women of such a revolution, are all seen as capable of being resolved within the existing framework of technical progress.

Unfortunately, a majority of the briefs presented by groups representing workers also adopted this view, calling for ways to compensate and adjust to the social costs of "progress," rather than asking the question as for whom progress was intended. Not surprisingly, the task force's recommendations are geared to adjusting the labour force to "inevitable" technological changes.... As one person wrote:

We are just now on the leading edge of a new technological wave. It is gathering volume and momentum and we cannot afford to fall off or flounder. We must stay balanced and afloat in the ride up to the crest.... Existing members of the labour force will very likely require support in the form of labour adjustment services to help in counselling, training, and to improve worker mobility in the process of adaptation.... Workers will need to recognize the need for, and value of, adopting new, more productive processes and procedures. (**Canada Commerce,** Supplement 1982)

With the above passage in mind, let's look at some of the recommendations the Microelectronics Task Force made:

Health and Safety: provide funding for research, especially in regard to VDTs; develop visual, general physiological, psycho-social and ergonomic standards for VDT use; amend the Canada Labour Code to ensure the existence of health and safety committees; and prohibit close electronic monitoring of people's work.

The Task Force further suggests that, until legislated standards appear, employers should accept the following guidelines concerning VDTs:

(a) In that pregnant women have the right to be reassigned to other positions without loss of pay, seniority and benefits; (b) in that the maximum time limit for VDT operators not exceed five hours per day; (c) in that rest breaks for VDT operators be provided hourly; (d) in that initial eye tests, followed by annual retesting, be conducted for VDT operators at the employer's expense; (e) in that corrective lenses specially adapted to the visual demands of VDT work be provided to the employee, where necessary (pp. 13-14).

The task force touches various union concerns about VDTs, especially the effect of radiation on health. It recognizes the validity of workers' subjective, nonexpert views, pointing out that their fears have not yet been allayed. It correctly lays the burden of proof on advocates of the VDTs and supports the assumption that no level of radiation is risk-free. The committee's concrete recommendations, unfortunately, are weak. Despite the fact that many researchers have questioned the safety of VDTs and that some European countries have developed VDT standards, this group could have at least called for the use of liquid-crystal screens rather than cathode-ray devices. Moreover, it could have demanded the pretesting of all machines for PCBs and other hazards as well.

The task force's procrastination will only ensure that workers become adapted to machines rather than the other way around. Of course, many VDT workers would benefit if the voluntary guidelines were followed, but even if these guidelines were legislated as standards, they would act only to reduce, not eliminate, the unhealthy effects of VDTs.

Regarding women, the task force recommended that hiring, training and promotion policies be developed to promote women's lot in industry and to avoid the further ghettoization of women inherent in electronic office pools. It also recommended using various means to improve women's educational position in the field of microelectronics.

Undoubtedly, women will suffer the most job losses due to the microelectronics revolution, since women's work in the service sector, such as filing and typing jobs, is a major target in the drive for productivity through technological change. The task force's report is totally unrealistic about women's chances of escaping this loss through retraining and job enlargment. Retraining costs, in general, must be borne by the worker, unless paid educational leave has been negotiated by an individual's union.

Nevertheless, it recommends some reasonable changes to the Labour Code. For instance, it wishes to broaden the definition of technological change, require 180 days notice from employers who plan technological changes, and establish joint technology committees to develop adjustment plans regarding retraining, relocation and severance payments. It would delete Part V of the Code, which provides for midcontract negotiations over the effects of proposed technological change. Following this suggestion, all disputes would be settled by binding arbitration. Further, provincial labour codes, as well as health and safety and education training policies, would be coordinated with federal legislation.

The report says that labour legislation should promote cooperation between workers and management, adding that current collective bargaining methods have failed to deal properly with technological change. By way of evidence it cites the absence of provisions for technolgical change in many collective agreements. It proposes eliminating Labour Code provisions for negotiations over technological change – which include the right to strike – during the term of an existing agreement, replacing them with required joint standing committees. These committees would discuss management policy and its effects; they would design plans to offset negative factors, consider work organization issues, and develop programmes to educate workers in a new technology.

The task force expresses regret that collective bargaining agreements continue to be "based on the notion of adversaries making gains determined by their relative economic strength" (p 43). It thus dismisses collective bargaining as a tool to resolve disputes about technological change. According to its report, there would be no legislation to sanction employers who ignore the work force's demands, and employers could give joint committees as much power as they wished to share. Arbitration, instead, would resolve all disputes, including those over committees. Unquestionably, a worker has a right to be concerned about the criteria upon which arbitrators' decisions would be made.

At present, arbitration is the court of last resort when disputes arise before the expiration of a contract. Experience shows, however, that arbitration is heavily weighted against workers' interests, even when the terminology has been clarified and agreed upon. In the Canada Codes, wherein vocabulary relating to technological change is disputed, fair and consistent arbitration seems difficult.

The report recommends deleting Part V of the Labour Code, proposing instead such ideas as a broader definition of technological change and a longer notice before an employer can enact certain changes. However appealing these may sound, workers would be well advised to be wary. According to my reading, employers would ultimately be able to introduce new conditions into the work place. Unions might negotiate "adjustment" clauses, but not conditions dealing with the technological change itself – unless it gained an outright veto clause.

Management is generally thought to possess all the residual rights not explicitly negotiated by a union. It relies on this concept to control not only technological change but also most aspects related to health, safety, and work organization. Perhaps if workers had the right to strike over technological change between contracts, they could regain a measure of the control they lost when midcontract strikes were prohibited in World War II for reasons of expediency. The union payoff was supposed to be arbitration. Although, theoretically, arbitration is an ideal way to resolve issues related to specific contract wording, it fails to deal properly with technological change.

It is worth noting that capitalism has survived in Saskatchewan, where there is no antistrike legislation. This factor may actually contribute to the province's industrial peace, since management must respect labour. As a result, many strikes between contracts are probably avoided. In contrast, strikes occur in other provinces despite their prohibition. Although the task force does not subscribe to this view about the right to strike, it is held by Paul Weiler, former chairman of the British Columbia Labour Relations Board. He has made this comment:

The real issue in current Canadian law is denial to trade unions of the right to strike about an issue...which is not reviewable in grievance arbitration because the parties have not agreed to any relevant standards in their contract.... The union should be free to strike to produce an acceptable compromise about such an issue. (**Reconcilable Differences**, p. 108, from **B.C. Worker's Health Newsletter**, No. 3, Jan.-Feb. 1983, pp.15-19)

IV. The Limits of Arbitration

In 1984 the Canada Labour Relations Board make a judgement about technological change at the Prince Rupert Grain Terminal in British Columbia. Decision No. 491 was granted to the Grain Workers' Union Local 333 on December 12, 1984. Here is what took place.

In the late 1970s a consortium of private operators, perceiving the need to increase grain elevator capacity in Prince Rupert, built a second terminal. Although rumours of the proposed construction abounded in 1981, the subject was not raised by either the operators or the grain workers in the 1982 contract negotiations; when it was formally discussed in 1983, however, the extra capacity was no longer needed. As a result, the consortium closed its old, inefficient terminal (which had been donated to them in 1980 by the British Columbia government for one dollar) and 100 persons were put out of work. Only 17 persons were needed for the new state-of-the-art, computed-controlled terminal. The company resisted union attempts to extend its collective agreement to the new terminal, although it offered conditional, voluntary recognition. It denied that the second terminal constituted a technological change under the Code, calling the terminal a "planned business change." Apparently the union concentrated its efforts on ensuring the continuation of its bargaining rights at the new operation.

The Board referred to the preceding case involving technological change, OC Transpo, declining comment on general issues. It ruled instead on the minimum number of issues necessary for resolution. According to the decision, the new terminal "unquestionably" met the two-part criterion of technological change. Closure of the old plant did not meet the definition, although operations at Prince Rupert were transferred to a second location. The Code's requirement for 120 days notice was said to be met when that period elapsed before work began at the new terminal. Since the company had given notice in August, the union was faced with a fait accompli: closure of the old terminal, arbitrary hiring of nonunion workers for technical positions, and a drastically reduced number of positions.

The Board thus ruled in favour of the union on all almost aspects of the case, extending its certificate. Nevertheless, the union did not gain much. Despite recent positive changes to the Canada Labour Code relating to technological changes, the outcome of this case was not affected. The Prince Rupert company was not obliged to consult its workers, and as a result of its changes, 75 percent of the workers lost their jobs.

V. THE STORY OF CANADA POST: A STRUGGLE AGAINST DECLASSIFICATION

Canada Post is a case in which automation was introduced not solely for profit motives but to break the workers' control over the production process. Automation was a tool with which management could fragment the workers' efforts. Trying to reduce the amount of human intelligence required, they introduced a new classification of codes. Perhaps because military men constituted the core of management, they sought to impose military control over the work process. Control seems to have been their goal, rather than efficiency, which actually declined following the changes. Here we reproduce excerpts from two documents written by the Canadian Union of Postal Workers (CUPW).

Automation and Postal Workers – Technological Change – CUPW – Past, Present and Future
The Technology: Scientific Management in the Post Office

The Post Office has been through various of these reorganizations along modern management principles. Obviously, in the past we have felt the impact of technological change or mechanization, particularly in mail handling and transport. Most of this, however, was simple mechanization which had relatively little effect on the relative control over work methods of management and workers. Conveyor systems, the switch from rail to air transport, and other such developments were not fundamental to the design and content of our basic jobs. The main thrust by Post Office management in the past has been organizational: the subdivision of sortation, the elaborate system of supervision and discipline, attempts at individual work measurement, and the like. The balance of control between postal workers and management has been relatively stable within this framework for a long, long time.

Postal Mechanization

The modernization and mechanization program is a totally new and qualitatively different bid for control by the management. In contains the attempt to reduce skills and substitute cheaper labour into mail processing in the time-honoured guise of lower classifications. This strategy is inherent in the very design of the equipment, which is the surest guide to management's true intentions. Let us examine the new system with a view to its impact on worker skills.

Postal Code

The uniting element of the whole new system is the alphanumeric postal code. The principal feature of the code is that it permits machine recognition of mail, making it possible for machines to perform functions which previously required human judgement. Our judgement. Human knowledge and judgement is the essence of skill.

Coding Suites

The coding suites and their operators substitute for traditional sortation, but the new job requires less skill. The postal clerk has to read, recognize, make decisions based on instant recall of knowledge, then sort with dexterity. The coding desk operator must read and duplicate on a keyboard with dexterity. Skill and dexterity are not the same thing. The human memory, knowledge and judgement factors have been largely removed from the sequence, and these are the essence of skill. What is left is dexterity, which can be learned faster and bought cheaper.

Optical Character Readers

The OCR's, in the case of properly coded mail, eliminate the need for both traditional sorting and the newer coding functions. What remains is a machine-tending and sweeping task, with skill requirements obliterated and dexterity requirements reduced.

Letter Sorting Machines

For properly coded mail, the LSM's can eliminate sortation skills entirely. They also have the potential to greatly reduce line-of-route sortation as detailed programs are developed by letter carriers.

Impact on Postal Workers

The effect of the massive quantities of new equipment will be both quantitative and qualitative. Clearly the introduction of 98 LSMs with a capacity of 23,500 pieces per hour each, 46 CFC's with a capacity of 23,000 pieces per hour and 39 OCR's rated at 30,000 pieces per hour will eliminate an enormous amount of manual manipulation of the mail by postal workers. Reduction in total manpower requirements will be aggravated by a further $157 million in planned improvements in handling equipment and facilities. Since June, 1975, additional plans for 25 FSM's have been revealed and smaller coding and LSM units are now under consideration. This is the quantitative aspect of mechanization on employment.

National Facilities Program Estimate (as of June 1975)

The qualitative effect is the impact on job design and job content. This affects our control of production and ultimately reflects on classifications and wage rates, job satisfaction and related matters. The first major manifestation of this was management's attempt to classify the coder jobs of level one, paid at $.50 per hour less than the level four Postal Clerk functions which were being replaced. This led to the strike of 1974.

At every turn, the effect of automation is a general degradation of skill requirements and a concerted attempt by management to cheapen our work, primarily by down classification. The degree to which management attains its objectives and the speed at which the changes occur is greatly variable. This depends on the performance of postal workers individually and through the union, but primarily through the union, since the whole nature of the changes is to reduce the control of the individual worker over his or her own labour.

Electronic Surveillance

A special feature of Canadian postal automation is the determination of management to introduce closed circuit television, monitoring the work area in association with the new production equipment. This is being explained as a measure to ensure the safety and security of the mails. More to the point, the electronic spying is part of the general thrust of management for total control of the work process... The reason for surveillance of every movement of the employees is that even the new automated system does not eliminate our ability to alter the pace of production, although it reduces the variety and nature of our opportunities to do so. Total electronic surveillance is designed to further reduce those opportunities and shift the balance of control over production still further in favour of management.

The History of the Conflict

Technological change has been a concern of our Union since the introduction in 1969 of the government report entitled "Blueprint for Change," which established the government's intention to cut costs through automation. A timely connection in the push for greater productivity emerged through John Mackay. From 1961 to 1969, Mackay was President of the Canadian Branch of ITT, the world's largest telecommunication company.

From 1970 to 1976, Mackay was the Deputy Postmaster General. Most of the mechanized equipment in the Post Office, including the computers, is manufactured by ITT.

In December of 1971, Post Office officials finally met with CUPW representatives to discuss the program of technological change. The Union was informed that 15 major centres would be mechanized at a cost of 96 million dollars. No meaningful consultation was held with the Union regarding the possible adverse effects on Postal Workers resulting from technological change. (These possible adverse effects have long since beome a reality that has never been sufficiently or properly dealt with.)

Post Office management (the government) regarded the introduction and use of technology as their sole right, and treated the Union's position of defending the members as simple audacity. Management's disregard for the workers was verified when, just seven months following the December meeting, the first mechanized facility was opened in Ottawa in the summer of 1972. The new equipment required a new position – coders. Management arbitrarily classified this new position as a P.O. 1, the lowest classifcation within the Union, at a pay differential 25 percent lower than what a manual sorter (P.O. 4) was receiving, even though, during an experimental program of mechanization in Winnipeg in 1971, coders had been classified and paid as P.O. 4's.

After months of talks to resolve this problem fairly – talks that fell on indifferent ears – the Union's response to this adverse effect was a national strike. The outcome of this strike eventually attained the up-grading of coders to the P.O. 4 classification. During this time, the Post Office had continued its automated program throughout the country, so that by 1975, 847 million dollars had been spent on 39 major facilities in 26 cities. At no time was the Union allowed input to eliminate adverse effects, thereby entrenching a militant and hostile setting for the future. The Union attempted to negotiate demands for job protection and direct benefits as a result of technological introduction – to no avail. The employer's obvious intention was to proceed with automation at all costs – without regard for the workers. The attitude of the employer forced the Union to become increasingly militant in its direction and policies, and may best be summarized by the following statement, released during this period.

Nowhere in North America has a Union successfully negotiated the right to prohibit the employer from entering into contracts for the research and development, or the purchase of new technology.

(Author's note: Until the recent experiment of CAITS in Britain, nowhere has the labour movement proposed its own alternative, for technological change.)

But, until this is possible, Unions will forever be on the defensive, attempting to eliminate the adverse effects of technology changes which management has unilaterally introduced by virtue of their power over investment. The employers purchase and install the machinery – the Unions are left to pick up the pieces and safeguard the membership....

In modern industry, the decisions to introduce new production techniques are made months and sometimes years in advance of the delivery of the actual machinery. It is not uncommon for investment of millions of dollars into research and development to be necessary before decisions are made by management as to whether to proceed with contracts to automate the workplace. These decisions are taken solely by management....

It is not unusual that workers will only learn of these decisions just a few months before the actual changes in the work place will begin. Usually by this time, the enterprise has committed enough finances that the very existence of the firm depends upon the success of the new technology. In other words, negotiations over the technological changes themselves are impossible – and the struggle to negotiate the effects of technological change begins.

(Postal workers are under a Federal Labour Code. Some provincial labour codes give different opportunities. The British Columbia Labour Code, for instance, gives the right to strike during a contract on technological change. The opportunity is seldom used by unions, however; the number of technological changes on which one can strike are few, and the number for which one can go to arbitration even fewer.)

Management's attitude was unbending, while professing to understand the problems and concerns put forth by the union. When it came time to take a positive position at the bargaining table – the employer abdicated any responsible concern for the workers by refusing the Union demands for protections and benefits. The result was a bitter 42-day strike in the late fall of 1975. While failing to receive direct benefits from technological change, the Union was successful in obtaining a new article in the collective agreement which was to commit the employer to eliminate all adverse effects and provide a mechanism to resolve problems arising from technological change. This provision – Article 29 – could well have been the foundation for industrial harmony – a means to correct past animosities and problems – and the means to introduce technology into the Post Office to the benefit of all. But, as was obvious from the beginning, management never intended to honour or live up to Article 29.

Management maintained their offensive strategy. Technological changes continued, with management claiming there were no adverse effects, and therefore no need for consultation....

Negotiations for a new contract began in April, 1977 – again calling for improvements in benefits and protections on technological change – achieving little or no results by the fall of 1978. In October, CUPW called a national strike, only to face legislation forcing them back to work ten days later. The eventual outcome was that the 1977 contract was finally imposed by arbitrator Lucien Tremblay in March of 1979. Though again defeated in a battle, C.U.P.W. did not give up the war against the Post Office approach to technological change. By increasingly publicizing their position and taking the forefront of solidarity action with other Unions, the CUPW received overwhelming support at the CLC Convention in Winnipeg in May, 1980. Just weeks later, the Treasury Board and the CUPW signed a contract which for the first time gave a tangible benefit from automation in the form of a reduced work week....

CUPW has shown that a union can stop lower classification. It also obtained one of the best contracts on technological change. It includes advanced notification (three months: date, number of people affected, equipment involved, impact on working conditions), a broad definition of technological change (including work methods and operations which alter one or more employees). The health and safety standards, however, are weak; the protection of casuals is also weak.

Collective Agreement – Canadian Union of Postal Workers

Article 29: Technological Changes

In this Article, technological changes means the introduction by the Post Office Department in the internal processing of mail, of equipment different in nature, type or quantity from that previously utilized by the Post Office Department, a change related to the introduction of this equipment in the manner in which the Post Office Department carries on the internal processing of mail and any change in work methods and postal services operations affecting one or more employees.

Adverse Effects to be Eliminated

When the employer is considering the introduction into any sector of the Canadian postal system a technological change: (a) the Employer agrees to notify the Union as far as possible in advance of his intention and to update the information provided as new developments arise and modifications are made; (b) the foregoing notwithstanding, the Employer shall provide the Union at least one hundred and twenty (120) days before the introduction of a technological change, with a detailed description of the repercussions on employees.

Pertinent Information Included

The notice mentioned in clause 29.03 (b) shall be given in writing and shall contain pertinent data including: (a) the nature of the change; (b) the date on which the Post Office Department proposes to effect the change; (c) the approximate number, type and location of employees likely to be affected by the change; (d) the effects the change may be expected to have on the employees' working conditions and terms of employment; and (e) all other pertinent data relating to the anticipated effects on employees....

Protection of Employees

In order to render effective the principle established in clause 29.02, the Employer agrees to the following provisions, which are designed to protect all employees covered by this Agreement: (a) Guaranteed Employment. Except as otherwise provided in this Agreement, the Employer guarantees continuous employment to all employees covered by this Agreement until the signing of the next Collective Agreement between the parties. (b) Guaranteed Classification. For the period of continuous employment guaranteed in the previous paragraph, an employee shall retain his classification and the corresponding wage scale, regardless of any reassignment to other duties or any reclassification of the duties performed by the employee at a lower level. The foregoing notwithstanding, an employee may accept a voluntary reassignment to another classification, but shall retain such new classification and the corresponding wage scale from the date of voluntary reassignment and for the duration of this Collective Agreement. Guaranteed Pay. To further clarify the intent of this clause, the Employer guarantees full pay and benefits for normal working hours as defined in this Collective Agreement for the full period of continuous employment guaranteed in paragraph (a) of this clause. Retraining. Any employee either voluntarily or compulsorily reassigned or reclassified as a result of these changes shall be provided with whatever amount of retraining he requires during his hours of work with full pay from the Employer and at no additonal cost to the employee. Any employee unable to follow a retraining course shall maintain his classification, or its equivalent, in the bargaining unit.

VI. JOB DISPLACEMENT AND CONTRACTING OUT

Harley Shaiken, a veteran machinist who now serves as a consultant to the United Automobile Workers, observed the delayed effects of technological change on employment. New technologies, he said, carry the threat of massive job displacement in the automobile industry. Without sophisticated automation, however, the auto companies raised productivity between 1955 and 1983; the average number of units built by a production worker per year rose from 12.8 to 17.7. Because sales also rose (they actually have doubled since 1961), the work force did not decline. But as the public becomes more demanding, vehicles are becoming more complex. Joseph Callahan, editor of **Automotive Industries**, believes that the North American car market is approaching its hypothetical saturation level, which will cause sales to level off. As a result, car production will decline and layoffs will follow (**In These Times**, Sept. 19-25, 1979). Hence new technologies will change work patterns in the auto industry at a period when companies may face lower demand, and thus need fewer workers. The work force has reason to be concerned.

Protecting Jobs Against Contracting Out
The Case of Telephone Workers

Telephone workers' unions across Canada have made a detailed study to determine how technological change affects their employment, as the following document shows:

Employment Trends and Technological Change in the Canadian Telecommunications Industry. A study by the Canadian Federation of Communication Workers, Toronto, Nov. 1, 1977

In the telephone industry, changes in technology are familiar and continuous. That process is still continuing in the industry. Technological change is not a new phenomenon to us. From magneto to battery switchboards, from manual to dial, from toll operators to Direct Distance Dialing and from step-by-step to crossbar, we thought we had seen it all. But there are new techniques threatening our members' job security. Now computerization has enabled the carriers to speed up toll switchboards through TOPS/TSPS, electronic switching is replacing electro-mechanical switching, and the combination of miniaturization and computerization is bringing us digital offices which require fewer people to install, and which can be maintained by fewer crafts people.

Marketing innovations like Directory Assistance Charging and Phone Stores are restricting job opportunities at the telephone companies as well. New speeded-up work methods are reducing clerical and manufacturing labour.

The greatest impact on telephone employment came with the substitution of dial telephones for manual service. Certainly that period saw the greatest reduction in staff. But it went relatively smoothly because it was foreseen well in advance, it happened during times of high employment and a growing economy so that those people displaced readily found other employment, and, furthermore, union agreements contained cushioning clauses. Also, we should admit that the people concerned were less well organized than other telephone workers, and less militant, too. Direct Distance Dialing caused a further reduction in operators, this time toll operators. There was a brief flurry of opposition to digit-dialing in the United States, where a considerable group of people fought the telephone companies before the regulators to preserve letters in their phone numbers, even going so far as to hire the famous Melvin Belli as counsel....

Directory Assistance Charging (DAX) was not a technological change but a marketing gimmick. It was expected that it would slightly reduce directory assistance calls and thus eliminate some operators. The original estimate was that calls would decrease by two-thirds. In the USA, the CWA (Communication Workers of America) reports that D.A. operators' jobs have decreased by 60 percent. Customers get less service at greater cost from fewer people. The program is a great success – for management.

Further reductions in traffic staff are predicted, due to further sophistication in the DAX program. At British Columbia Telephone, for example, centralizing of Directory Assistance and the use of a computerized information retrieval system will reduce the directory assistance operator positional requirements by 25 percent, according to the company's estimate. The further spread of Automatic Number Identification (ANI) will produce further labour savings, to use B.C.'s Telephone's phrase. It is true that automatic recording of the calling number does provide improved customer service.

TOPS/TSPS

The new computerized system of individual toll operator positions is known as Traffic Operator Position Systems (TOPS) by Northern Telecom and is in use at SaskTel and Bell Canada. The similar system manufactured by Automatic Electric is known as Traffic Service Position Systems (TSPS) and has been introduced in B.C. Telephone territory. TSPS, or TOPS, is nothing more nor less than our old friend, the speed-up, aided by computerization.

The first installation in Canada was in Vancouver. By December of 1976 B.C. telephone was able to make the following claim:

In Vancouver, the computerized operator switchboard system reduced our positional requirements significantly and has made it possible to provide service with an operating staff 22 percent less than would have been required using previous technology.

TSPS will be extended to New Westminster in 1978. The company expects a 40 percent reduction in workload there. They expect attrition and transfers will take care of surplus operators. There is no retraining program because of TSPS.

At Bell Canada, the company estimates that there will be a reduction of 35 to 40 percent in necessary operators in offices converted from 3CL cord switchboards. There will be a loss of 475 operators in Toronto by the end of 1978, 59 in Hamilton by the end of 1979, and 518 fewer in Montreal by the end of 1982. An operator is expected to handle 35 to 40 percent more calls at a TOPS position as compared to a cord board. The company will spend up to $25 million per year until 1981 on this program. Training is provided for displaced operators.

One would expect that other telephone companies will have similar reductions in traffic jobs with the introduction of this system.

Clerical Functions

It is difficult to get the facts about the fluctuations in clerical jobs at the telephone companies. We do know about the great reductions in office staff by Northern Telecom in Quebec – down from 2,600 in 1971 to 1412 in 1977 – which affected the COEU bargaining unit. In operating companies, a drop in service representatives and general clerical jobs has been offset by gains in marketing and engineering. No one knows how many jobs disappeared when the companies shut down small-town business offices and contracted-out the work to Woolworth Company and the banks. We do know how many payroll jobs were eliminated by computerization. Job evaluation took its toll too.

The net loss of clerical jobs due to the Phone Store concept is unknown. We do know, however, that the centralized automatic loop reporting system will require 85 fewer clerical and craft jobs by the end of 1978....

Phone Stores

One of the areas that has received a lot of attention from our affiliates is the area of Phone Stores.... The first Phone Center was opened in Florida by Southern Bell in early 1973. It proved profitable and spread rapidly throughout the United States. A requirement of the Canadian Department of Communications, that a telephone line must terminate in a ringing device, prevented phone store installations here. Sometime in 1973 that requirement was dropped by the Department of Communications without prior notice.

In January, 1974, the program, called Phone Mart, began in Vancouver. The union fought it through wildcat strikes, arbitration, appeals under the Labour Code, and complaints to the Canadian Transport Commission. The CTC replied: "Neither of these measures will have a detrimental effect upon the rates which B.C. Telephone subscribers will have to pay. Indeed it is our opinion that the Phone Mart approach and the charge for Directory Assistance calling may well prove to be effective measures of cost control."

The new regulator, the Canadian Radio-television and Telecommunications Commission (CRTC), has continued its favourable stance toward the Phone Mart. In May of 1977 it permitted installation charges to rise from $18 to $23, saying, "Cost-cutting programs such as Phone Mart... are positive steps toward encouraging savings for the Company and customers alike."

The CRTC also permitted Bell Canada to increase the spread in service charges, thus encouraging the use of the Phone Centre. In 1977 B.C. Telephone has six Phone Marts in operation, with three scheduled for 1978 and one for 1979.

The Phone Store experience indicates that the new CRTC is as unresponsive to the needs of telephone workers as the old Commission was.

Electronic Switching

Changing technology in central exchange offices will decrease the number of craft jobs required to maintain the new systems and also decrease jobs in manufacturing and equipment installations. Obviously, operating equipment in good working order is not scrapped when new equipment is developed. The new technology is used in new offices, for extensions or for replacements when the other equipment is finally disposed of. Consequently, a great variety of types of central office equipment are in use simultaneously. For example, at the end of 1975, Bell Canada had 597 step-by-step switching systems in use, 432 crossbar systems, 11 Electronic Switching System (ESS) offices, and 31 SP-1 (Stored Program) offices.

Whatever other advantages the move to electronic switching brings to the telephone company, a reduction in maintenance man-hours is clear. B.C. Telephone has declared regarding Electronic Common Control (ECC): "The main reason for ECC conversion is to provide improved service capabilities and reduce operating costs. A major element in cost reduction is the cost of labour required, so that the result will be a reduction in labour cost." B.C. Telephone expects savings to balance capital costs by 1980 and then save as much as $34.6 million in 1985. Fifty percent of local customers will be converted to electronic switching by 1980 and 75 percent by 1985. Bell Canada has been replacing SXS by electronic switching by about 40,000 lines per year. Studies by B.C. Telephone, of small SXS offices replaced by ECC machines, showed dramatic reductions in maintenance workers per 10,000 lines. For example, in Houston, from 9.4 to 3.75, and in Port Hardy, from 11.0 to 1.7.

Digital Technology

Digital technology is already in use on toll routes and in the SL-1 PBX. About 12 percent of Bell Canada toll trunks are on digital carrier (Ld-1, Ld-4 or DUV-digits under voice). Digital Multiplex Systems (DMS) will cover about 15 percent of Bell exchanges and 50 percent of toll trunking by the mid-1980s. Bell Canada says the emphasis is on digital techniques because of cost savings. A portion of that saving is in reduced labour cost. A Dms-100 (a medium to large machine, handling from 6,000 lines and up) relative to SP-1 is expected to reduce the maintenance effort by 0.4 person-years for every 10,000 lines.

The introduction of digital technology has meant a reduction of the work force in both manufacturing and installation. A Northern Telecom spokesman has said: "The company is reducing its work force. Causes are the shift to less labour-intensive digital products and reduced telephone expansions." New products are produced by newer, more highly automated machines. The new products use more miniature and transistor units, which reduce the size of the modules which then can be installed by fewer equipment installers. Northern Telecom (NC) has managed to increase its profits fantastically by high Canadian productivity (up by 71 percent from 1970 to 1976, compared with the national average of 20.8 percent). Those profits have been used to establish factories in other countries. In the United States those plants are usually in low wage, non-union areas. We find the situation now where NT brings in telephone housings from plants in Ireland and Tennessee, crossbar frames from Turkey, and fuses from Malaysia.

Interconnect

Interconnection is usually used to refer to two different things. The attachment of subscriber-owned (or leased from a supplier other than the telephone company) equipment to the telephone network is one part of the problem. Interconnection of the telephone network with rival, competing networks is the other part of this phenomenon.

The interconnect menace has yet to hit Canadian telephone workers with the effect we have seen in the United States. There the president of SWA has estimated that 100,000 jobs have disappeared from the industry. The United States Federal Communications Commission has a policy of introducing competition into the telecommunications industry. The famous "Carter phone" decision of 1968 cleared the way for the marketing of the interconnect apparatus. Microwave companies now offer carrier services. There are several corporations offering digital data networks, including ITT and Datran. There is a satellite through a "dish" on the customer's premises. Private value-added networks lease transmission facilities and link them to their own minicomputers. The situation in the United States has been described as "a competitive free-for-all, apparently for the sake of competition, not for the sake of public benefit" (Eldon Thompson, Trans-Canada Telephone System)....

Fibre Optics Technology

The new technology of fibre optics is being tested. The first field trial in Canada began October 20, 1977, when a cable of six glass fibres was run between two Montreal switching centres. The technology consists of carrying information via laser beams through thin glass fibres. Bell-Northern Research has 35 people working on optical communications now, with prospects of building to 50 in 1978. Northern Telecom has set up an optical system division in Lachine with a very small work force. That work force will grow, but the use of copper wire will, of course, diminish. Copper wire will not be obsolete for many years, because, for one thing, optical fibres cannot transmit the electricity needed to ring a subscriber's bell. Fibres are still very fragile and almost impossible to splice. The present cost is from $2-3 a metre, compared with five cents for a similar-capacity copper line. However, optical fibres have some big advantages. They are small and lightweight; they carry 50 times the information 20 percent faster; there is no induction, hence no electrical interference, cross-talk or possible taps; fewer repeaters are needed...

Any study that deals with the effects of technological change on employment must be precise. If the same product is made by fewer workers, the argument can always be made that the change in numbers will result in unemployment in the long run. Sometimes one industry might gain employment, to the detriment of another industry; for instance, electronic mail may provide an increase in jobs but a loss in post office positions. The whole labour movement, therefore, must address the issue of the effects of technological change on employment.

As a whole, the Telephone Workers Union in British Columbia obtained employment guarantees against technological change in a 1981 contract. It gives the TWU workers a one-year notice, protecting all employees with at least two years of service, employer-paid retraining, and a guarantee against the contracting-out of union jobs. Such a gain at the negotiation table required that the workers operate the telephone exchanges themselves, thus proving to the public that management was not indispensable. The contract also needed active support from the Vancouver public and the rest of the British Columbia labour movement.

In such cases, benefits may be transmitted to consumers by lower prices. This assumes, however, that lower costs are transmitted by producers to consumers, which does not always happen. If there is a monopoly, duopoly, or oligopoly (the control of production by one, two, or a few), the absence of strong competition within the industry may enable manufacturers to keep their prices high, even though their costs have been reduced. Furthermore, even if the prices are lowered, consumer demand may not increase. Most product demands are responsive to price decreases. A decrease in the price of cars or meat will increase demand, but this is not the case in most "first-necessity" goods, or those goods for which our needs are quickly saturated. Hence if no sales increases come out of price decreases, cost-reducing innovations are not likely to create more jobs in other industries.

Excerpt from the **Collective Agreement between the Telecommunications Workers Union and British Columbia Telephone Company.** Effective January 1, 1980. Signed March 12, 1981.

ARTICLE XX – LAY-OFFS

Whenever economic or force conditions are considered by the Company to warrant the laying off of regular employees, such force adjustments as the Company may deem necessary shall be effective among all employees covered by the Collective Agreement, subject to the following conditions.

(a) Temporary employees shall be laid off first.

(b) Lay-offs shall be according to seniority and shall be on the basis of employee's seniority standing at the time of lay-off without regard to classification.... The Company shall have the right to deviate from seniority only when it is necessary to do so in order o retain employees with particular training and special qualifications necessary in the work operations involved. In that event it shall first notify the Vice-President of the Union involved one month prior to the lay-off of the employees involved taking effect. If the Union objects to the deviation from seniority proposed by the Company, it shall notify the Company accordingly within fourteen days of being so notified and in the event that no agreement can be reached within a further fourteen days the matter shall go to arbitration.... The employees affected by the proposed deviation from seniority cannot be laid off unless the Company establishes that it is necessary to deviate from seniority in order to retain employees with particular training and special qualifications in the work operations involved.

(c) The Company will, at all times, endeavour to rehire laid-off regular employees according to seniority of such former employees without loss of seniority, provided, however, that the period of lay-off of such former employees does not exceed one year. In the event the period of lay-off does exceed one year, regular laid-off employees, on re-employment at first opportunity, shall obtain their seniority back after one year of re-employment with the Company. The Company agrees to supply on request of the Union the names of the laid-off employees contacted in the filling of a particular vacancy and that of the engaged employee.

(d) A former employee must keep the Company informed of the address at which he can be reached and any offer of re-employment shall be made in person or by registered letter addressed to the latest address so furnished by the former employee. When an offer of employment has been so made, the former employee shall inform the Company of his acceptance and shall report for duty within twenty-one days from the date such re-employment was offered or such longer period as requested by the Company.

(e) A laid-off employee who declines an offer of regular employment or who fails to report for duty in accordance with provisions of paragraph (d) shall be considered as no longer subject to recall....

(i) The Company agrees to inform the Union of any contemplated lay-offs of regular employees, giving twelve months' notice where the lay-off is necessitated through technological change as defined in the Canada Labour Code. In the event that a lay-off is necessitated for economic reasons the relevant notice provisions of the Canada Labour Code shall apply, provided that in any event a minimum of one month's notice shall be given. Affected employees will receive two weeks' additional notice upon expiry of the foregoing notice.

(j) Coincident with the Company notifying the Union of any contemplated lay-off of regular employees, the Company will immediately cease all new hiring....

(k) In the event of a lay-off due to technological change, the Company shall pay all costs incident to re-training and relocation of affected employees for positions within the Company.

(l) In the event of a lay-off due to technological change, any employee choosing to accept a job in a lower classification shall not have his wage rate reduced but shall continue to be paid the same rate until the applicable rate in the lower job equals or is higher than what he is receiving. Thereafter, he shall progress on the applicable scale in the lower group.

(m) An employee who has been downgraded as a result of technological change will be given the first opportunity to qualify for a position in his former classification or equivalent prior to outside recruitment.

ARTICLE XXI – CONTRACTING OUT

The following jobs may be contracted out without notification to the Telecommunications Workers Union: ... (Here follows a description of jobs not regularly performed by classifications of the Collective Agreement.)

(a) The Company shall not contract out work regularly performed by the classifications set out in this Agreement without the prior approval of the Joint Standing Committee on Contracting Out and Technological Change. Such contracts shall not be awarded until the Committee has given its approval or until a decision to allow the contract has been made by the Chairman of the Committee.

(b) The Committee shall be comprised of 8 representatives, 4 appointed by the Company, 4 appointed by the Union, and a Chairman.

(c) The Chairman shall be appointed jointly by the parties from the 3 names submitted by the Union and the 3 names submitted by the Company. If the parties are unable or fail to agree on the appointment of the Chairman within 30 days from the execution of this Agreement, either party may apply to the Chief Justice of the Supreme Court of British Columbia to appoint a person to the position of Chairman....

(f) The Company agrees that it will not contract out work normally performed by employees within the bargaining unit if such contracting out would cause any employee in the bargaining unit to be terminated or laid off unless no present or laid-off employees are capable of doing the work....

VII. Work Intensity and Pacing

Speed on the production line has become a legitimate bargaining issue in certain factories in Great Britain. Employers introducing technical change often subsequently speed up the pace of production. A mechanic, Harvey Shaiken, told how robots were used to speed up production work:

It is the potential use of robots and robotic technology to control and pace workers on the job. One way of doing this is to design robotic systems that pace work, currently done on the bench by individual workers, at their own pace, on the assembly line. Another way is to use robots to actually pace work once it is on the assembly line.

An example of both these approaches is a new system being developed by General Motors Corporation called the PUMA, programmable universal machine for assembly. This is a combination of robots, parts feeders, transfer machines, and people. The role of people in the system is what is so unusual. According to American Machinist Magazine, a leading trade journal, GM thinks that robots and people can work together in assembly lines, and that they should be interchangeable. I think we must seriously ask ourselves, is this type of system mandated by the production process, or is it in fact a form of managerial control? Does it free workers from drudgery? Or does it create a new form of pressure and drudgery? In fact, it may be the ultimate reflection of considering people as cogs in a machine to actually make them cogs in a machine. Robots, however, are only one part of an increasingly computer-integrated workplace.

Pacing Workers

As in the above caricature, many machines have pacing devices which have no relation to the technical function but are used to control human activity. For instance, word processors are sometimes fitted with instruments that record the number of digits typed by the operator to help supervisors monitor their workers.

Hierarchical computer systems control industrial presses, turn on the lights to guide machine tools... Here, too, computer technology can be designed in a way that creates new pressures. I would like to look at how this is done in factory management systems.

With many factory management systems a central computer is linked directly to a minicomputer placed in a production machine on a shop floor. Every time the machine makes a part it registers in the computer. When the machine does not make a part within the allotted time, generally two minutes, it is immediately obvious. This information is displayed on a video screen in the supervisor's office and it is recorded on a computer printout. The foreman is instructed to go to the machine and investigate the problem. The printout, however, is forwarded to higher management for analysis.

Every minute of the worker's time must be accounted for. The records state how many minutes he was back late from lunch or break, how many minutes the machine was down without explanation, how many breakdown minutes were recorded, regardless of whether the production that worker was supposed to produce in that given day was present or not. This results, of course, in a 7-day-a-week, 24-hours-a-day, 60-minute-per-hour time study.

The role of the foreman changes as well in this system. He no longer decides whether or not to discipline the worker. He only carries out the automatic decisions of the system, and this, of course, eliminates, as one top manager puts it, "the cozy relationship with operators and managers on the top floor."

In one plant where this system was installed, the workers quickly devised a way to take a break, leaving the machine to "cut air." For a while everyone was happy: the workers could pace their jobs, and the computers recorded their numbers. But then management compared the number of parts recorded to the number of parts produced, noting the discrepancy. They countered by linking the computer directly to each machine's motor. When a machine cuts metal, it draws more power than when it runs idle. Hence, management could determine when parts were actually being produced. There were no more unauthorized breaks after that.

Some guarantees against imposed speed-up can be gained by careful wording in the contract. Clauses that require negotiation about work pace can also be written. The only ultimate guarantee, however, is the control of machines by operators on the shop floor.

VIII. Job Complexity and Retraining

As we saw earlier, coding and lower job classifications were introduced into the Post Office at the same time. When employers introduce such changes, they usually intend to eliminate a skill and/or the machinist's control over the work pace.

David Noble has argued that the complexity of a job increases with the complexity of a worker's machine. Melvin Kranzberg, another historian of technology, has noted that automated machines are no threat as long as human knowledge increases at the same time. Labour thus can play a role, to ensure that this does happen. If the work force hopes to regain its control over the labour process, retraining should enable workers to monitor, delay, adjust and repair their new equipment. When computer technology is involved, this means that programmes must be written and training in systems design must be provided.

The social advantage of such an arrangement is obvious. The application and use of new techniques is unlikely if workers' skills are not upgraded. When upgrading does enable workers to have control of their jobs, however, new technologies can be implemented and economies realized.

IX. Collective Agreements and Job Control

Few unions have technological change clauses in their contracts. Since this is a new matter for negotiation, there will be many modifications in future contracts, which, in turn, will bring about many social changes.

The major change aimed at seems to be the control of jobs and work processes on the part of workers. Collective agreements may facilitate workers' initiatives on the shop floor in the future, although most contracts, and even official union proposals, do not reflect this goal. In view of this, we have included a recent agreement made by Rolls Royce, in Great Britain, concerning the use of computers.

ACTSS/APEX (United Kingdom)

Management and Unions recognize that the introduction of computer-based systems in clerical areas is vital to the commercial and business interests of Rolls Royce, with the aim of achieving greater efficiency and providing increased job opportunities for all present and future employees.

(1) Consultation: All information which is relevant to decision making, planning or implementation of technical change will be made available to the Union in the area concerned prior to ordering new equipment....

(3) Shiftworking: ... Training programmes will be established for those employees who will be using new equipment/systems. Such courses will be reviewed regularly to ensure their relevance to any developments which may occur in the use of a particular piece of equipment/system...

(4) Appropriate forms of training will be given to employees redeployed to other jobs demanding new or different skills as a result of the introduction of new equipment/systems.

(5) Benefits:... Where skills and working practices change as a result of introducing computer-based systems, such changes will be evaluated by Job Evaluation within the trial period. At the end of the trial period the equipment or system would cease to be used until agreement is reached. The Unions reaffirm their commitment to work towards a shorter working week and improved holiday and retiral arrangements. Such matters would be the subject of normal bargaining procedures.

(6) Health and Safety: Both parties recognize that the environmental standards, location and use of computer-based equipment are subject to continuous research. Improvements designed to safeguard the health and safety of operators will be introduced after consultation at any appropriate time....

Of particular importance is the clause that specifies that each section of the union is required to negotiate work conditions on the shop floor:

Each area/department of ACTSS/APEX will be responsible for negotiating appropriate arrangements within the framework of this agreement. The introduction of new methods or equipment and any consequential changes in working conditions shall be the subject of consultation in accordance with domestic and national procedures. A review of this document will take place on an annual basis.

VDTs: Health and Safety Factors

The following guidelines about the use of Video Display Terminals have been gathered from recently published materials. They are general measures for avoiding health hazards in the work place. Since work stations vary, specific solutions must be based on given conditions; the following recommendations will serve as a general framework.

Luminance: (1) There should be a minimum screen luminance of 75 cd. In most VDTs, this is variable from 0 (zero) to well above 150 cd. (2) Brightness must be adjustable. (3) Contrast control should be provided where available.

Colour of Display: (1) Colours such as red/green or orange/black should be avoided. (2) Colours must be restful to the eye, while allowing the symbols to stand out.

Matrix Size: (1) For character definition the dot matrix will not be less than 5x7 , with character size not less than 3mm. (2) The preferred size, in some instances adjustable, is at least 4.5mm.

Refresh Rate (frequency of flicker): (1) The refresh rate should be a minimum of 50 hertz. (2) Existing equipment with less than this should be replaced or upgraded when circumstances permit.

Radiation: (1) The equipment should comply with the Health and Safety at Work Act 1974, regulations concerning Building Operation and Work Engineering Construction. (2) In addition, the supplier of such equipment should confirm that there is no occupational health hazard caused by the terminals.

Explosion/Implosion: All VDTs must provide protection for the operator against the risk of implosion.

Heat: Heat output from a VDT should be kept to a minimum.

Noise: Noise levels shold be as low as possible and should conform to accepted Health and Safety levels.

General Machine Design: (1) Surface of machines should be matt, and shining decorations should be avoided. (2) Bright reflection in the table screen should be avoided, and the employee's field of vision should not include a source of glare. (2) Ambient lighting in areas in whch VDUs are used should not exceed 300 LUX.

Static Electricity: Steps should be taken to reduce the incidence of static.

Positioning of Screen, Keyboard, and Papers: (1) The screen and paperwork should be on the same level. (2) The distance of reading material to eye and screen to eye should be the same; about 700 mm is recommended.

Seats: All seats should be adjustable in height.

Machine Maintenance: (1) VDTs should be maintained in accordance with manufacturers' specifications. (2) Tubes should be replaced at regular intervals, and not allowed to deteriorate until they cease to function. (3) VDT screens should be kept clean. (4) VDTs should be switched off when not in use.

Access: (1) VDT work stations would be located so they are equally accessible to all users. (2) At each station, access and regress should be easy. (3) Walkways, floor areas, and work spaces should be clear of unnecessary obstructions.

Work Surfaces: Work surfaces should be sufficiently large to accommodate telephones, documents and any other aids necessary for efficient task performance....

Health: (1) Medically approved eye tests should be available for all VDT operators prior to their working on VDTs. Employees with unsuitable eyesight will not be required to become full-time operators, and if necessary, will be redeployed. (2) Eyesight retesting should take place every two years. (3) Employees suffering from migraine, epilepsy, or nervous complaints should not be required to operate VDTs. (4) Detailed working practices should be evaluated within the trial period. There should be no agreement on workload until the trial period has been completed.

X. Work Environment: Norwegian Legislation and Swedish Woodworkers' Practice

An interesting principle, the parity of people with machines, was recently advanced by industrial draughtspersons in Great Britain. Since much sophisticated computer equipment is very sensitive, it must be handled carefully, sometimes in clinically clean settings. In many industries, the care lavished by employers on their machines contrasts glaringly with the comparatively primitive conditions reserved for their workers.

In June, 1973, designers and draughtsmen who were members of the AUEW/TASS union, employed by a large Birmingham engineering firm, officially claimed "Parity of environment with the CAD Equipment" in the following terms:

This claim is made in furtherance of a longstanding complaint concerning the heating and ventilation in the Design and Drawing Office Area, going back to April 1972. Indeed to our knowledge these working conditions have been unsatisfactory as far back as 1958. We believe that if electro-mechanical equipment can be considered to the point of giving it an air-conditioned environment for its efficient working, the human beings who may be interfaced with this equipment should receive the same consideration.

In 1964 a placard at Berkeley, California, read: "I am a human being: Please do not fold, spindle or mutilate."

The work environment is usually defined very restrictively. Yet it encompasses all aspects of health and safety. It includes not only the workers' relationships with their daily working conditions and work processes, but also the effects of these relationships on individual lives. The work place is also the most visible example of interpersonal relationships shaped by technology. It may be the springboard from which working people start to redesign not only their places of work but also their personal and community ways of living.

The work environment permeates collective agreements. Such legislation can be improved, however, only through political action; the public will support improved legislation.

The following excerpt gives an example of Norwegian legislation, which is considered one of the most progressive in the industrial world. An article from the International Woodworkers of America (IWA), has also been reproduced. The IWA was impressed by the control over total work environment some Swedish woodworkers attained.

Excerpt from the Norwegian ACT RELATING TO WORKER PROTECTION AND WORKING ENVIRONMENT

Chapter I. Objectives and Scope of the Act.

The objectives of this Act are (1) to secure a working environment which affords the employees full safety against harmful physical and mental influences, and which has safety, occupational health and welfare standards that correspond to the level of technological and social development of the society at large at any time; (2) to secure sound contract conditions and meaningful occupation for the individual employee; and (3) to provide a basis whereby the enterprises themselves can solve their working environment problems in cooperation with organizations of employers and employees, and under the supervision and guidance of the public authorities.

Scope of the Act.

1. Provided that it does not expressly state otherwise, this Act applies to all enterprises that engage employees. 2. (Exceptions follow....) 5. The King may direct that technical apparatus and equipment shall be subject to supervision pursuant to this Act though not used in enterprises covered by the Act. The same applies in respect of work not covered by this Act when such work takes place under conditions that may involve a hazard to life or health.... 6. **Compulsory registration.** Every enterprise covered by this Act shall register in writing with the Labour Inspection....

Chapter II. Requirements concerning the working environment

General requirements .... 1. The working environment in the enterprise shall be fully satisfactory when the factors in the working environment that may influence the mental and physical health and welfare of the workers are judged separately and collectively....

(8) **The workplace.** 1. The workplace shall be arranged so that the working environment is fully satisfactory as regards the safety, health and welfare of the employees. In particular it shall be ensured that: (a) workrooms, passageways, stairways, etc. are suitably dimensioned and equipped for the activities being conducted; (b) good lighting is provided, if possible with daylight and a view; (c) climatic conditions are fully satisfactory as regards

volume of air, ventilation, humidity, draughts, temperature, etc.; (d) pollution in the form of dust, smoke, gas, vapours, unpleasant odours and radiation is avoided, unless it is known that the pollution cannot lead to undesirable effects upon employees; (e) noise and vibration is avoided or reduced to prevent undesirable effects....

(Author's note: Note that in the passage "unless it is known that the pollution cannot lead to undesirable effects upon employees," the contrary is assumed. The burden of proof therefore lies on the producer of the new pollution.)

Living quarters made available to employees by the employer shall be properly constructed, fitted out and kept in repair. Any house rules shall be drawn up in consultation with employee representatives. The Directorate of Labour Inspection may issue regulations prohibiting house rules that have unreasonable effects upon employees....

(9) **Technical apparatus and equipment.** 1. Technical apparatus and equipment in the enterprise shall be designed and provided with safety devices so as to protect employees from injury and disease. When technical apparatus is being installed and used, care shall be taken to ensure that the employees are not exposed to undesirable effects from noise, vibrations, uncomfortable working positions, etc. Technical apparatus and equipment should be designed and installed so that it can be operated by, or be adapted for, use by employees of varying physique. Technical apparatus and equipment shall always be maintained and attended....

Toxic and other noxious substances. 1. In enterprises where toxic or other noxious substances are manufactured, packed, used or stored in a manner that may involve a health hazard, the working processes and other work shall be fully satisfactory so that employees are protected against accidents, injury to health, and excessive discomfort. Containers and packaging for the substances shall be clearly marked, giving the name of the substance and a warning in Norwegian. The enterprise shall keep a record of such substances, showing the name of the substance, its composition, physical and chemical properties, as well as information concerning possible poisonous effects (toxicological data), elements of risk, preventive meansures and first-aid treatment. The enterprise shall have the necessary equipment to prevent or counteract injury to health due to such substances. **Such substances shall not be used if they can be replaced by substances less hazardous to the employees** (author's emphasis).

In enterprises that manufacture, pack, use or store toxic or noxious substances in a manner that may involve a health hazard, the working environment and the health of the employees shall be kept under continuous control.... 13. The Directorate (of Labour) may require the employer to carry out special studies or submit specimens for study. The cost of studies required under this secton shall be borne by the party under obligation to carry out the study or submit the specimen. The Directorate of Labour Inspection may direct that a record shall be kept of all employees who are exposed to specified noxious ubstances in enterprises covered by this Act. 14. The Directorate of Labour Inspection may forbid the manufacture, packaging, use or storage of noxious substances in enterprises covered by this Act. Moreover, the Directorate may impose further conditions for the use or production of any substance....

Planning the work. .... 1. Technology, organization of the work, working hours and wage systems shall be set up so that the employees are not exposed to undesirable physical or mental strain and so that their possibilities of displaying caution and observing safety measures are not impaired. Conditions shall be arranged so that employees are afforded reasonable opportunity for professional and personal development through their work.

Arrangement of work. The individual employee's opportunity for self-determination and professional responsibility shall be taken into consideration when planning and arranging the work. Efforts shall be made to avoid undiversified, repetitive work and work that is governed by machine or conveyor belt in such a manner that the employees themselves are prevented from varying the speed of the work. Otherwise efforts shall be made to arrange the work so as to provide possibilities for variation and for contact with others, for connection between individual job assignments, and for employees to keep themselves informed about production requirements and results.

Control and planning systems. The employees and their elected union representatives shall be kept informed about the systems employed for planning and effecting the work, and about planned changes in such systems. They shall be given the training necessary to enable them to learn these systems, and they shall take part in planning them.

Work involving safety hazards. (a) Performance premium wage systems shall not be employed for work where this may materially affect safety. (b) If work is to be carried out in the enterprise that may involve particular hazard to life and health, a special directive shall be issued prescribing how the work is to be done and the safety precautions to be observed, including any particular instruction and supervision. (c) When the work is of such a nature that it involves danger of a disaster or disastrous accident, plans shall be drawn up for first-aid, escape routes, and so on. (d) Employees shall be informed of the regulations safety rules relating to the area concerned and of the plans and measures mentioned under (c). When satisfactory precaution to protect life and health cannot be achieved by other means, employees shall be provided with suitable personal protective equipment. Employees shall be trained in the use of such equipment and if necessary shall be ordered to use it....

Occupationally handicapped employees. 1. Passageways, sanitary facilities, technical apparatus and equipment... shall, to the extent possible and reasonable, be designed and arranged so that the enterprise can employ occupationally handicapped persons. 2. If an employee has become handicapped in his occupation as the result of accident, disease, overstrain or the like, the employer shall, to the extent possible, effect the necessary measures so as to enable the employee to be given or to retain suitable work. Preferably the employee shall be afforded opportunity to continue his normal work, possibly after special adaptation of the work, alteration of technical apparatus, rehabilitation or the like. 3. In the event that, in accordance with the rules of subsection (2) above, there is question of transferring an employee to other work, the employee and the elected union representative concerned shall be consulted before any decision is made. (The institutional mechanisms of the Law follow....)

Working environment committees. 1. Enterprises which regularly employ more than 50 employees shall have a working environment committee on which the employer, the employees and the safety and health personnel are represented. Working environment committees shall also be formed in enterprises having between 20 and 50 employees when so required by any of the parties at the enterprise. Where working conditions so dictate, the Labour Inspection may direct that enterprises having less than 50 employees shall establish a working environment committee....Notices shall be posted at the workplace giving the names of the persons who are members of the committee at any time. The employer and the employees shall have an equal number of representatives on the committee. Representatives of the employer and of the employees shall be elected alternately as chairman of the committee. Safety and health representatives on the committee have no vote. When votes are equally divided, the chairman has the casting vote....

Duties of working environment committees. 1. The working environment committee shall consider: a) questions relating to the company health service and the company safety service; b) questions relating to training, instruction and information activities in the enterprise that are of significance for the working environment; c) plans that require the consent of the Labour Inspection ....d) other plans that may be of material significance for the working environment, such as plans for building work, purchases of materials, rationalization, work processes, working time systems and preventive safety measures. Questions relating to work for occupationally handicapped employees may also be considered by the committee....The committee shall study all reports relating to occupational disease, occupational accidents and near accidents, seek to find the cause of the accident or disease, and ensure that the employer takes steps to prevent recurrence. As a general rule the committee shall have access to Labour Inspection or police inquiry documents. When the committee considers it necessary, the committee may decide that inquiries shall be conducted by specialists or by a commission of inquiry appointed by the committee. Without undue delay the employer may submit such decision to the Labour Inspection for decision. The committee shall study all reports relating to occupational health inspections and test results....If the working environment committee considers it necessary in order to protect the life or health of employees, it may decide that the employer shall effect concrete measures to improve the working environment, within the framework of the provisions stipulated in or by virtue of this Act. To determine whether a health hazard exists, the committee may decide that the employer shall have the working environment explained or tested. A time limit for effectuation of the decision shall be imposed by the committee. If the employer finds that he is unable to effectuate the decision, the matter shall be submitted without undue delay to the Labour Inspection for decision. Each year the working environment committee shall submit a report on its activities to the administrative bodies of the enterprise, to employee organizations and to the Labour Inspection....

Safety delegates. 1. Safety delegates shall be elected at all enterprises covered by this Act. At enterprises having less than five employees, the parties may agree upon a different system or agree that the enterprise shall not have a safety delegate. At enterprises having more than 10 employees, more than one safety delegate may be elected. 2. The number of safety delegates shall be determined according to the size of the enterprise, the nature of the work and working conditions in general. Enterprises that consist of several separate departments, or where employees work shifts, shall as a general rule have at least one safety delegate for each department or each shift team. Safety areas shall be clearly marked and shall not be larger than that, so the safety delegate can have full control and attend to his duties in a proper manner. 3. Enterprises having more than one safety delegate shall have at least one senior safety delegate, who shall be responsible for coordinating safety delegate activities. The senior safety delegate shall be elected from among the safety delegates or other persons who hold or have held offices in the enterprise.... (The duties and procedures of safety delegates follow.)

If the Swedes Can Do It... by Matt Witt

In some ways, it was just like an American or Canadian sawmill, with conveyors moving past the saws which reduced logs to cants, cants to boards. But to the visitors from the International Woodworkers Association (IWA), there was something very different about this sawmill in Sweden. It was so quiet that they didn't need ear plugs in much of the mill, and they could actually talk to each other over the sound of the machines. It was so clean that no dust had accumulated on the floor or equipment. Bright lights reduced both the stress on workers and the chance of accidents. Enclosed booths for machine operators looked like offices, with comfortable seats and little or no vibration in the floor.

It wasn't paradise, but the work environment in the Anebyhus Company's sawmill was much better than in mills in North America. And it was just one of many impressive work sites visited by eight IWA members and staff and two government officials during a two-week study tour of the wood products industry in Sweden. (The tour, which was made possible by a grant from the German Marshall Fund, also included visits to West Germany and Austria.) IWA group members met dozens of local and national officials of government, management and unions, who taught them not only about wooden shoes, fermented herring, and Swedish drinking songs, but also about the Swedes' highly effective program for job safety and health. The North Americans had a chance to see with their own eyes work environment improvements in sawmills, logging, board plants, and pulp and paper mills. And they were able to ask probing questions about the laws, union contracts, and overall philosophy that made those improvements possible.

The Swedish system they saw has three main features. First, Swedish workers have won real power to prevent hazards, as well as the training to enable them to use that power. Second, the unions have a major voice in research programs on safety and health problems. Those programs are conducted through cooperative efforts of employers, manufacturers of industrial equipment, university researchers, government experts and rank-and-file workers. Research generally is designed to find specific solutions which can be put into practice. Third, the Swedish unions are trying to improve the total work environment, not just safety and health in the narrow North American sense. They recognize that physical safety hazards, health hazards such as noise and chemical exposure, and stress from heat or cold, speed-up, or boredom are not separate, unrelated problems. They are aware, for example, that noise, stress, or chemically-induced headaches may contribute to accidents, and that stress over long periods of time is often a health hazard.

The Swedes are concerned about not only injuries and illnesses but also discomfort and lack of job satisfaction. They believe that all workers – not just corporate executives – are entitled to a humane work environment and as much control over their jobs as possible.

A Real Role for Workers

In North America, labour-management "cooperation" on safety and health is usually an empty slogan, because the employers have virtually all the decision-making authority. But in Sweden, cooperation works because the unions have real power.

The key to the Swedish system is the safety committee. Under a combination of national laws and contracts, every Swedish workplace with 50 or more emloyees must have a labour-management safety committee – **with more than half of the committee members elected from the union**. In smaller workplaces, where the workers feel a committee is necessary, one must be created. Otherwise, a **regional safety representative** from the union plays the same role as the union committee members in a larger operation. The union-dominated committees (or the regional representative) have the right to veto any plans for new machines, materials, or work processes for safety and health reasons. Three examples will show the trend: in a forestry operation visted by the IWA group, the union safety committee members were involved in choosing the model of chainsaw the company would purchase; pentachlorophenols are no longer used as wood preservatives because of worker complaints; and workers at a logging company said they have refused to work with the herbicide 2.4D in situations in which thinning could be accomplished manually with brush cutters.

Decide how to spend the company safety and health budget

The size of that budget is negotiated at each operation, and was considered too small by each local union the IWA group visited. But union control meant that the budget was being spend on solutions to the most serious work environment problems – control of noise, dust and chemicals – rather than being siphoned off from projects to improve productivity.

Approve the selection and direct the work of the company doctor, nurse, safety engineer, or industrial hygienist

At the Ala Company sawmill, for example, the fact that the doctor and nurse report to the safety committee seemed to allow them to worry more about the health of the workers than about company profits. "We have the advantage that when we treat a worker, we know what his working conditions are," explained Dr. Bertil Jonsson. "And it is part of our job not just to treat the patient but to recommend ways to change the working conditions so the health problem won't happen again."

Review all corporate medical records, monitoring results, and other information on hazards

The Swedish unions have made access to information such a high priority that often when the group met with top company officials and a local union safety committee member at the same time, the managers would refer most questions to the union representative, because he was more knowledgeable about safety and health. "The whole idea of the Swedish system is that workers have the right to be involved in workplace planning and design so hazards can be prevented," explained Denny Scott, the IWA researcher who led the study tour. "The system is set up to minimize the number of cases in which workers must either accept hazards or lose wages while something is corrected," he said.

To monitor conditions on a daily basis, enough union safety stewards must be elected to cover each work area on each shift at all Swedish workplaces with five or more employees. These stewards, as well as individual workers, have the right to shut down any dangerous operation until it can be corrected – without fear of punishment. The mere threat of shutting down an operaion seems to be quite effective, because stewards have had to actually use that power only about 25 times per year since it was established by law in 1974.

Union stewards, safety committee members, and regional representatives have the right to determine how much time they need to carry out their duties. Although chosen by the union, all are paid from employer funds. Providing training for these union personnel is considered a cost of doing business in Sweden. In 1971, the unions won passage of a law creating a national Work Environment Fund. It is financed by a 0.1 percent payroll tax on all employers, and guided by a union-dominated board. The Fund has paid for the training of more than 4,000 safety stewards from the Swedish Woodworkers Union, which represents 67,000 workers in sawmills, board mills, and other wood products manufacturing plants. Training has been provided to about 2,000 stewards from the Forestry Workers Union, which has 25,000 members.

Classes are given during normal work hours, with employers paying lost time. In the two-and-a-half years ending in June 1979, woodworkers' employers paid $1 million in lost time wages for safety training. Forestry employers have been required to spend more than $700,000. The 40-hour basic courses cover such topics as workplace planning, noise, ventilation, toxic substances, illumination, "ergonomics" (the science of fitting the job to the worker rather than the worker to the job), and "psychosocial factors" such as job satisfaction. Courses are taught in "study circles" rather than with the formal classroom approach usually used in North America. Trained study circle leaders, who generally are workers rather than safety technicians, guide the discussions.

Safety stewards say the study circle method teaches them to work together and to rely on experts only for technical advice. Written material and filmstrips explain basic principles, which are then applied by the students during special workplace inspections. A study circle graduate goes back to work with lists of conditions which must be corrected.

Lennart Olsson, chief safety steward at a large government-owned hardboard mill, told the IWA group that the basic course "worked vary well."

Practical Research

Both the forestry and woodworking industries have national work environment research committees, run jointly by the employers and the unions. Much of the research is financed by the union-dominated, employer-financed Work Environment Fund. The committees review all proposals from researchers to the Fund. The Fund is now spending more than $1 million to teach Swedish union representatives both to evaluate those proposals and to develop more of their own.

One work environment research group has been working in 15 sawmills, a similar group has concentrated on woodworking factories such as furniture and prefab housing plants, and a third has worked in forestry under another $1 million Fund grant. These groups have succeeded because they include not only engineers, professors, doctors, and psychologists, but also representatives of the unions, employers, and equipment manufacturers. They have demonstrated methods for controlling noise, dust, chemicals, and other hazards, as well as for redesigning jobs to make them less stressful.

In contrast to the North American system, in which research is mainly distributed to other researchers, the Swedish groups' achievements are being explained to the unions; regional safety representatives – at Work Environment Fund expense – and the representatives will, in turn, educate local union stewards.

Bengt Ager, a professor who has served as leader of these research groups, told the IWA visitors that "We are forming a circle of communication between those who study and design industrial equipment, those who make it, those who buy it, and those who use it every day."

Throughout their two-week tour in Sweden, IWA group members had many chances to see how the process Ager described has paid off in reducing workplace hazards:

Noise and Dust

The Swedish standard for average exposure to noise over an eight-hour shift is 85 decibels – almost a quarter as damaging to the ear as the 90 decibels allowed in the U.S. and Canada. Noise control in logging has been achieved mainly by mechanization. With smaller trees to work with than in western North America, the Swedes are able to do much of their felling, bucking, loading, forwarding, and hauling by machine. Operators are provided fully air-conditioned cabs, which reduce noise and dust and allow them to do the job comfortably and efficiently in all seasons.

At the Anebyhus sawmill, work environment researchers have helped the safety committee make dramatic improvements. Accoustical tile and a concrete-wood sound absorbent mixture are used on the ceiling and walls to reduce the spread of sound from conveyor belts. For purposes of both noise and dust control, saws are completely enclosed in housings the size of small rooms, which are entered only for maintenance. Wood dust levels in the mill air are below one milligram per cubic metre.

Saw blades at Anebyhus are chosen for the best design for noise control; adjustments in the angle of teeth can mean a reduction of 5 decibels when cutting, 10 when idle, according to research engineer Anders Soderqvist.

"A lot of things we want, like controls for your noise or your dust, were simple things anybody could understand," reported tour member Joel Hembree of IWA Local 3-536. "Research doesn't have to be some complicated thing, only for what you'd call 'experts'," he said. "A lot of what they're doing is just common sense. And if they can do it, so can we."

At a Wood Research Centre established by the employers and unions in order to find cheaper hazard control methods for small businesses, the IWA group was shown a demonstration system for exhausting dust from a saw. The guard was placed as close as physically possible to the blade so dust would have no way to escape. The suction hose was placed below the saw at the point where the blade's centrifugal force was throwing off the dust. Suction occurred only when the saw was cutting; when it was in ideal position, the suction cut off.

This system effectively reduces both dust and noise levels. There is less noise from ventilation when the saw is idle. Proper placement of the suction hose means that ventilation noise when the saw is cutting is also reduced because the amount of air needed is less.

"We are not preoccupied with standards, standards, standards," said Rolf Ottosson, employer representative on the centre's board. "Standards are necessary, but they only tell you the state of scientific knowledge today, and they may always beome more strict tomorrow when our knowledge changes. So we are trying to use our design expertise now to anticipate problems and to find ways to modify our processes in the best way possible."

Accidents

The Swedish National Safety Board, similar to OSHA in the U.S. and the provincial workers' compensation boards in Canada, does issue standards, and its research shows that they make a difference. For example, chain saw-related hand and wrist injuries in the logging industry were reduced by 90 percent between 1967 and 1976, primarily as a result of new requirements for hand guards. A foot and leg injury reduction of more than 50 percent was achieved in one year through the introduction of chain brakes.

Researchers from the College of Forestry didn't have to dig very far to find that slips and falls while climbing onto equipment are a major cause of injuries. Employers traditionally have argued that the only answer to the problem is pep talks to encourage workers not to be so "careless." Ladders leading up to the cab are often either not provided or jerry-rigged so that they are easily broken. With some prodding, Swedish manufacturers have solved the problem. They now build into logging machines a set of hydraulic stairs which is raised and lowered automatically as the machine is turned on and off.

"In the past, we only worried about the work environment after a machine was built," said Ake Ullman, safety director for the Osa forestry equipment company. "Now we find we can discuss work environment ahead of time and put it right in at the design stage."

Physical stress

Studies in the forestry industry confirmed workers' reports that large numbers of loggers, especially older workers, suffer back problems. Employers, union members and researchers together developed a system for using one log as a bench and then felling other trees on top of it. Under this system, buckers don't have to bend over so far. Noting that his technique might not always be practical, tour member Verna Ledger, IWA Region I safety director, commented, "The point is not whether we can adopt every solution the Swedes have found. The point is that we can adopt their way of thinking and then find our own answers."

"Their concern for older workers and people with back trouble is typical of their concern for the total work environment and for the total worker," she said. "That's what we have to learn from."

Psychological stress

At the Ala Company sawmill, the IWA group saw a booth in the trimming plant that was constructed for use by two operators monitoring a conveyor belt. The two-person booth protected the workers from noise and dust without forcing them to spend an entire shift totally isolated from other people. When IWA tour members entered the booth, the workers were talking and listening to a radio. The operators' controls were embedded in the arms of their chairs, so that the workers' arms were supported all day. The two men rotated with a third worker who was physically handling lumber on the belt, so that each operator was in the booth for 40 minutes and outside of it for 20.

At a large, cooperatively-owned forestry company, schedules of eight hours' work plus a total of an hour for lunch and breaks had been changed to reduce operator stress. Under the new system, each operator worked three hours on the machine, three hours off it, and then three hours on. Workers told the IWA group that because of the three-hour break they could produce as much in six hours on the machine as in eight under the old system. One of the company's shifts began three hours after the other, so the equipment was in use for 12 hours.

"You can't keep cutting or bucking for an entire shift without getting tired and making mistakes," said a young worker operating a timber-bucker. "It's bad for your health because of all the pressure, it's bad for safety, and it's bad for production."

Unsafe payment systems

A wildcat strike by Swedish forestry workers in 1975 ended the piece rate system in many companies. A Work Environment Fund study found that the new hourly stystem resulted in 30 percent fewer accidents and 35 percent less lost time. Yet there was no evidence of a decline in productivity.

Uncomfortable protective gear

Swedes, like workers all over the world, do not like to wear uncomfortable protective clothing. College of Forestry researchers surveyed 2,000 loggers to find out their specific complaints. Not surprisingly, the workers said their hard hats were too heavy, eye protection blocked their vision, and ear muffs created too much pressure. Following the survey, equipment manufacturers were persuaded to design much more comfortable gear than is generally used in North America.

Work environment and politics

Why have Swedish employers accepted expensive work environment programs? One reason is that they had to. The basic structure of the system was created under the labour-backed Social Democratic party, which until 1976 had been in power for 44 years. About 90 percent of Swedish workers are unionized, compared to 20 percent in the U.S. and 31 percent in Canada.

Most employers also see work environment improvement as a way to reduce absenteeism, wildcat strikes, and other results of worker unrest. When many North American employers resort to the stick, their Swedish counterparts often try to use the carrot. "When we have a national absentee rate of 10 percent, we have to start asking questions about the motivation of the 90 percent who do come to work," said Dr. Rolf Lindblom, a work design specialist for the Swedish employers' confederation. "What can we do to make work more rewarding, more satisfying, and with less danger?"

In addition to increasing worker motivation and productivity, some employers hope that work environment improvement will take the steam out of growing union demands for control over the Swedish economy. A new law provides for co-determination, or employer consultation with unions in making busines decisions, and the Swedish labour movement is proposing eventual union control of all of the country's businesses, 90 percent of which are now privately owned. "Our goal is to reduce conflict," said C.G.S. Danberg, an employers' confederation psychiatrist. "Whenever there is a concentration of resources, or power, you get a 'we and them' psychology. We want to improve communication, to solve problems people have, so this kind of conflict will not occur."

Ironically, Swedish unionists saw the work environment movements as part of their overall drive toward "economic democracy." They want not only to save lives, but to improve the quality of life on the job as well. "The fight to have more power in the workplace was the logical next step for Swedish workers," said Birger Viklund of the Swedish unions' Work Quality Centre. "For decades we fought for social democracy, or security for every person to have a job, health care, and a place to live. Now we want economic democracy, which means not only a larger share of the wealth but also more control over working conditions...."

XI. THE RIGHT TO INFORMATION BEFORE DESIGN OF TECHNOLOGY: INFORMATION STEWARDS

In December 1983 the Belgian FGTB (the equivalent of the Canadian Labour Congress) gained a general agreement concerning information rights.

Such agreements are vital, since we are going through a protracted period of technical change, and the work force will bear the consequences of implementing many new technologies. After investment decisions are made it's too late: unions can only wage defensive resistance. Thus workers and their unions should be participants at the ground level.

Unions must bring about a radical change in the area of information if they expect to redirect technological change. They must have such rights as access to data bases, consultants' reports, the choice of alternative consultants, separate meetings with them, and answers to questions pertaining to their research. (Suitably informed, they can avoid certain collision with firms. Companies often have tacit standing agreements with suppliers, even though they are not supposed to be linked corporately with them. The information which management shares with unions should cover technical changes and alternatives, projects being studied by a company's Research and Development, and the current status of Research and Development programs both in and out of a specific company. Unions must also be involved in the testing of new technology, have the right to stop work, and they must be given some responsibility for the maintenance and control of equipment.

Some Scandinavian unions have obtained special information standards. They have also found it necessary to have information stewards to meet technical change. These stewards receive paid educational leave to learn about a new technology. Such changes are desirable, but the right to information is useful only if the technical change is postponed until everyone is properly informed, and agreements about its implementation have been reached well in advance.

XII. CONTROL OF CHOICE AND DESIGN

The following excerpt, written by David Noble, shows that some unions in Norway have managed to participate in the selection of technologies.

Social Choice in Machine Design

The situation is quite different in the state-owned weapons factory in Kongsberg, Norway, a plant with roughly the same number of employees, a similar line of products (aircraft parts and turbines), a similar mix of commercial and military customers, and, most, important, the same types of CNC machinery (although here they tend to be European-made rather than than Japanese, as at G.E.). The similarity ends with the way in which these machines are used. Here the operators routinely do all of the editing of programs, according to their own criteria of safety, efficiency, quality, and convenience; they change the sequence of operations, add or subtract operations, and sometimes alter the entire structure of the program to suit themselves. When they are satisfied with a program and have finished producing a batch of parts, they press a button to generate a corrected tape which, after being approved by a programmer, is put into the library for permanent storage.

All operators are trained in N/C programming and, as a consequence, their conflicts with programmers are reduced. One programmer, who, like most of his colleagues had received training in programming while still a machine operator, explained the justification for having programmers at all by the fact that the programmer specialized in programming and thus got more proficient at it (he also dealt directly with customers and did most of the APT programming of highly complex aircraft parts). Yet, when asked if it bothered him to have his well-worked programs tampered with by the operators, he replied, without hesitation, that the operator knows best; he's the one who has to actually make the part and is more intimately familiar with the particular safety and convenience factors; also, he usually best knows how to optimize the program for his machine.

This situation, it should be pointed out, is rather unusual even for Norway. It is a product of many factors. The Iron and Metalworkers Union in Norway is the most powerful industrial union in the country, and the local club in Kongsberg is a potent force in the industrial, political and social life of Kongsberg, representing a cohesive and rather homogeneous working class community. The Vapenfabrikk is important in state policy, as a holding company in electronics, and the plant is an important centre of high technology engineering. Also, Social Democratic legislation in Norway has encouraged worker participation in matters pertaining to working conditions and has given unions the right to information. But most important, the local club here has been involved for the last seven years in what has been called the trade union participation project, an important development in workers' control which focuses upon the introduction of computer-based manufacturing technology.

In 1971, the Iron and Metalworkers' Union, faced with an unprecedented challenge of new computer-based information and control systems (for production, scheduling, inventory, etc., as well as machining), took steps to learn how to meet it. They succeeded in hiring, on a single-party basis (that is, without management collaboration), the government Norwegian Computing Centre to conduct research for them on the new technology. As the direct result of this unprecedented effort, computer technology was demystified for the union, and the union – and labour in general – was demystified for the computer scientists at the Centre; the union became more sophisticated about the technology, and the technical people became more attuned to the needs and disciplines of trade unionists. In practical terms, the study resulted in the production of a number of textbooks on the new technology, written by and for shop stewards, the creation of a new union position, the data shop steward, and, in time, the establishment of formal data agreements (between individual companies and their local clubs and between the national union and the employers' federation), which outlined union rights to participate in the decisions about technology.

The Kongsberg plant was the first and primary site of such trade union participation. Here the data shop steward, a former assembly worker, is responsible for keeping abreast of, and critically scrutinizing, all new systems; another man is assigned the job of supervising the activity of the data shop steward to ensure that he doesn't become a 'technical' man, that is, captive either to the technology or to management, and out of touch with the interests of the people on the shop floor. The responsibilities are enormous; that is not a situation in which the union and the management are partners in harmonious cooperation, nor is it a management-devised job enlargement scheme to motivate workers. The task of the data shop steward, and the union in general, is to engage, as effectively as possible, in a struggle over information and control, a struggle engaged in, with equal sophistication and earnestness by the other side.

When management plans to introduce a new computer-based production system, for example, the union must assume as a matter of course (based upon long experience) that the proposed design reflects purposes which are not always consonant with the interests of the workers. Thus, the data shop steward and his colleagues must learn about the system early enough and investigate it thoroughly enough to ensure that it contains no features that make possible, for example, the measurement of individual performance or any monitoring of shop floor activities that would restrict worker freedom or control. As it turns out, all new systems invariably contain such features (since they are often camouflaged attempts to introduce control mechanisms that, in other forms, have been successfully resisted by the workers); thus it is up to the union to identify them and demand that they be eliminated. It is the union's responsibility to its members, in short, to struggle to recondition the system so that it meets their own, as well as management's, specifications. At Kongsberg, for example, after a long battle, the union has succeeded in securing for all of the people on the shop floor complete access to the computer-based production and inventory systems. Just as CNC has made automatic machining more accessible to shopfloor control, so computer-integrated production systems have made it possible to eliminate certain managerial functions by simply extending the reach of the people on the shop floor. How this technology will actually be employed in a plant depends less upon any inherent nature of the technology than upon the particular manufacturing processes involved, the political and economic setting, and the relative power and sophistication of the parties engaged in the struggle over control of production.

The potential inherent in new technologies like CNC has not been lost on everyone except the Norwegians. At the Edgewick plant of Alfred Herbert, Ltd. in Coventry, England, for example, the political and economic situation is strikingly different from Kongsberg, as is the physical appearance and social organization of the factory. Here the strength of the machinists' union, the traditon-bound and craft-based Amalgamated Union of Engineering Workers, has been preserved, and shop floor control over production has been retained, largely as a consequence of technological backwardness. Herbert, for a century one of the world's premier machine tool builders, had for a long time enjoyed something of a monopoly in a particular market for special custom-made machinery. As a result, the company had no incentive to invest in new production methods, and the Edgewick plant still resembles a nineteenth-century pre-Taylorite machine shop; the products, sophisticated electronically-controlled machine tools (such as the famous batchmatic), are painstakingly constructed by highly skilled craftsmen. Standardization of parts is the exception rather than the rule; the lead-time is long and the costs are high.

During the last decade, the management did begin to introduce some tape-controlled N/C machines – primarily some of their own machines which they hadn't been able to sell – and to hire some programmers to prepare tapes. Inevitably, the programmers came into conflict with the workers on the floor who ran the machines that they programmed. Moreover, when the programmers (who are unionized) went out on strike for better wages, the workers feared that they might some day be in a position to hold the entire company for ransom.

In recent years, the company's monopoly position has steadily deteriorated as its traditional market has been flooded with lower-priced Japanese and European machinery. In response, Herbert has been developing a new machine with which it hopes to penetrate the relatively untouched job shop market: a fully programmable CNC lathe that eliminates much of the overhead and support staff traditionally associated with N/C. The company sees the new machine as its salvation. The people on the floor, meanwhile, see the machine as their salvation too. CNC, they fully realize, will enable them to retain the full shop floor control over production that they have long been accustomed to. With this technology, the shop steward convenor, a sixty-year-old highly skilled fitter, explained, the programmers are superfluous; they're through, finished. Then he hesitated for a moment, cocked his head to one side, and, with a slight grin, added reassuringly, "Of course, we won't toss the poor fellows out onto the street. We'll phase them out through attrition, let them retire."

(From a mimeographed text)

XIII. UNION-DIRECTED RESEARCH

One condition of the Norwegian unions' success was the existence of a strong research arm. Unions know specifically what their needs are, what research is useful to them. A large measure of success in research depends on formulating the right questions. Social scientists looking at research productivity have noted that the best research results are obtained when users are involved from the very start. This applies as well to labour research.

In the following excerpt, David Noble describes how the Norwegian Union of Iron and Metal Workers set up their own research, making sure it answered their needs.

At the national congress of the Iron and Metal Workers' Union (Norwegian Union of Iron and Metal Workers) in the spring of 1970 these problems were discussed and a resolution passed which stated that the **trade unions had to start up research of the own** (author's emphasis), like the employers had been doing for a long time.

The newly elected board reacted immediately and applied to the Royal Norwegian Council for Scientific and Industrial Research for money to finance a project to study planning, control and data processing systems, evaluated from the point of view of the workers. This application came as quite a shock, and many people associated with the Research Council regarded it as a political demonstration. Money was, however, appropriated and the Iron And Metal Project was started in January 1971 and was completed in August 1973. The Iron and Metal Workers' Union asked the Norwegian Computing Centre (NCC) to provide research staff, and the institute was willing to assist.

The Norwegian Computing Centre is a governmental research institute, supervised by the Research Council, working within data processing, operational research, applied mathematics and statistics. The Institute takes on jobs for customers and also does basic research. The Iron and Metal Project was the institute's first project for a trade union, and also the first Norwegian project with a trade union as the only customer....

When the project started in the beginning of 1971, the following project organization was established: a steering committee, a working group, and four associated local union clubs at four companies. (In Norway all blue-collar workers in a company are organized in one, single company club.)

The steering committee consisted of the national chairman of the Iron and Metal Workers' Union, two from his staff, a representative from the TUC secretariat (the present chairman), three representatives from other research institutions and three from the NCC, including the two researchers. Later on, a representative from the four local clubs joined the committee.

The working group consisted of the two researchers and the two staff members from the national union, among them Jan Balstad (now national vice-chairman), who played an important part in all stages of the project.

The four local clubs were at these four companies: Kongsberg Vapenfabrikk (government-owned, situated at Kongsberg, 2,000 employees, the technologically most advanced company in the job shop industry, also producing computers and control systems); Norsk Elektrisk & Brown Boveri, Div. Skoyen (NEBB: Norwegian branch of the Swiss Brown Boveri, producing electric generators, etc., 1,200 employees from the important clubs in Oslo); Jonas Oglaend, Sykkelfabrikken (bicycle factory in Andnes on the west coast, assembly lines and part production, 500 employees); and Hydraulik, Brattvag (dominant company in a small community on the northwest coast, produces high quality hydraulic equipment for ships and offshore activities, 350 employees).

The plan was that actual work should be done by the research workers in very close contact with the two other members of the working group. The steering committee was not expected to do very much more than such committees usually do. The clubs were included to act as reference environments, providing case studies, contacts on the shop floor, comments and criticism. It turned out that the organization worked well, but rather differently from what was originally intended.

The initial research plan was developed during the first three months of the project. The main components of the plan were (1) a study of a few, typical computer-based planning and control systems being used in one or more of the four companies; (2) discussions with the clubs to clarify and tentatively formulate trade union objectives in relation to such systems; (3) a more comprehensive opinion survey, based on these discussions, among a larger, representative sample of the union members; (4) an evaluation of the selected planning and control systems from the points of view expressed in the opinion survey; and (5) a discussion of the **possibilities of changing existing systems and designing new systems to conform better to the objectives of the trade union members** (author's emphasis).

After six months of work, however, the research workers began to question this plan.... The most important research problem for the union was to study the design of a process which would "build up knowledge and activity at all levels of the union's organization," with the main emphasis at the club level. The initial research plan would not help in this respect, since the main result would be that a few experts had gained some insight.

The research workers presented these considerations to the steering committee and asked for permission to reevaluate and possibly redesign the research plan for the project. This request initiated a serious and penetrating discussion in the steering committee, and from then on the committee took an active part in the project. It became the forum in which strategy problems were debated and all-important decisions made. As a result, the union at all levels participated more directly and the insight gained was more rapidly assimilated in the organization.

The new research strategy was developed during the autumn of 1971.... The project became much more oriented towards the participating clubs and their building up of understanding as a platform for action. During the spring of 1972 the four clubs gradually became more and more important partners in the project.

The research workers had to be made acquainted with the working conditions, the production and administration in the companies of the four clubs. The clubs had to start the building up of knowledge about planning, control and data processing. An important outcome of this effort was the production of the first version of a textbook. So far, only the key members of the clubs had been active in the project. During the next phase a larger group had to be involved, and written educational material was needed.

For three main reasons it was necessary to produce a new textbook, different from existing ones. Firstly, the language used had to be understandable for the union members. Secondly, the fact that planning, control and data processing systems are designed to further the objectives of those who are in power, and thus are not neutral and objective, had to be emphasized as a basis for understanding. Thirdly, **the starting point should be the members' own conception of their work and interests, not the system analyst's understanding of reality** (author's emphasis).

The textbook has since then been further developed as a result of experience. Today it is used, fully or in part, in the numerous courses given by national unions and by the TUC. It is also used in the other Scandinavian countries (and even in university courses). The current 3rd edition of the textbook also contains examples and experiences from the Iron and Metal Project itself and later Norwegian trade union activities.

The next major step in the project was the establishment of working groups consisting of members and shop stewards in the four clubs.... The club at Kongsberg Vapenfabrikk in their report made an analysis of two of the production planning and control systems at their company: the IBM planning system CLASS, and the KUPOL system then being developed within the company. KUPOL is an information system based upon a central data bank and two-way terminals (typewriters) located on the shop floor. It collects state information and distributes control information about the production.

Useful new insights into the effects of the CLASS system were obtained. The analysis of the KUPOL system resulted in a number of proposals for changes in that system. The proposals were later on negotiated with the management. In these negotiations the club succeeded in many cases, lost in others.

At NEBB the club made a survey of the state of the methods being used in their production planning and control. Then it discussed the interests of its members in relation to the systems being used, and, in particular, in relation to the new kinds of systems which management probably would want to introduce, in the near future....

At Johas Ogland the club report contained three separate discussions: an evaluation of its experience from its participation in the planning of a new plant; a proposal for the reorganization of one of the main assembly lines to provide less monotonous work; and a survey of some important planning and control systems in the company....

Since the Iron and Metal Project was concluded in 1973, the activity has been spreading within the union and to other national unions. For the time being, research projects of a similar nature are carried out by the Norwegian Union of Employees in Commerce and Offices and the Norwegian Union of Chemical Industry Workers. The research projects only represent a small fraction of these activities. A much larger and increasing number of unions and many of their local clubs are engaged in work related to planning, control and data processing systems. In relation to the total number of unions and clubs, the situation is not yet at all satisfactory, considering the importance of these systems to the trade union members. (From a mimeographed paper)

Perhaps the most important aspect of this action was the discussion about the clubs' responsibility within the companies as representing the interests of the local community, for unless the work force clearly appears to have interests other than its own, their chances of success are severely reduced. The public often rightly perceives the interests of organized labour as narrow and egotistical. Looking back, we can conclude that organized labour's support of jobs in the nuclear power industry was shortsighted for themselves as well as their children and the community at large.

If the work force ever wants to present alternative social and technical designs, it has to think about more than its own interests; it must consider the welfare of the community. Polish Solidarity, for instance, is known to have blocked the construction of a new factory in Sceztzin because the site was on unstable ground, even though it would have given workers more jobs. Unfortunately, examples of such vision are rare.

XIV. TECHNOLOGICAL RESEARCH AND DESIGN: FACTORY UNIVERSITIES

During the Chinese Cultural Revolution in the late 1960s, an interesting idea was tried out in the Shanghai Machine Shop. (Although the pressures and violence that marked this Revolution were deplorable, some positive, innovative initiatives did emerge in this tumultuous period.) In the Shanghai Machine Shop, research in new technologies was carried out in "factory universities" by workers elected from the ranks. Those who were elected were not destined to become professional technicians; rather, they were expected to return to their work in the shop. The following account is translated from the French.

THE MACHINE TOOL FACTORY IN SHANGHAI

Translated by Chris De Bresson from Benjamin Coriat, **Science, Technique et Capital**, 1st ed., pp. 209-235 (Paris: Seuil, 1976). (Deleted from the second edition.)

Here the fight on the technical front has started early, since successes today do not come out of the sky. They were prepared for by initiatives that were imposed at the time of the liberation in 1939. To limit ourselves to the main point, it is necessary to distinguish two main periods.

Between 1953 and 1965, 250 factory workers, from a group 600, were formed as technicians; that is, about 40 percent. Several methods were used. First, an amateur school was set up after working hours so workers could come and train themselves in difficult manipulations and assemblies. With the help of factory technicians and cadres, they improved their knowledge in various disciplines. It seems this method gave good results, because an amateur school like this still exists today.

A second method was to send experimental workers (design officers) into the technical offices of the factory. They were taken in charge by firm technicians, who put them on study programs and research into technical innovation. This training was complemented by other studies, supervised again by the technicians. Thus the workers progressed, rapidly becoming technicians.

The third and more classical method consisted of organized training periods complemented by classes in different technical schools located in the same district.

This was the state of things in 1966, when the Cultural Revolution started. Major changes occurred in many domains, including the factory. As for the training of technicians, one can safely say that the principal change was the establishment of an institution for higher education of a new type: a factory university. Following the July 21, 1968, directive, it took a major place in the educational revolution. Three main elements characterized this institution: (1) recruitment; (2) the nature and methods of schooling; and (3) the composition of the teaching staff.

Recruitment

From now on, students at the 21st of July University (managed by the factory and dependent on it) will be chosen from workers of the same type factories. Three generations of students have already been recruited and formed. In the first group of 52 workers, the mean age was 29 and seniority was twelve years. The second group was comprised of 98 workers, 58 of whom were from the factory itself and 48 from other factories. The mean age was 27 years and the mean seniority eight years. The third generation comprised 109 workers, 60 of whom were from other Shanghai factories. Here the mean age was 26 years and the seniority seven.

Not all problems were resolved. For instance, certain factory shops were unwilling to release key men for studies....Nonetheless, considerable progress was made, because the system of one-by-one has been done away with....The previous conception... meant that the engineer's role was to use his talent while the worker used his hands. Now the engineer was supposed to give ideas and the worker make them realities. In other words, the factory university has blown away the old conception that those who supply mental effort are rulers of the people, and those who use their hands are those to be governed. In order that the earlier state of affairs not reproduce itself, a number of guarantees were taken. The most important of these hinged on the conception of schooling itself.

A new type of training

At least two elements differentiate this system from the old. They concern the choice of subjects taught and the means of linking theory with practice. To understand the scope, I believe that we must remind ourselves that training here is done for the workers' sake; it is not aimed solely at making them competent technicians. Training also should allow for the existence of a new type of power, a worker's power in the domain of management and technical research. In other words, the aim is not to replace some experts with other experts, but to break the monopoly of a handful of experts in technical know-how in all domains....

The new subjects of study are not different from those of the university. The classical manuals of mechanics, dynamics, electricity and so forth exist and are at the workers' disposal, of course. But they do not start their schooling with them. Instead, mixed groups of workers and technicians are asked by veteran and qualified workers to identify production problems. The important point here is that theoretical, conceptual problems are not separated from the practical problems of making things....

We might think this is just some tinkering or "productivist" idea of building knowledge. However, the participation and initiative of simple workers at least guarantees that courses will be transformed. The idea also offers an opportunity for workers to exert a certain control over technicians.

Means of linking theory and practice

....The first period of basic training is an elementary survey of primary materials for training. The accent is put on theoretical training and basic, professional techniques. This lasts for eight to nine months. The second period is called learning by doing. The students go back to their shops, where they are integrated into existing units called Triple Union Groups for Technological Innovation. These contribute directly to the advancement of research and development programs, up to and including manufacturing techniques. During this period the teachers continue their instruction, but on the shop floor rather than in a classroom, and in relation to production difficulties that arise. The third period is dedicated to a new advance in formal knowledge. New theoretical studies are made, and difficult problems that have not yet been met are resolved. The fourth period, finally, is dedicated again to practice; but this time the working technicians are able to analyze problems independently. They contribute to the conception and making of many complex machines.

The Training Staff

After considerable evolution, the staff is composed of 22 permanent members. They come from three different origins: eight are workers and technicians from the factory itself; two accomplished workers and six working technicians were formed on the shop floor; four come from technical schools in Shanghai; and the last ten are teachers from state universities....

We can now understand better the difference between the old methods used at the University of Peking, where the old system presented three elements: the teacher, the course and the book. This led to a closed system. The know-how found in the pages of books was not understandable. Learning implied going from idea to idea and from book to book without really ever knowing how things worked out, how peasants cultivated, and how merchandise was circulated. In other words, this schooling led to a separation from productive work. It was given by elitists to continue the elite class. People who came out of these universities were promoted to positions of responsibility....

Some modifications in the organization of industrial work is exemplified by the Triple Union Groups for Technological Innovation.

Setting up groups for a choice of technological innovation is one of the key responses the Chinese made (at that time) to technological change. Instead of relying on a handful of expert technicians, engineers and professional researchers for technical innovation, the Chinese tried to give workers control over choice. Each factory set up one or several groups where workers, technicians and cadres collaborate. Some factories have many groups....

There is a constant fight to prevent workers from being used as simple doers. A well-known case is that of some Shanghai dock workers who reproached management for not having accepted their suggestions for innovation, aimed at lightening their work. These ideas were refused because they were estimated to be too costly. Nevertheless, despite such limitations, the triple union is better than no worker participation....

A modification of the social relationships of work inside the factory is extended to the training of technicians. The two contribute to the appropriation of technical know-how by workers and their exercise of effective power.

The interesting aspect of the previous example is not so much that workers' initiative in technical change was encouraged – many managers know how to do this occasionally – but that the control by experts and the traditional division between manual and intellectual labour was challenged.

Cases where workers develop alternative technologies which are implented are also rare. We should not underestimate, however, those alternative technical systems which do materialize. A notable case is that of **Compost, Fertilizer and Biogas Production from Human and Farm Wastes in the People's Republic of China**, described by Michael G. McGarry and Jill Stainforth in an IDRC publication in 1978 (IDRC – TS8e). This company grew out of a system developed by workers on a commune; it was an integrated, biological management of human and farm wastes. This system has since spread to other regions because it reduces dependence on more complex systems and is less costly.

XV. LABOUR'S ALTERNATIVE CORPORATE PLANS

Redirection of technical design is not limited to China and the Scandinavian countries. Lucas Aerospace workers in England are also a case in point. Much of their plant production has been for the defence industry. The unions wanted job security but opposed defence production. (A strong antinuclear movement in England has influenced the labour movement.) When an aircraft contract fell through, the Lucas Aesospace workers proposed to reorient their company to nonmilitary activities and preserve their jobs in a productive occupation that was more socially meaningful to them. As many craft unions coexist in Lucas Aerospace, the shop steward's committees play a role similar to those in industrial unions. Organized into a combine, or association, at the corporate level, the stewards promoted their own plan. Here are some extracts from their proposal.

Development of the Combine Committee, now known as the Lucas Aerospace and Defence Systems Combine Shop Stewards Committee, took approximtely four years. In its early stages it lacked cohesion and strength. The Company was, as a result of this, able to embark on a rationalization programme in which the work force was reduced from 18,000 to the present 13,000. However, at the last attempted sacking of 800 workers in January-February 1974, the Combine Committee was well enough organized to resist this....

Gradually the Combine Committee set up a series of advisory services for its members....One included a Science and Technology Advisory Service which provided technical information on the safeguards to be campaigned for when new equipment was being introduced or when health hazards were possibly involved....

Corporate Plan

The object of the Corporate Plan is twofold. Firstly to protect our members' right to work, by proposing a range of alternative products on which they could become engaged in the event of further cutbacks in the aerospace industry. Secondly to ensure that among the alternative products proposed are a number which would be socially useful to the community at large.

The idea of proposing alternative products on which the work force could be engaged as an alternative to the redundancy arising from cutbacks in the aerospace industry is not new in Lucas Aerospace; as far back as 1970, when the Company was attempting to close the Willesden site, a number of projects were put forward at the negotiations which took place on that occasion. However, the idea of preparing an overall Corporate Plan for Lucas Aerospace arose in the first instance at a meeting in November 1974 with Tony Benn, the then Minister of Industry. That meeting took place at the request of the Combine Committee to discuss the nationalisation of Lucas Aerospace. In the course of the meeting Mr. Benn suggested that there was the distinct possibility of further cutbacks in certain aerospace and military projects.

Even if this did not occur the rate at which new projects woud be started was likely to be reduced. Accordingly he felt that the Combine Committee would be well advised to consider alternative products, not excluding intermediate technology on which our members could become engaged in the event of a recession.

The problems of the aerospace industry have of course been further compounded by the energy crisis. It is also likely that in order to make its austerity measures somewhat acceptable, the government will at least make a gesture towards cuts in defence expenditure....

Indeed it is the national policy of almost all of the unions the Combine Committee represents that there should be cuts in defence expenditure. However, when these cuts are made our members are placed in the position of being made redundant or fighting for their continuation. We ourselves have done this in the past and will support our colleagues in the rest of the aerospace industry in doing so in future. Indeed, recently when the campaign to protect the H.S.146 was at its height our members at the Wolverhampton plant seized drawings in support of their colleagues at Hawker Siddeley's.

It has to be recognized, however, that the traditional method of fighting for the right to work has not been particularly successful. It is not suggested in this report that Lucas Aerospace is suddenly going to cease to be deeply involved in the aerospace industry. We recognize, whether we like it or not, that the aerospace industry is going to remain a major part of the economic and technological activity of the so-called "technologically advanced nations." The intention is rather to suggest that alternative products should be introduced in a phased manner such that the tendency of the industry to contract would firstly be halted and then gradually reversed as Lucas Aerospace diversfied into these new fields.

It is also evident to us that when the three sectors of the aerospace industry are nationalized the relationship between them and Lucas Aerospace may well change....

The desire to work on socially useful products is one which is now widespread through large sectors of industry. The aerospace industry is a particularly glaring example of the gap which exists between that which technology could provide and that which it actually does provide to meet the wide range of human problems we see about us. There is something seriously wrong about a society which can produce a level of technology to design and build Concorde but cannot provide enough simple urban heating systems to protect the old-age pensioners who are dying each winter of hypothermia. (It is estimated that 980 died of hypothermia in London alone last winter, which was a particularly warm one.)

Further it is clear that there is now deep-rooted cynicism amongst wide sections of the public about the idea, carefully nurtured by the media, that advanced science and technology will solve all our material problems....

It is our view that these problems arise, not because of the behaviour of scientists and technologists in isolation, but because of the manner in which society misuses this skill and ability. We believe, however, that scientists, engineers and the workers in those industries have a profound responsibility to challenge the underlying assumptions of large-scale industry; they must seek to assert their right to use their skill and ability in the interest of the community at large. In saying that, we recognize that this is a fundamental challenge to many of the economic and ideological assumptions of our society....

Our intentions are... modest, namely... to make a small contribution to demonstrating that workers are prepared to press for the right to work on products which actually help to solve human problems rather than create them....

Perhaps the most significant feature of the Corporate Plan is that trade unionists are attempting to transcend the narrow economism which has characterized trade union activity in the past and extend our demands to the extent of questioning the products on which we work and the way in which we work upon them. This questioning of basic assumptions about what should be produced and how it should be produced is one that is likely to grow in momentum.

Worker participation or worker directors

This Combine Committee is opposed to such concepts and is not prepared to share in the management of means of production and the production of products which they find abhorrent. Indeed at times of Company crisis the real role of the so-called directors becomes self-evident. Thus in spite of one-third of the seats on the Volkswagen board being filled by union representatives and those voting with socialist politicians on the board, which in practice is said to give a 50-50 say in the running of the plant, this in no way helped the workers during the massive redundancies which took place in Volkswagen recently.

There cannot be industrial democracy until there is a real shift in power to the workers themselves. Trade Unionists at the point of production, through their contact with the real world of manufacturing and making things, are conscious of the great economic power which workers have. This growing sense of confidence by working people to cope with the technological and social problems we see about us is in glaring contrast to the confusion and disarray of management, particularly in the highest echelons of industry....

We believe this Corporate Plan will provide an opportunity for Lucas Aerospace to demonstrate whether it is really prepared to take its social responsibility seriously or not.

Job redesign

The past seventy years have seen systematic efforts to de-skill jobs, to fragment them into small narrow functions and to have them carried out at an increased tempo. This process, which oddly is known as Scientific Management, attempts to reduce the worker to a blind unthinking appendage to the machine or process in which he or she is working.

In Scientific Management, as its founder, Frederick Winslow Taylor, tells us, the workman is told minutely just what he is to do and how he is to do it, and any improvement he makes upon the orders given to him is fatal to success. Taylor was not unaware of the implications of what he was doing, and once said that the requirement of a man for a manual job is that he shall be so stupid and so phlegmatic that he more nearly resembles in his mental make up the ox than any other type.

The tendency to destroy skill and job interest is now evident in all fields of manufacturing, including Lucas Aerospace; but human beings are not oxen and are rebelling against such a system in many ways. In Volvo in Sweden, the labour turnover in 1969 was 52 percent and the absentee rate reached 30 percent in some plants. In the United States the reaction has been even more dramatic; in General Motors Lordstown's plant the computer-controlled production line and the products on it have been directly sabotaged by workers who felt completely oppressed by their working environment....

In fact workers have always known that it is far better if people work in teams and know what each other is doing. They know that if they are engaged in work which is challenging to them, this results in better products or higher quality. However modern industry continues to move in the opposite direction: a gradual replacement of human beings by machines, a change in the organic composition of capital in which industry is made capital-intensive rather than labour-intensive. Not only does this give rise to serious problems of structural unemployment but it also causes serious problems as far as quality of products is concerned, and more importantly, quality of life.

It is clearly evident from some of the Lucas Aerospace plants that attempts to replace human intelligence by machine intelligence (e.g. overemphasizing the importance of numerically controlled machine tools as against human skill) have had quite disastrous results. It is intended to campaign for quite radical job re-design which will protect our members from this.

The idea of a Corporate Plan of this kind is an entirely new initiative by industrial workers. It is, to our knowledge, the first time that such a plan has been proposed in the United Kingdom. There have, of course, been some developments of this kind abroad, notably in Italy, where at Fiat the work force put forward a series of social demands in addition to the straightforward economic ones (such as wages). Whilst the Combine Committee is unanimous in its desire to have the Corporate Plan produced, there is by no means universal agreement on the tactics for its introduction. This is because of the industrial dangers which arise in a project of this kind. There is obviously the danger that the discussions with the Management about the implementation of the plan (if it were agreed that such discussion should take place) could gradually degenerate into a form of collaboration. There is also the danger that, even if collaboration were carefully avoided, the Company might simply take parts of the Corporate Plan and have all this technology free. The plan has taken a very considerable length of time to prepare, and involved many evenings and weekends of work. It has also meant that outside experts have been prepared to give generously of their detailed knowledge in order to help the development of the Corporte Plan.

In these circumstances the greatest care will have to be taken to ensure that the Company does not succeed in drawing off the money spinners from the plan, and perhaps even having these produced abroad, whilst declining those products which would be socially useful. It is even conceivable that whilst the Company would take sections of the plan, our members may still be confronted with the perennial problem of redundancy. Because of these dangers it is suggested that the correct tactic would be to present only part of the plan to the Company, and then to test out in practice the manner in which the Company will attempt to deal with it.

Approximately 150 products were proposed for the Lucas Corporate Plan. Twelve of these were selected for presentation at this stage and are suitable for use. Each of these major areas is supported by a file of some 250 pages of detailed technical and economic supporting information.

While the Corporate Plan was being prepared, unemployment problems arose at the Hemel Hempstead and Marston Green plants. Separate minicorporate reports were prepared for these plants, and they are being handled by the local shop stewards' committees. Such participation of workers has, or course, a double edge. It can either contribute to productivity in such a way as to foster incessant change, and management may well benefit from this as well, or, if structural changes do result at the end of this effort, they will benefit a general movement for working people's control over technological designs.

Paid educational leaves and retraining may be positive for labour, but they can also serve management's ends of endless rationalization and constant change, for the purpose of wresting control away from the work force.

Employee Development

During the past five years the Lucas Aerospace work force has been reduced approximately 25 percent. This has come about either by direct sackings or by a deliberate policy of so-called natural wastage, i.e., by not replacing those who leave, or encouraging early retirement. The net result has been that highly skilled teams of manual workers and design staff have been seriously diminished and disrupted; we cannot accept that such a development is in the long-term national interest.

Coupled with this development has been one inside the Company, in which the attempt to replace human intelligence by machine intelligence, in particular, the introduction of numerically controlled machine tools. It has, in a number of cases, proved to have been quite disastrous, and the quality of the products has suffered in consequence. In many instances the Company has fallen victim to the high-pressure salesmanship of those who would have us believe that all problems can be solved by high-capital equipment. We have allowed our regard for human talents to be bludgeoned into silence by the mystique of advanced equipment and technology, and so forget that our most precious asset is the creative and productive power of our people.

When we reviewed the work force we now have, our concern centred on four points. Firstly very little is being done to extend and develop the very considerable skills and ability still to be found within the work force. Secondly the age group in some of the factories is very high, typically around 46-50 years average. Thirdly there is little indication that the Company is embarking on any real programme of apprenticeships and the intake of young people (it is in fact sacking apprentices as they finish their time). Fourthly the Company is making no attempt to employ women in technical jobs, and apart from recruitment of these from outside, there are many women doing routine jobs well below their existing capabilities. Quite apart from the desirability of countering these discriminatory practices, the employment of women in the male-dominated areas would have an important humanizing affect on science and technology. In that section of the report dealing with specific recommendations we propose a number of steps which should be taken in this direction.... Firstly retraining and re-education would mean that we were developing the capabilities of our people to meet the technological and sociological challenges which will come during the next few years. Secondly, in the event of work shortage occurring before alternative products have been introduced, the potential redundancy could be transformed into a positive breathing space during which re-education could act as a form of enlightened work sharing....

It is our view that the entire workforce, including semi-skilled and skilled workers, are capable of retraining for jobs which would greatly extend the range of work they could undertake. This would provide opportunities which they may have been denied, for a number of reasons, at an earlier stage in their lives. Such courses could best be organized in local technical colleges and polytechnics.

It is our view that universities are too rigid in both their entrance requirements and teaching methods. The courses would have to take into account that many of those involved would not have had traditional forms of education and paper qualifications, but could bring to the course a wealth of experience through actual work in industry.

It would further mean that those teaching these courses would have to develop new teaching methods and have a real respect for people who have had industrial experience. Such an arrangement would not be without its advantages for the polytechnic and technical colleges involved, as such trainees could bring to these institutions a much more mature and balanced view about productive processes in general, but also about wider political, social and economic matters.... (From a mimeographed document)

The Lucas Corporate Plan then proposes many alternative technologies in fields as diverse as vehicles for seabed mining, aquatic agriculture, medical equipment, alternative energy, and braking devices. In the following section we reproduce only the excerpts pertaining to braking devices, for which the skills of Lucas Aerospace are so well known.

BRAKING SYSTEMS

The increased speed of both road and rail vehicles and the larger payloads which they will carry, both of passengers and goods, will give rise to stringent braking regulations during the coming years. This tendency will be further increased by Britain's membership in the EEC. The EEC is now introducing a range of new braking regulations. These specify not only stopping distances but call for minimum standards of braking endurance over a continuous period. In addition the regulations lay down conditions for braking balance between axles in order to prevent a dangerous sequence of wheel locking.

Many individual EEC countries have, in addition, their own national braking requirements. In France, for example, since the mid-1950s, auxiliary braking systems have been compulsory for coaches operating in mountainous terrain. A fundamental weakness of normal mechanical brakes is that when subjected to long braking periods they overheat, and the braking linings, at elevated temperatures, tend to temporarily lose their gripping qualities. This problem can be greatly reduced, if not totally overcome, by using a retarder. A retarder is basically an electro-magnetic dynamometer which is fitted usually to the prop shaft between the engine and the back axle. To reduce speed, its coils are excited by an electrical supply direct from the vehicle battery, thereby inducing a braking force as the disc rotates in the magnetic field.

At the Willesden plant some 25 years of design experience exists in this field of dynamometry. Attempts by the design staff some 10 years ago to get the Company to develop and simplify these eddycurrent dynamometers for mass production as retarders failed. It is felt, however, that the time is now opportune to reconsider this whole project.

In Britain public attention has been dramatically focused on the weaknesses of existing braking systems by the Yorkshire Coach disaster, which claimed 32 lives in May of this year. The Sunday Times of June 1 stated: "Last week's crash might have been avoided if the coach had been equipped with an extra braking device, such as an electro-magnetic retarder, which is being fitted to an increasing number of coaches in this country." In fact it would appear that only 10 of Britain's 75,000 buses and coaches actually have retarders fitted to them. There is, therefore, clearly a vast market available to Lucas if it adopts an imaginative approach to this problem. It is not suggested that Lucas should simply produce dynamometers; rather what is proposed is that they should analyze the whole nature of braking systems through a wide range of vehicles, including buses, coaches, articulated lorries, underground and overhead rails as used by British Rail.

It is proposed that a braking system analysis and development team should be set up to take an overview of this problem. The team should make an analysis of the actual requirements for the different applications, and at the same time should analyze any patent problems which might arise with respect to the French Labinal retarder, which is marketed in this country as "Telma." Simultaneously a development team should develop an existing Lucas Aerospace dynamometer, using a unit capable of being fitted in the conventional position, i.e., in the prop shaft between the engine and the back axle, capable of absorbing 600 brake horsepower, and the weight of approximately 200 kilograms. Once this unit has been designed and developed, discussions should take place with Girlings to arrange for its mass production under a licensing arrangement from Lucas Aerospace. Although a vast potential market exists for dynamometers of this kind, this unit should be seen only as the first step in evolving a total braking system capability.

The second stage would be a combined electro-magnetic braking system coupled directly to a traditional mechanical brake based on a Girling disc. The control system would have to be designed such that by moving the brake pedal the dynamometer would initially operate and the further depression of the pedal would gradually increase the current and hence the braking load, until finally the mechanical brake could be applied if necessary. Use of the dynamometer between the prop shaft and the back axle clearly limits its range of application. To overcome this, discussion should take place with manufacturers of gear boxes to arrange to have them fitted on the output side of the gear box, such that they could be used on the tractors of articulated vehicles.

A further development would be to design and produce units which could be fitted to each individual axle. Work in this field is already being carried out in France, but based on traditional dynamometer units. An elaborate control system would be necessary to ensure that as each of the individual axles is braked it still meets the new EEC (European Economic Community) requirements concerning the sequence and the effects on individual axles and their proper synchronisation to remove the risk of unstable skidding or jackknifing. This work would dovetail conveniently with existing work being undertaken by Girlings on anti-skid systems. It is important that this programme should not be carried out in the usual piecemeal short-term manner. A longterm overall plan should be worked out and each stage of the development programme should be a tactical step towards a long-term strategy.

Part of that long-term strategy should be the provision of radar-applied braking systems. All the necessary components should be designed to produce a flexible range of systems options. Dynamometers lend themselves ideally to this as the load is applied electrically. The 1975 Society of Automotive Engineers Congress held in Detroit reported that the National Highway Safety Association's 1971 statistics showed that 8 of the vehicles on the road were involved in rear-end accidents. They represented 25 percent of the accidents, out of 8 million vehicles. The medium- to long-term aim should be to provide radar-applied braking systems, particularly for use on motorways.

The **Financial Times** of May 7, 1975, stated that the longer-run electronic station keeping devices, which use a form of radar to apply brakes automatically to cars travelling along motorways when they approach too close to a slowly moving vehicle ahead, may be adopted. If they were introduced, compulsory for traffic, they would certainly lead to a substantial reduction in the number of lives lost through motorway accidents in fog.

R. A. Chandler and L. E. Woods, of the U.S. Department of Commerce Institute for Telecommunication Sciences, have said at the conference quoted above: "While significant problems exist in the development of generally acceptable radar sensors for automobile braking, no insurmountable difficulties are evident." Applications more complex than mere station keeping should also be considered, but these give rise to a series of technological problems which, although they could be overcome, may only be solvable with very expensive equipment. However, both Chandler and Woods had the following to say: "Both pedestrians and cyclists are detectable, radiation hazards are minimal, small radius corners give a problem in false alarms, inter-system blinding is a problem, and the effects of rain scattering are serious." Spokesmen for the National Highway Traffic Safety Association have stated that research in radar braking fields warrants continuation, but the decision to implement such devices should be made only after cost benefit studies and acceptable hardware performance has been verified. It is clear that now is the stage for Lucas to become involved in these developments.

It is proposed that a similar long-term overview should be taken of braking requirements for rolling stock railways and underground. Already British Rail has introduced, on an experimental basis, velocity monitoring systems, which indicate to the driver if he is travelling at a velocity considered to be dangerous for an oncoming curve, junction or other impediment. With these velocity sensing devices already installed, it would be a logical step to use this information to feed into braking systems such that the train was automatically slowed down to meet the travelling requirements already determined for other sections of the track if the driver fails to respond due to illness or whatever. Such overall braking systems would require many computers and microprocessors. The use of these would fit in with suggestions made elsewhere in the Corporate Plan.

TRANSPORT SYSTEMS
Road vehicles

There will be an increasing requirement for battery powered vehicles during the next 20 years. However, the numbers involved are not likely to be substantial until alternative forms of battery power storage and battery production have been developed, and until means of charging these, other than using conventionally produced electricity have been developed.

In the meantime there is likely to be growing interest in hybrid systems which make the best use of battery storage and coupled that with the optimum performance of internal combustion engines. It is therefore proposed that a hybrid system be evolved utilizing the internal combustion engine running at a permanent and optimum power setting and connected to a generator. The generator would charge the batteries, which in turn supply the power to the electric motor driving the vehicle. Viewed in the wider company context, it may be desirable to use the diesel engine with its inherent advantages of better fuel consumption characteristics. Initial calculations suggest a 50-litre fuel saving in such a hybrid.

The Ground Support Equipment Group of the Aerospace division already has considerable experience in the packaging of coupled prime movers and generators. In addition it has developed considerable expertise in the silencing of units of this kind without greatly impairing the efficiency of the engine. This would mean not only could atmospheric pollution be greatly reduced, in that the toxic emissions would be reduced by some 70 to 80 percent by the permanent power setting, but the noise pollution could be greatly reduced as an added advantage.

The Lucas battery powered vehicles could be used as a test bed for this generator package. It is therefore proposed that designers from the Ground Support Equipment Group ally themselves with their colleagues in the Lucas Electrical Company and CAV so that a specification can be drawn up for the hybrid package. A prototype should then be built by the Ground Support Equipment Group and tests carried out on the vehicles already in existence....

Railway Systems

The structure of railway coaches is based on a design philosophy which is about 100 years out of date. Strength and weight of railway coach structures depends essentially on the characteristics of a rigid wheel on the track and its power transmissions through that. R. Fletcher, of the North East London Polytechnic, pointed out that for a number of years these problems could be overcome if pneumatic wheels were used. The entire suspension system of the vehicle could then be much lighter, as could the overall payload bearing structure. This work is currently supported by a Science Research Council grant. If Lucas were to accept the proposal for braking systems made elsewhere in the Corporate Plan they could extend that idea by providing a complete wheel and axle unit which would embody a pneumatic wheel, a retarder and disc brake. Aerospace would provide the automatic braking system and the micro-processors to operate the unit.

With the overcrowding on roads such a lightweight train could be used to great advantage on suburban lines and might even be used on some of the lines now closed by the Beeching Plan. It is therefore proposed that contact should be made with R. Fletcher to establish in which way the braking systems could be incorporated into an overall design philosophy for these lightweight railway vehicles.

Approximately 10 years ago Lucas Aerospace spent vast sums of money on developing a railway actuator. Basically the idea was that a vehicle could be taken directly from a railway and run on wheels suitable for conventional road surfaces, these wheels to be actuated into position by a system provided by the Rotax Division. It is suggested that the system should now be re-examined in light of current transport requirements. It should be particularly re-examined in light of the proposals above for a lightweight vehicle.

The (Scottish) Highland and Islands Development Board has already shown considerable interest in such a hybrid road-rail system. A section of track has been located where the tests can be carried out. The hybrid prime mover and the braking system proposed above should be incorporated into the final model.... (From a mimeographed document)

The model of Lucas Aerospace workers was later followed by the Vickers National Combine Committee of Shop Stewards, who produced two similar mimeographed documents: **Building a Chieftain Tank and the Alternative** and **Alternative Employment for Naval Shipbuilding Workers – A Case Study of the Resources Devoted to the Production of the ASW Cruiser.**

What has happened since the events described in these texts? The story is told in a fascinating book written by Hilary Wainwright and David Elliot, called **The Lucas Plans: A New Trade Unionism in the Making?** London and New York: Allison & Busby, 1982. The influence of the Corporate Plan was not limited to the United Kingdom. A meeting held June 22-24, 1984, in Boston drew 700 North American and European labour and peace activists, who considered projects similar to the above plans. (See **Labor Notes,** July 26, 1984, p. 12.)

XVI. MORATORIUM, VETO RIGHTS AND STOPPING TECHNICAL CHANGES

Alternatives are of little use if they cannot be implemented. Very often management either takes from a worker's creativity whatever it finds useful or ignores proposed alternatives entirely. Meanwhile management continues, relentlessly, to promote its own technological designs. Eventually the issue boils down to how the undemocratic imposition of management's chosen techniques can be stopped. Sometimes it does happen.

In the late 1970s, for instance, Manitoba provincial employees obtained a temporary stop pause in the introduction of word processing techniques until a full study could be completed. Around the same time, workers belonging to social movements in the North Thompson and Okanagan valleys of British Columbia obtained a seven-year moratorium on nuclear mining, after intervention by Premier Bill Bennett (whose constituency was being threatened), a moratorium which the new premier, Bill Van Der Zalm, terminated in 1987. One important consideration, however, is what happens during this moratorium, which only buys time. The future of nuclear mining in these areas depends on how the moratorium time is used.

As another example, Danish workers in one municipality have obtained "veto rights" over technological change. This makes sense; those who spend their lives and risk their health using new techniques should have the right to refuse them. If managers want to use a certain technique, alone, it may be all right, as long as using the technique does not affect the community at large. But since most contemporary techniques do affect the whole community sooner or later, workers must be alert to acquire and exercise properly the right to modify the pace of technical change.

XVII. A BILL OF RIGHTS CONCERNING TECHNOLOGICAL CHANGE

In May 1981, the International Association of Machinists in the United States issued a proposal called "A Technology Bill of Rights." Its scope is limited. Although we do not intend to discuss its contents here, we call attention to the document in order to affirm society's growing perception of the need for instating the political rights of citizens, and working people in particular, concerning technical choice. We have already discussed this idea in Chapter 15.

XVIII. A PROPOSED NEW INSTITUTION: SOLIDARITY'S "SOCIAL ENTERPRISES"

This book is dedicated to the Polish Solidarity movement started in 1980, which survived General Jaruselski's Moscow-backed martial law of December 1981. The Solidarity experience influenced this book in a number of ways, some of which are already apparent. Solidarity was not content with being just a labour union; it championed democratic, human and collective rights, as well as national rights for all Poles. It has a social vision for Poland as a whole, not just for its trade union members. Therein lies its social power.

Solidarity has taken positions on ecology, mutual disarmament by the nuclear powers, self-management and indicative planning systems, and government through renewed social contract. The means by which it has promoted its views – neither violence nor passive resistance – are similar to those of Gandhi and Martin Luther King. This tactic is interesting not only because it has worked, at least as well as other, more violent methods (which at best lead to new military dictatorships), but because the nonviolent resistance has promoted an alternate mode of self-government.

But perhaps the most interesting contribution of Polish Solidarity is not yet known to most Western readers: at its second convention, a few days before martial law was imposed, Solidarity proposed a new form of productive organization in a paper called **Draft for an Act about Social Enterprise.** (This is the first time that large extracts of this document are being mass reproduced in the West, and we thank Marek Garztecki, editor of **The Voice of Solidarity** in London, for allowing us to do so. For a complete relation of this discussion and related documents, see **Solidarity Sourcebook,** 1982, Vancouver: New Star, edited by Stan Persky and Henry Flam.)

The problem addressed by the proposal, made by the Network of Solidarity Organizations in the Leading Factories, is central to all past attempts of the labour movement, namely, how workers can participate in self-management without creating a state bureaucracy around which a new group of socially privileged people will coalesce. The Polish people, who have lived with state-owned enterprises since 1946, have learned to distinguish between state ownership and social control. In Canada, our experience of state-owned crown corporations has led to similar problems. But powerful ideas make their way eventually, even when their promoters are consigned to prison camps for a year or more, decimated, and deprived of their civil rights.

By way of presenting some of these powerful ideas, I will summarize the main points of a the 25-page document, **Draft for an Act about Social Enterprise,** written originally in Polish.

Summary of Solidarity Proposal
(November 1981)

I will summarize the main points of this 25-page document.

Social enterprises are independent centres of initiative. Instead of being private, they are socially controlled.

> Article 1. A social enterprise is the basic organizational unit of national economy; it functions independently on the basis of economic calculation, it is endowed with legal status, comprises its organized workforce, administers the part of national property which is entrusted to it and is run by the employees' self-management body.
>
> Article 2, section 1. A social enterprise carries on economic activities aimed at achieving intended economic and social results, making rational use of the means at its disposal.
>
> section 2. The enterprise carries on activities to model among its employees a conscientious attitude towards performing their duties and observing the principles of social coexistence.

These enterprises would be basically self-financed, although they could request loans from banks, like any other enterprises.

> Self-financing
>
> Instead of subsidizing "planned deficits" it is necessary to introduce the principle of self-financing consisting in the enterprise covering all it expenses from its own profits (or possibly bank credits). This means that enterprises functioning better will be able to develop and those functioning badly may even go bankrupt.
>
> Wages of the employees should depend on profits of the enterprise, so the workers could directly benefit from their good work. This would mean however that in unprofitable enterprises, and especially decaying ones, wages would be lower or even become endangered....
>
> In order for profit to become the main stimulus of economic activity of an enterprise it is necessary to stop automatic crediting of any unprofitable, even if planned, activity. The old principle that credit is given only to those who can guarantee solvency, (sic) should be rein-

troduced. This requires changes in the banking system. Central Bank would be responsible for economic and market equilibrium, and would control the emission of money; remaining banks should work as self-financing institutions, interested in giving credit only to those who are profitable and guarantee the return of the loan.

In other words, the social enterprises would be motivated to maximize their profits, sales, market shares and growth. Aside from the Central Bank, only transport and mail services would remain state run. The social enterprises would set their prices (Article 52, section 2), and the Parliament would have to regulate the economy by legal means. The market system is re-established as being a lesser evil than the totalitarian discretion of bureaucracies.

State Supervision

Art. 52, section 1. The state extends its influence over the functioning of the enterprise by means of legal regulations and specific economic parameters (taxes, custom duty, credits) settled in a general manner.

section 2. Setting of prices which are not reserved for decisions of state bodies is within the powers of the enterprise.

Art. 53. State bodies may intervene in the internal affairs of the enterprise only within limits set by parliamentary acts.

Art. 54. The functioning of the enterprise is subject to control of state control bodies.

Art. 55. The enterprise has the right to appeal within 7 days against any decision of state bodies. The appeal suspends the execution of the decision....

Regulations and specific parameters mentioned in section 1 present an opionion as to the advisability of founding the enterprise.

A social enterprise is controlled by the workforce, which approves of its Charter. The State property is entrusted the the enterprise, which is not owned by the workers (as in a cooperative) or by private individuals (as in a corporation with stocks).

Charter of an Enterprise

Art. 9, section 1. The charter of an enterprise is approved by its workforce in a referendum....

Principles of Managing the Enterprise

Art. 10, section 1. The enterprise is managed by its workforce by means of their self-management body.

section 2. The workers self-management consists of all employees of the enterprise.

section 3. Self-management bodies with the exception of the general meeting of the workforce are elected. Members of self-management bodies are responsible before their electors and may be recalled only by them....

section 7. The managing director of the enterprise, as an executor of the resolutions of self-management, effectively manages the enterprise according to the principle of one-man managment.

The equivalent of the stockholders' representative in the Social Enterprise is the Workers' Council, elected by the work force. The council elects an executive and appoints a managing director.

Workers' Council

Art. 16... section 2. Elections to the council are general, equal, direct and secret.

section 3. The council's term of office is 4 years.

section 4. Active electoral rights belong to each employee of the enterprise.

section 5. Passive electoral rights belong to employees working in the enterprise for at least 2 years. This last limitation does not refer to newly organized enterprises....

Art. 19. It is within the powers of the council to:

1. pass resolutions concerning basic trends of economic activity and development of the enterprise,

2. vote on the plan of the enterprise,

3. resolve the organizational structure of the enterprise,

4. pass resolutions concerning the division of profits,

5. appoint or recall the manager,

6. express opinions on the candidates for deputy managers and head accountant,

7. pass resolutions concerning changes in the profile of production or services,

8. pass resolutions concerning the acceptance of annual balance of payments and account of results, as well as grant vote of acceptance to the managing director,

9. pass resolutions concerning economic agreements and cooperational contracts with other enterprises,

10. sign agreements of cooperation with state administrative bodies,

11. establish principles of personnel policy,

12. establish work regulation,

13. control the overall activities of the enterprise,

14. elect the chairman and members of the presidium of the council,

15. pass resolutions concerning the purchase, sale and mortgaging of immovables and other permanent assets,

16. pass resolutions concerning social, material and cultural matters of the enterprise workforce,

17. pass resolutions concerning import and export contracts,

18. approve proposals to confer medals and state distinctions,

19. administer the information media of the enterprise....

The Managing Director

...Art. 42, section 1. The managing director is appointed by the workers' council following a public competition....

If the above **Act About Social Enterprise** had been accepted by the Polish Communist Party and its Parliament, Solidarity would have limited itself to the duties of an independent, democratic union. The social vision of the Solidarity movement, however, has promoted the idea of a social innovation which should be considered seriously.

GLOSSARY

ABUNDANCE

Abundance of a resource, relative to another country, will usually manifest itself in lower prices and attract techniques which make much use of the resource.

ADAPTATION

The modification of an existing technique to suit a specific task and environment.

ADOPTION

Adoption of an existing technology — as is. Not quite synonymous with adaptation.

APPRENTICESHIP

Learning a new technique through practical production experience, sometimes along with formal learning of theory in a class environment.

APPROPRIATE TECHNOLOGY

Appropriate technology to given goals and specific economic and social contexts of a given institution. See also "adaptation".

ASSEMBLY LINE

A system of production organization wherein all phases of the process are simultaneous and in synchrony, each worker performing only a small segment of the work. See also "line production."

ASSIMILATION (of technique)

Personal assimilation of technique through direct productive experience allows to manage the production process without outside assistance.

AUTOMATIC MACHINE

A machine with control and self-feeding mechanisms.

AUTOMATION

The process of replacing people in the work process through self-controlling devices. See control instrument.

AUXILIARY TECHNIQUE

In any technical system, a core technique is helped in its function by auxiliary techniques which allow it to work smoothly. See also support technique.

BANAL LAW

An edict (ban) issued by feudal lords in the middle ages concerning who was allowed to do what in society, thus defining monopoly rights.

BATCH PRODUCTION or PROCESS

The production on order (or slightly in excess of the order) of a set quantity of a given product.

BIO-ENGINEERING or BIO-CHEMICAL ENGINEERING

The artificial reproduction and creation of living organisms by manipulation of the DNA.

BOOLIAN ALGEBRA

An algebra which allows for only two numbers: 0 and 1 — or yes and no.

BOTTLENECKS

In economic analysis, areas where supply does not match demand, or vice-versa.

BUREAUCRACY

A situation in which civil servants define their own prerogatives. Also a system of government in the USSR.

CAMS

A revolving part of machinery to impart an alternating or variable motion.

CAPITAL GOODS

Machinery or other equipment that lasts beyond a production period. Although its duration is varied, it tends to be long-term.

CATALYST

In chemistry, a substance which simply by its presence enables certain syntheses to occur without directly being part of the synthesis.

CHOICE OF TECHNIQUE

The act of choosing one particular technique, in relation to various economic and other considerations, amongst a set of possible ways of solving technical production problems to produce a given good and earning revenues from the activity.

CIRCULATING CAPITAL

The money and goods that move in each production run by opposition to fixed capital.

CLAN

A hierarchical relationship within a large extended family network.

CLUSTER

A higher than normal statistical concentration of any given phenomenon.

COLLECTIVE KNOW-HOW

A sharing of knowledge by all participants when a productive task requires the collaboration of more than one person, each doing a specific task in coordination with the other.

COMPETITION

A situation in which firms compete against each other in the marketplace, as opposed to a situation of monopoly or oligopoly, in which case a few are protected against competition and the entry of new firms is barred.

COMPLEMENT

Some products need one another in order to be used: they are complements.

COMPLEMENTARY TECHNIQUE

Some techniques need others to function.

COMPUTER AIDED DESIGN

The design of products on a screen with the aid of computer programs which check the compatibility of each feature and the consistency of the system.

COMPUTER AIDED MANUFACTURING

A generic word created by the U.S. Air Force to refer to the automatic processes commanded by computer. Very few are in operation in 1987.

COMPUTER CHIP

A microprocessor element which wires into a semi-conductor some of the operations of the computer.

COMPUTER DIGIT

In a computer each information is written in a yes/no binary language and stored on an electronic bit — or digit.

COMPUTER LOGIC

The electronic wiring of the computing functions, programmes and operation procedures.

COMPUTER MEMORY

The part of the electronic bits reserved to store information temporarily during sequential operations.

CONNECTING ROD

In a cranshaft the rod which connects the piston rod to a fly wheel. See crankshaft.

CONSENT

In order to work, a technique which involves many people or many classes of people requires the intelligent consent of all participants.

CONSPICUOUS CONSUMPTION

The consumption of goods chosen so that they will be noticed by others and seen as a sign of status and wealth.

CONTROL INSTRUMENTS

An instrument to control the working operations of a machine.

CONVEYOR BELT

Mechanism to bring the work to the work station and avoid movements of workers and unnecessary movement of goods in an assembly line.

COOPERATIVE

An institution owned jointly and operated jointly either for distribution, production or banking.

COST-BENEFIT ANALYSIS

An analysis of all direct and indirect costs, cash flow requirements and generation, as well as rates of return of alternative investments.

COST-PLUS CONTRACTS

Contracts, common in defence, where the client agrees to pay automatically a certain percentage of profits above costs and pay all the costs billed.

CRANKSHAFT

Mechanical device to convert rotary energy into linear energy or vice-versa.

CRYSTALLOGRAPHER

A physical chemist studying the physical structure of chemical compounds through the use of the diffracting properties of crystals and with X-rays.

CULTURAL VALUES

As contrasted with material culture, the ideas, feelings and hierarchy of values held by a group of people with a common history.

CULTURE

See material culture and cultural values.

CUMULATIVE CHANGE

The accumulation of small incremental modifications of a technique may amount in the end to significant overall change.

CUSTOM SHOP

An industrial institution which produces only on order to specified requirements of clients. See also machine shop.

CUSTOMIZED PROCESS

The production on order and on specification of a given client for a product for his own private needs.

DEBUG

The adjustment and repair of a new technical artefact.

DEIST

A believer in one non-human God of rationality.

DESIGN

The conception, representation and projection of a possible product, process or social organisation.

DESKILLING
The reduction of skills of the workforce through a change in operations assigned.

DETERMINISM
The belief that human choice cannot modify the historical outcome.

DEVELOPMENT POLES
The point around which innovative and inventive activity concentrates in the economic system.

DIFFUSION
The progressive sequential adoption of identical techniques to new geographic or industrial areas.

DISCOVERY
The finding of a truth immanent in nature or of a continent.

DIVISION OF LABOUR
The seperation of tasks amongst different individuals.

DNA
A double helix molecule which reproduces itself and transmits genetic features.

DYNAMICS
By opposition to static and equilibrium, phenomena which gather speed and more force than was present at the outset.

ECOLOGY
The balance and sustainability of complex biological systems.

ECONOMIC
To do with the allocation of scarce means to a given end — whatever that end may be.

ECONOMIC EFFICIENCY
Technically efficient solutions which will yield at least the normal profits, if not more.

ECONOMIC POWER
The capacity to invest, acquire production factors or control a market. Distinct from technical power.

ECONOMIC SYSTEMS
Institutions, property rights and rules of economic production and distribution.

ECONOMIES OF SCALE
Economies which result from a decreasing average or marginal unit cost with scale of production.

ECONOMIES OF SCOPE

Economies which result from a decreasing average or marginal unit cost of producing jointly more than one product with the same inputs.

ECONOMIES OF SPEED

Economies resulting from the reduction of average or marginal unit time required for production and the reduction of the share of the time financial resources are immobilized without making profits.

EFFECTIVE DEMAND

A need or want which is backed by money and a willingness to buy certain quantities at set prices.

ELECTRICAL

Using electric energy and conductor materials. Different from electronic.

ELECTRICAL CONTROL

Control instruments which use electrical devices as command mechanisms.

ELECTRONIC

Use of electrical power in relatively small quantities with semi-conductive materials. Different from electrical.

ELECTRONIC CONTROL

Control instruments using electronic command devices.

ENGINEERING

One who contrives, designs or invents, usually on paper, a product or process which then has to be applied in practice.

ENTREPRENEUR

A person who takes the initiative of a new form of organization, launching a new product, process, opening a new market, exploiting new resources, or just combining existing factors of production in a new way. See also initiative.

ENTREPRENEURIAL PROFITS

Exceptional profits, well above normal profits or next best return on investment in the same industry.

ENTROPY

The state of disorganization of matter; low entropy being more organized and capable of generating energy and high entropy disorganized.

EVOLUTION

A slow process of change, adjustment, differentiation and change.

EXPERIENCE

See know-how, working knowledge.

EXTENDED FAMILY

A family organization beyond the immediate parents, brothers and sisters.

EXTRA-PROFITS

See entrepreneurial profits.

FACTORY

An industrial production establishment with machinery and power source with many workers with technical division of tasks.

FEED-BACK LOOPS OR PROCESSES

Processes where each factor is sequentially the cause of the other.

FEED MECHANISM

Ways to automatically feed a machine with feed stocks and primary materials.

FIXED CAPITAL

Capital, usually machinery, equipment and buildings which stay immobilised during the flow of production.

FIXTURES

An element securely fastened in position which fixes the process for a particular task.

FLUID FLOW PROCESS OR PRODUCTION

A continuous process in chemical processing which enlarges the controlled experiments of the laboratory. See also line production for other industries.

FOREMAN

Person who oversees workers in production without working himself.

FORMAL KNOWLEDGE

Theoretical, literary or mathematical knowledge acquired in books and in class settings.

GENDER DIVISION OF LABOUR

Division of tasks along sex lines which is not based on biological differences.

GOING IN THE HOLE

Not performing the assigned work in the time allotted by management.

GRAVY WORK

A job for which too much time was allotted by management and in the process of which the worker may "bank time" and provide slack for the situations described above.

HAND TOOLS

Any tool for which the direction of the operations are guided by the human hand, including power tools.

HANDICRAFT

Production by hand without power.

HARDWARE (computer)

The physical artefact of the technique. In computer technology, the computer itself.

HUMAN MACHINE

The organization of coordinated differentiated human work in a machine like fashion which yields substantial results due only to the organization, coordination and collective discipline and not to the artefacts used — as in the building of pyramids or hand-made dams in China.

HYDRAULIC CONTROL

A control instrument where hydraulic devices are used for commands.

HYDRAULIC STATE OR SOCIETY

Societies based on the control of flood water and the irrigation of agricultural lands, often involved in rice culture, and controlled by an educated bureaucracy in the cities which surveys the land, stores the grain, controls the water levels and taxes the farmers.

IMPLEMENTATION (of a technique)

First application and use of a technique previously used elsewhere or conceived on paper.

IMPLEMENTS

Simple technical artefacts in agriculture and handicraft.

INCENTIVE SCHEMES

Financial reward systems existing in certain firms for participation of workers in the increase of productivity or communication of ideas for the improvement of technology.

INCREMENTAL CHANGE

A minor improvement, addition or modification on an existing technical system.

INDUCEMENT EFFECT

Economic incentive stemming from expectations as to medium to long term evolution of demand, relative price variations or scarcities of factors directing technical efforts to the supply of growing demand, the use of abundant and the saving of scarce factors.

INDUSTRIAL ENGINEERING

The conception and design of work flow and production organization.

INDUSTRY

In the larger sense of the work, all productive activity. In the more common modern restrictive sense, production in factories and workshops.

INITIATIVE

The will and skill to start up any new institution, product or process. See also entrepreneur.

– INNOVATION

A new or improved commercialized product, process, organization, market or resource, which may involve invention but need not necessary require technical novelty, that provide extra-profits well over the normal returns on investment.

INPUT-OUTPUT ANALYSIS

The analysis of all first order and second order inputs for the production of a given good which enables to determine the total derived demand from any production and the flow of goods through the economy.

– INSTITUTIONAL INNOVATION

The first use of a new institution or form of organization for production of distribution. See also social innovation.

INSTRUMENTS

Instruments are artefacts which enable precise measurments and sometimes command operations.

INTERACTION

A two way causal process where each factor affects the other, usually in sequence. See also feed-back loops.

INTERACTIVE (technologies)

Like the telephone or certain computer programmes, technologies where the machinery process allows human beings to intervene in the course of the process.

– INVENTION

The creation of a new device. In contrast to innovation, an invention may never be commercialy used. See also patents.

INVESTORS

People disposing of financial resources and savings who acquire production facilities in order to reap financial earnings.

KNOW-HOW

The often tacit knowledge of how to make things work which is acquired through experience. See experience, working knowledge.

LASER CONTROLS

A control instrument which uses an optical laser device to measure and command a process.

LATHES

A machine for rotating materials against tools in order to give them a certain shape.

LEARNING-BY-DOING

See know-how and learning curve

LEARNING CURVE

The acquisition of know-how through production increases productivity proportionately to the cumulative amount of productive experience and time.

LICENSE

The right to produce certain products with certain processes, conferred either by the government or the inventors. See also patent.

LINE PRODUCTION

Production in a coordinated and synchronous sequence where the product will simultaneously be at each stage of production at any given time. Line production can be semi-continuous, continuous, automatic. Assembly lines and fluid flow systems are examples of continuous line production.

LONG ECONOMIC CYCLES OR WAVES

The idea that new lines of technology, or other factors, create every 40-60 years recurent cycles of prosperity and depression.

MACHINE

A tool linked to a power source and control instrument for production.

MACHINE ARCHITECTURE

The spatial design of a machine, in particular as it relates to the way in which its operator will be located.

MACHINE SHOP

A job shop which produces or fixes machinery, engines or metal products on order and specifications of clients.

MACHINE TOOLS

Machines for the production of other tools, implements and machinery.

MACHINE'S LIFE

The duration of use of machinery, which is determined by economic considerations as well as physical durability.

MANAGEMENT

The organization of production and the distributing of work to others.

MANUFACTURING

Originally, production by hand. Now, production with machines in factories and workshops.

MARKET
The organized locus for the exchange of goods where sellers and buyers negotiate prices and quantities exchanged voluntarily.

MASS PRODUCTION
The production of large quantities of a standardized good.

MATERIAL CULTURE
The set of ways in which we lead our daily lives, eat, dress, lodge ourselves, interact socially and work.

MATRIX
A table with similar values on both the columns and the lines which enables one to measure the interactions of all the variables with one another.

MECHANIZATION
The replacement of human operations by machines.

MICROPROCESSOR
The wiring of computer functions (input, output, operations, logic) into the transistors.

MONOPOLY
The production of the industry is performed by only one firm.

MORATORIUM
The postponement of implementation of a decision.

NATURAL SELECTION
The survival of the fittest and most adapted specie within an environment with limited resources leads to the extinction of the less adapted ones.

NECESSITY
See needs.

NEEDS
A want for a good or service or satisfaction, which may or may not be backed by financial means.

NEGATIVE CONSTRAINT
Factors blocking the occurence of a phenomenum and determining what cannot, or is unlikely to be.

NORMAL PROFIT
Profit which would be made with an alternative investment decision without benefiting from any long term advantage or rent.

NUCLEAR FAMILY
The minimum family size structured around the parents and children.

NUMERICAL CONTROL

A control instrument which can be programmed by the digital transcription and geometrical representation of spatial operations for machine commands.

NUMERICAL CONTROL MACHINE TOOLS

A machine tool with above system of controls and commands.

OLIGOPOLY

The control of the majority of production by a few large firms with a fringe of small firms producing for a small share of the market.

OPTICAL CONTROLS

Control instruments which use optical devices to measure and command operations.

ORGANIZATION OF WORK

The inter-personal and hierarchical relations in the work process.

OSTENTATIOUS CONSUMPTION

The buying and consumption of goods for purposes of display to signify to others one's status, rank or wealth.

PARADIGMS

Originally an exemplar, a pattern. Now also a set of scientific hypotheses and questions percieved at an epoch as being relevant, while others are no longer of interest. See also world views.

PATENTS

A temporary (17 years) monopoly right awarded by the government for the exclusive application of an invention. See also invention.

PATRIARCHAL FAMILY

Family dominated by the male at the top of the hierarchy.

PLURALISM

The promotion and support of a variety of beliefs, philosophies, values and institutions within a society.

POLITICAL

Originally the affairs of the city (polis) or of civil society. Refers to the governance of society, laws and regulations, as well as the power of some over others in society. See also power.

POLITICAL SYSTEMS

The rules, prerogatives, rights and institutions of regulation of society and the forms of government.

POWER

Power of some over others. This may include power of influence, political, economic or technical power. See also political.

POWER TOOL

A hand tool linked with a power source (e.g. electrical) but which is guided by the human hand.

PRIVATE ENTERPRISE

Type of enterprise which is owned by a private individual or a group of individuals.

PROBLEM SOLVING

A form of learning derived from concrete challenges to resolve a problem.

PROCEDURES

Every production technique involves a set of proceedures and sequence of operations to be followed which reflect the technical know-how about the best way to do things. In contrast to process equipment.

PROCESS

The proceedures, sequence and operations of production.

PRODUCT

A good sold to a customer outside the firm.

PRODUCTION SYSTEMS

Inter-related production proceedures and equipment.

PROGRESS

The idea that each progression from one technique to another is advantageous to all of society and humanity.

PROPERTY RIGHT

The definition by laws and convention of who has a right to what within a given political system. See proprietary rights, patents.

PROPRIETARY RIGHTS

Some techniques are subject to proprietary rights either through trade secrets or, temporarily, through patents.

PROTOTYPE

The first model of a new technique for the purpose of demonstration, testing and evaluation.

RADICAL INNOVATION

An innovation which, retrospectively, is seen as having made a critical departure in the way of doing things.

RATE OF PROFIT

The proportion of earnings on initial investments once all costs have been deducted.

RATE OF RETURN

See above.

REDUCTIONISM

Theories which try to explain all phenomena with only a few assumptions and hypotheses.

REGULATION

The rules of conduct, written and unwritten, through which conflicting interests establish a social compromise.

RESEARCH AND DEVELOPMENT

Basic scientific research, applied research and exploratory development for the purposes of economic application.

RETAIL

Sale directly to the individual consumer.

ROBOT

A computer programmed machine performing a set task automatically. See also numerical control.

SCARCITY

Insufficient availability and supply of goods or services to satisfy demand.

SCIENCE

The explanation of why phenomena occur with theories, hyptheses and controlled experiments.

SCIENCE BASED INDUSTRY (OR INVENTION)

Industries related to the research in a scientific field.

SCIENTIFIC INSTRUMENTS

Measurement instruments for the purposes of scientific research, explorations, tests and discovery.

SCIENTIFIC KNOWLEDGE

The organized and systematic explanation of the regularities of measurable phenomena by the help of theories and controlled experiments.

SEDENTARIZATION (of agriculture)

The settlement of nomadic people in one place for the growing of crops around the flood waters of major rivers around 6,000 B.C.

SELF-MANAGED FIRMS

Firms where workers elect and/or rotate their management and minimize its functions.

SEMI-CONDUCTOR

A material which is conductive only in one direction.

SET UP

The adjustment of a machine for a specific job.

SEQUENCE OF PRODUCTION
The order of production operations.

SKILLED WORKER
A worker who has acquired experience and know-how in a specialty and may have formal papers recognizing those special skills.

SOCIAL BIAS
The preference of a social group for certain technical designs which are to its advantage but which are not shared by other groups.

SOCIAL DIVISION OF LABOUR
Division of labour which results in different professions forming and different social groups being dedicated to specialized tasks.

SOCIAL EVALUATION OF TECHNIQUES
See social impact assessment.

SOCIAL IMPACT ASSESSMENT
The evaluation of the advantages and disadvantages to be gained by different social groups in society.

SOCIAL INNOVATION
The initiation of new social relationships. See also institutional innovation.

SOCIAL SYSTEMS
A set of interdependent social relationships.

SOCIAL TRANSFORMATION
The slow but irreversible change of basic relationships on which society is based.

SOFTWARE (computer)
Human knowledge about proceedures, the systems operations and programming of computers.

SOLID STATE PHYSICS
A scientific field concerned with the physical composition of materials, in particular of semi-conductors.

SOLVENT DEMAND
See effective demand, or demand.

SPECIALIZED PRODUCTS OR PROCESSES
Products or processes which are used only by a few for specific applications which do not recur often.

SPECULATIVE INVESTMENT
The buying of a good (land, gold) in order to make money from its eventual resale due to the expectancy that the value of the good will rise.

SPEED SKILLS

The capacity and knowledge of how to perform the work faster. See also economies of speed.

STANDARDIZED PRODUCTS OR PROCESSES

An uniform design, standard and norm for a product, allowing mass production, and perhaps interchangeable parts.

STATE ENTERPRISE

An enterprise owned and managed by the State.

SUBSTITUTE

A product or process which, although different, has similar attributes or can perform an equivalent service and thus may compete for the same market.

SUPERVISOR

See foreman.

SUPPLY

The production of goods and services to meet some demand.

SUPPORT TECHNIQUE

A technical system will often be assisted by the existence of repair, maintenance and improvement techniques. See also auxiliary technique.

SYNERGY

The combination of two convergent factors which result, in interaction, in a greater effect than the addition of the two.

SYSTEMS

Interdependent components which form a whole. There are political, social, economic and technical systems.

TECHNICAL ACCUMULATION

The slow accumulation of know-how through productive experience and the incorporation of this working knowledge in new and improved equipment.

TECHNICAL ADAPTATION

The modification of an existing technique for a special application to suit the environment. See also technical variation and technical application.

TECHNICAL APPLICATION

The transposition of a technique to solve a problem. See also technical variation and technical adaptation.

TECHNICAL ARTIFACTS

The implements, tools, power tools, machinery and control instruments — or hardware.

TECHNICAL ASSESSMENT

The evaluation of a technology and its alternatives with comparative performance analysis, cost benefit analysis and social impact assessment.

TECHNICAL CHOICE

See choice of technique.

TECHNICAL DIVISION OF LABOUR

The seperation of tasks amongst different workers within the same factory.

TECHNICAL EFFICIENCY

A precondition of economic efficiency but not all technical efficient solutions are at a given time economically feasible or profitable. See economic efficiency.

TECHNICAL EVALUATION

See technical assessment.

TECHNICAL OPPORTUNITIES

The set of technically feasible alternatives.

TECHNICAL PERFORMANCE

Measured in physical terms and in relation with physical inputs.

TECHNICAL POWER

The power to design, choose and implement a technique that others will have to work with and which will determine their social and interpersonal relationships. Distinct from economic power.

TECHNICAL PREROGATIVES

The right to initiate, design, choose, invest, promote, modify and use a technique.

TECHNICAL RIGHTS

See above: technical prerogatives.

TECHNICAL VARIATION

The different version of the same technique due to special application and context of use. See also technical adaptation and technical application.

TECHNICS

The set of technical artefacts.

TECHNIQUE

A way of doing things.

TECHNOLOGY

Science related techniques.

TECNE

The Greek word for art, techniques and science.

TELEOLOGY
The explanation of the present events by an assumed future outcome.

TIME AND MOTION
The decomposition of human work movements into small segments and time fragments for the purpose of reducing the time allowed for a set job.

TOOLS
See hand tool.

TRADESPEOPLE
Skilled workers who have official recognition of their skills and are often organised in a profession. See also skilled worker.

TRANSISTOR
A semi-conductor which allows the transistor from positive to negative and back to positive.

TROUBLE SHOOT
The rapid solution of a technical problem for which few have experience and which is relatively unknown.

TURNOVER TIME
The time necessary from the initial investment to the time of the sale.

UNSKILLED WORKER
A worker will little experience, or experience which is not recognized.

USUFACTURE
The production for use by the producers themselves.

UTENSILS
See implements.

VACUUM TUBES
A semi-conductor device similar to a light bulb with which the first ENIAC computer was built.

VALUE ADDED
The increase in prices between the end product and all the input costs due to production in a firm.

VALVES (electronic)
See vacuum tubes.

VARIABLE CAPITAL
Those costs of production and factors which vary with each production run and are more or less related to the output: throughout materials, energy, labour.

VETO RIGHTS
The right to stop a new technique from being used.

WANTS
See needs.

WHOLESALE
Sales of large quantities to retailers.

WORK ORGANIZATION
See organization of work.

WORK STATION
The position at which a worker is to stay to perform the tasks he has been assigned.

WORKING KNOWLEDGE
See know-how and experience.

WORK SHOP
The area reserved for tools, machines and work.

WORLD VIEWS
Overall images and representations of the world influencing the values and goals of behaviours. See also paradigms.

SUBJECT INDEX

AUTHOR INDEX

ACKNOWLEDGEMENTS

This book was first written as material for a Labour Studies course called "The Challenge of Technological Change" at Capilano College in Vancouver, British Columbia. Without this course, the material would have had no purpose. I am indebted to Ed Lavalle, Betty Merrall and the union workers who participated in this course. I am particularly grateful to Ken Hansen, already very knowledgeable about technological change when he participated in the course, who spent many hours carefully reading the manuscript to suggest improvements.

Margaret Benston, Willem van Hoorn, and Melvin Kranzberg read the 1981 course materials and made sound recommendations. Rick Coe proposed the organization of this book; Janet Giltrow, Phil Hall, and Tom Wayman gave me advice about writing. Jim Petersen generated some of the text about learning on the job (Chapter 6). I appreciate his input, since he has first-hand experience in industrial production.

Catherine LeGrand's constant social concern sustained my belief in the worth of this project. Willem van Hoorn and Kees Bertels graciously permitted me to choose illustrations from the beautiful collection they have assembled at Leiden University in Holland. Other illustrations come from the Dibner Library and Museum of American History, Smithsonian Institution collection in Washington, D.C. The editor of The Voice of Solidarity, Marek Garztecki, enabled me to reproduce the Draft for an Act about Social Enterprise. Ken Hansen, David Noble, and many unions kindly authorized the reproduction of extracts from their documents.

Although this book was not originally intended for use in universities, I drew from the work demanded of me during 1974-84, when I studied for a Ph.D. in economics at the Université de Paris. The multidisciplinary tradition that the French Annales School of History promoted at Section VI (Sciences Economiques et Sociales) of the Ecole Pratique des Hautes Etudes en Sciences Sociales proved an ideal setting to force me to think beyond the field of economics. If I had known what I was getting into, I might not have begun that decade of work. In retrospect, however, I realize that these studies forced me to decide what I thought about certain issues.

In this work I benefited from the uncompromising theoretical criticisms of François Chesnais. Joe Townsend served as my model of perseverance, precision and patience in my laborious apprenticeship as an historian of technology. Jim Petersen, another working intellectual, in more ways than one, provided regular feedback. Stanley Ryerson found ellipses and raised questions (which I am not sure of having answered satisfactorily). Without Professor Henri Aujac's generous and relentless prodding, I might never have completed my thesis. After completing this requirement, I was encouraged by Professors René Passet and François Perroux to further refine the ideas about which I had written.

I want to thank Debbie Seed and Richelle Houtakker for editing my manuscript. My thanks also to Brent Murray for checking all references and preparing the index. I am grateful to the friends and colleagues whose names do not appear here, but who have helped me in many ways, directly and indirectly.

Ironically, I started this work as a skeptic about research. But I have come out of the exercise believing that perhaps analysis and social criticism can contribute to historical action. I hope that working people will find it useful in their attempts to shape and control technological change. I invite comments, criticism and suggestions, so the next text on this subject can be substantially improved.

January 1986

2ND REVISED EDITION

TURNING THE TIDE

The U.S. and Latin America
by Noam Chomsky

Regarding U.S. policy in Latin America, *Turning the Tide* succinctly provides the most cogent available descriptions of what is going on, and why. It will be a central tool for everyone who wants to promote peace and justice in the Americas.

Noam Chomsky reveals the aim and impact of U.S. policy in Latin America by examining the historical record and current events. With this as backdrop, he also shows the connection between Latin American policy and broader nuclear and international politics and explains the logic and role of the Cold War for both super-powers. Finally, Chomsky looks at why we accept Reaganesque rhetoric in light of the role of the media and the intelligentsia in the numbing of our awareness. He concludes by describing what we can do to resist.

Turning the Tide is a succinct volume ideal for understanding the broad factors governing U.S. policy in Latin America, the role of the Cold War, and the role of the media and intellectuals with respect to each.

Noam Chomsky is professor of Linguistics and Philosophy and Institute Professor at M.I.T.; recipient of honorary degrees from the University of London, University of Chicago, Delhi University, and four other colleges and universities; fellow of the American Academy of Arts and Sciences, member of the National Academy of Arts and Sciences, and member of the National Academy of Sciences; author of numerous books and articles on linguistics, philosophy, intellectual history and contemporary issues.

Paperback ISBN: 0-920057-78-0   **$14.95**
Hardcover ISBN: 0-920057-76-4   **$29.95**

THE COMING OF
WORLD WAR THREE

Volume 1
From Protest to Resistance / the International War System

Dimitrios I. Roussopoulos

This book is <u>not</u> about the arms race,
it is about the peace movement. In presenting
an analysis of the strengths and weaknesses
of actions for peace,
Dimitrios Roussopoulos shows us what
we must really do to prevent a third world war.

ISBN: 0-920057-02-0 $14.95

BLACK ROSE BOOKS

Write for free catalogue of more than 110 books:

Black Rose Books
3981, boul. St. Laurent
Montréal, Québec
H2W 1Y5

Printed by
the workers of
Ateliers Graphiques Marc Veilleux Inc.
Cap-Saint-Ignace, Qué.
for
Black Rose Books Ltd.